BLEST ARE WE

Series Authors
Rev. Richard N. Fragomeni, Ph.D.
Maureen Gallagher, Ph.D.
Jeannine Goggin, M.P.S.
Michael P. Horan, Ph.D.

Scripture Co-editor and Consultant
Maria Pascuzzi, S.S.L., S.T.D.

Resources Consultants
Janaan Manternach, D.Min.
Carl J. Pfeifer, D.Min.

SILVER BURDETT GINN RELIGION
A SCOTT FORESMAN IMPRINT
PARSIPPANY, NJ

BLEST ARE WE

Multicultural Consultant
Angela Erevia, M.C.D.P., M.R.E.

Contributing Writers
Theresa Flynn-Nason
Dr. Craig O'Neill
Kathleen Whaley, M.A.

Contributing Authors
Catholic Schools in America:
  Robert Kealey, Ph.D.
Family Time: Steve and Kathy Beirne
Feasts and Seasons: Marianne K. Lenihan;
  Louise Timko, Ph.D.
*Unit Organizers and Reviews, Our Catholic
  Heritage*: Joyce A. Crider
We Care: Richard Reichert, M.A.

Advisory Board
William C. Allegri, M.A.; Patricia M. Feeley,
S.S.J., M.A.; Edmund F. Gordon; Patricia A.
Hoffmann; Rev. Daniel Kelly; Cris V.
Villapando, D.Min.

Consultants
Joy Villotti-Biedrzycki; Margaret J. Borders,
M.R.S.; Kelly O'Lague Dulka, M.S.W.; Diane
Hardick, M.A.; Debra Schurko; Linda S. Tonelli,
M.Ed.

Music Advisors
GIA Publications: Michael A. Cymbala, Alec
Harris, Robert W. Piercy

Nihil Obstat
M. Kathleen Flanagan, S.C., Ph.D.
Ellen Joyce, S.C., Ph.D.
Censors Librorum

Imprimatur
✠ Most Reverend Frank J. Rodimer
Bishop of Paterson
February 5, 2003

The *nihil obstat* and *imprimatur* are official declarations that a book or pamphlet is free of doctrinal and moral error. No implication is contained therein that those who have granted the *nihil obstat* and *imprimatur* agree with the contents, opinions, or statements expressed.

Acknowledgments
Excerpts from *The New American Bible* © 1970 by the Confraternity of Christian Doctrine, Washington, D.C., including the revised *New Testament* © 1986 by the Confraternity of Christian Doctrine, Washington, D.C., used with permission. All rights reserved.

All adaptations of Scripture are based on *The New American Bible* © 1970 and 1986

Excerpts from the English translation of the *Rite of Penance* © 1974, International Committee on English in the Liturgy, Inc. (ICEL); excerpts from the English translation of the *Rite of Confirmation*, Second Edition © 1975, ICEL; excerpts from the English translation of *The Roman Missal*, © 1973, ICEL; excerpts from the English translation of the *Rite of Christian Initiation of Adults* © 1988, ICEL. All rights reserved.

Music selections copyrighted and/or administered by GIA Publications are used with permission of GIA Publications, Inc., 7404 So. Mason Avenue, Chicago, IL 60638-9927. Please refer to songs for specific copyright dates and information.

Chapter II from *Thoughts in Solitude* by Thomas Merton, p. 79, Copyright © 1956, 1958 by The Abbey of Our Lady of Gethsemani. Reprinted by permission of Farrar, Straus & Giroux, LLC.

Excerpt from Anthony Stern, *Everything Starts From Prayer: Mother Teresa's Meditations on Spiritual Life for People of All Faiths*. Ashland, Oregon: White Cloud Press, 1998, p. 132. Used with permission.

In appreciation: Beau Veste, Butler, NJ; Blessed Kateri Church, Sparta, NJ; Church of the Assumption, Morristown, NJ; Our Lady of Mercy Church, Whippany, NJ; Our Lady of the Lake Church, Sparta, NJ; St. Ann Church, Parsippany, NJ; St. Joseph Church, Croton Falls, NY; St. Peter the Apostle Church, Parsippany, NJ; St. Thomas More Church, Convent Station, NJ; San Alfonso Retreat House, Long Branch, NJ; ILP Publications, Nashville, TN; GIA Publications, Inc., Chicago, IL; WLP Publications, Schiller Park, IL; Craig Baker, www.schooluniforms.com

Our Commitment Prayer

Name Megan Murray

School Holy Name of Jesus

Leader: This year, we will learn about the words and actions of God in the world by studying his holy word, the Scriptures. God's word came about through the inspiration and wisdom of the Holy Spirit.

All: Holy Spirit, with you as our guide, we will focus our thoughts on your holy word.

Leader: In the Old Testament, the Lord called the Hebrews to be his people. The Gospels tell us that we are the new people of God. From the beginning, God's creation has been accomplished through the power of the Holy Spirit.

All: Holy Spirit, we will appreciate the gifts you have created in us.

Leader: Jesus Christ, the Word of God, was conceived by the power of the Holy Spirit and became man, God among us.

All: Holy Spirit, we will be open to the Word of God among us.

Leader: The Catholic Church had its birth at Pentecost, when the Holy Spirit came upon the first disciples, filling them with faith, hope, and love.

All: Holy Spirit, come to us as we begin this year. Help our faith grow as we learn about our ancestors in faith in the Old Testament. Fill us with hope, and teach us to love as Christ has loved us. Amen.

CONTENTS

Blest Are We

Words and Music by David Haas
Spanish translation by Ronald F. Krisman

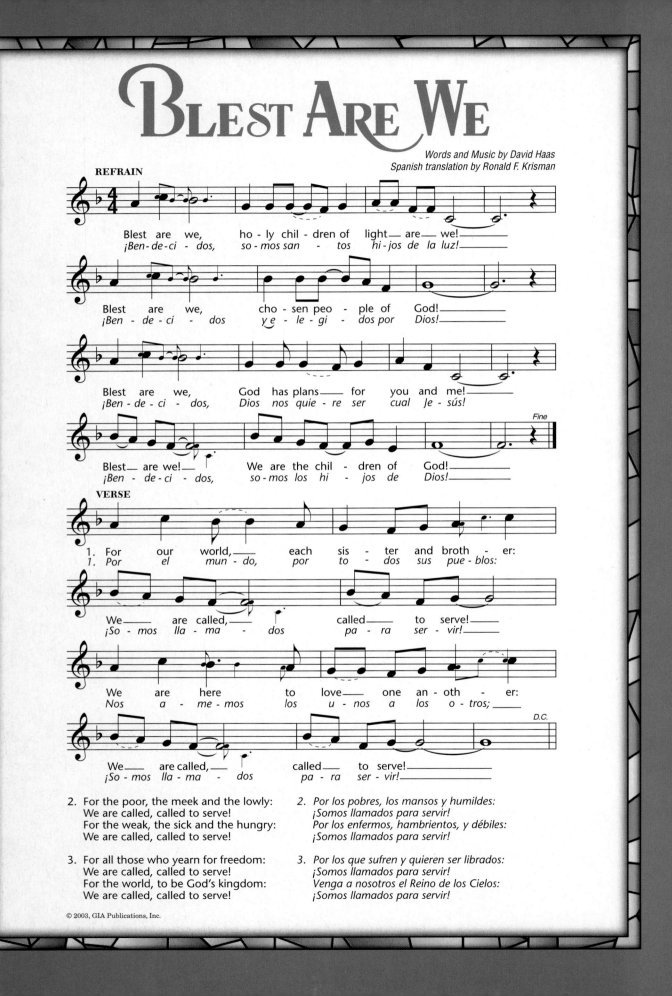

REFRAIN

Blest are we, ho-ly chil-dren of light are we!
¡Ben-de-ci-dos, so-mos san-tos hi-jos de la luz!

Blest are we, cho-sen peo-ple of God!
¡Ben-de-ci-dos y e-le-gi-dos por Dios!

Blest are we, God has plans for you and me!
¡Ben-de-ci-dos, Dios nos quie-re ser cual Je-sús!

Fine

Blest are we! We are the chil-dren of God!
¡Ben-de-ci-dos, so-mos los hi-jos de Dios!

VERSE

1. For our world, each sis-ter and broth-er:
1. Por el mun-do, por to-dos sus pue-blos:

We are called, called to serve!
¡So-mos lla-ma-dos pa-ra ser-vir!

We are here to love one an-oth-er:
Nos a-me-mos los u-nos a los o-tros;

D.C.

We are called, called to serve!
¡So-mos lla-ma-dos pa-ra ser-vir!

2. For the poor, the meek and the lowly:
We are called, called to serve!
For the weak, the sick and the hungry:
We are called, called to serve!

2. Por los pobres, los mansos y humildes:
¡Somos llamados para servir!
Por los enfermos, hambrientos, y débiles:
¡Somos llamados para servir!

3. For all those who yearn for freedom:
We are called, called to serve!
For the world, to be God's kingdom:
We are called, called to serve!

3. Por los que sufren y quieren ser librados:
¡Somos llamados para servir!
Venga a nosotros el Reino de los Cielos:
¡Somos llamados para servir!

A GREAT BIBLE EXPEDITION

A LOOK INSIDE THE BIBLE

If you were to look at the last page number in the Bible, you would see that the Bible is more than 1,000 pages long! What's inside? There are stories, songs, poems, family histories, letters, wise sayings, parables, prophecies, and many other kinds of writing. Some of the writings date back to about 3,000 years ago. Even the most recently written parts of the Bible are about 2,000 years old. But the Bible is one of the best-selling books of all time, because everything in the Bible has something to reveal about God, human life, and the world.

The Bible is a collection of 73 books. The word *Bible* comes from the Greek word *biblia*, meaning "books." The Bible is also known as *Scripture*, a word that means "word of God" or "sacred writings." This year you will take a great expedition through Scripture.

You will explore the writings in the first part of the Bible, which is called the *Old Testament*. These writings describe how God revealed to the Hebrews or Jewish people knowledge about himself and his ways. As Catholics, we seek to learn about God with an understanding of our link to the Hebrews. They were the first to hear the word of God and to form a special relationship with God. That is why we sometimes refer to them as "our ancestors in faith." The Old Testament is a collection of 46 books that tell us about the experiences of our ancestors in faith.

You will also study the *New Testament*, a collection of 27 books that are very important to Catholics and all Christians. These books tell us about the life and teachings of Jesus Christ. He fulfilled the promises God made to our ancestors in faith in the Old Testament.

What Is Your Bible IQ?

How much do you know about the Bible? Take this fun quiz to find out!

II

1. The writers of the Bible wrote down stories that were
   (a) completely made up.
   (b) originally passed down by word of mouth.
   (c) all told by Jesus.
   (d) scientifically correct.

2. The first part of the Bible is the
   (a) New Testament.
   (b) Old Testament.

3. What body of water parted so the Israelites could escape Egypt?
   (a) Jordan River
   (b) Red Sea
   (c) Dead Sea
   (d) Mediterranean Sea

4. Who was Jacob's favorite son?
   (a) Cain
   (b) Abel
   (c) Joseph
   (d) Moses

5. What animal told Eve to eat the fruit of the Tree of Knowledge?
   (a) a serpent
   (b) a wolf
   (c) a bird
   (d) a mouse

6. What sign did God send to tell Noah there would not be another Great Flood?
   (a) a dove
   (b) a burning bush
   (c) sunshine
   (d) a rainbow

7. According to the Bible, how long did it take God to create the world?
   (a) six days
   (b) five years
   (c) one day
   (d) seven days

8. The man who received the Ten Commandments from God was
   (a) Abraham.
   (b) Jesus.
   (c) Peter.
   (d) Moses.

9. Which Jewish holiday celebrates the Exodus? (Hint: It occurs around the same time as Easter.)
   (a) Hanukkah
   (b) Rosh Hashanah
   (c) Passover
   (d) Yom Kippur

10. Who was left in a basket beside the river as a baby?
    (a) Isaac
    (b) Deborah
    (c) Moses
    (d) David

11. When Mary and Joseph lost the boy Jesus, they found him
    (a) talking to John the Baptizer.
    (b) fishing with the Twelve Apostles.
    (c) changing water into wine at Cana.
    (d) talking to teachers in the Temple.

Check your score on page xiv!

THE HISTORY OF THE BIBLE

1. THE PATRIARCHS (2000–1700 B.C.)

In 1800 B.C. the patriarch Abraham, a nomadic shepherd, left Mesopotamia for a land called Canaan, following the guidance of God. His son Isaac and grandson Jacob were patriarchs who also followed the guidance of God. At this time, the patriarchs' experiences of God were passed down through the generations by word of mouth.

2. THE EXODUS (1700–1200 B.C.)

Jacob's son Joseph was taken to Egypt as a slave but became a great ruler. His father and brothers moved to Egypt. Their descendants thrived there until Pharaoh made them slaves. Moses helped them escape Egypt around 1300 B.C. They journeyed through the desert. God gave them the Ten Commandments. Joshua led them to the promised land, and they conquered Palestine around 1200 B.C. The Bible was not yet written.

3. THE KINGDOM (1200–900 B.C.)

The Israelites (descendants of Jacob's family) settled in Canaan. Leaders called *judges* helped rule the Israelites between 1200 and 1000 B.C. Around 1000 B.C. David became king of the southern part of the land. Jerusalem was its capital. David's son, Solomon, was king of most of Canaan between 965 and 928 B.C. He built the Temple. Scribes began to write the Bible's histories of the kings, story of the Garden of Eden, and parts of stories about Abraham, Joseph, and Moses.

The Twelve Tribes

A TIMELINE OF BIBLE EVENTS

IN THE BIBLE	**1800** Abraham journeys to Canaan.	**1700** Joseph and family live in Egypt.		**1300** Moses and Hebrews leave Egypt.	**1200** Israelites conquer Palestine.	**1200–1000** Judges rule.	**1000** King David captures Jerusalem.
	THE PATRIARCHS 2000–1700 B.C.		**THE EXODUS 1700–1200 B.C.**			**THE KINGDOM 1200–900 B.C.**	
IN THE WORLD	**2000** Stonehenge is built in England.	**1600** First Chinese civilizations develop.	**1350** Mediterranean peoples migrate to Canaan and Egypt.		**1200** Iron Age begins in Middle East.	**1150** Olmec civilization in Central America develops.	

x

4. THE PROPHETS AND THE EXILE (900–500 B.C.)

After Solomon's son became king, the empire divided into Judah in the south and Israel in the north. Prophets such as Isaiah and Micah guided people. People added to the stories of Abraham, Joseph, and Moses. In 722 B.C. Assyria destroyed Israel and took its people captive. Hezekiah and Josiah were Israel's kings. Hezekiah made changes to early stories about Abraham, Joseph, and Moses. Josiah's scribes included early versions of stories in new works such as Deuteronomy, Joshua, Judges, 1 and 2 Samuel, and 1 and 2 Kings.

The Babylonians destroyed Jerusalem and the Temple in 587 B.C. Judaens were exiled to Babylon. Joshua, Deuteronomy, Judges, 1 and 2 Samuel, and 1 and 2 Kings were rewritten. In 539 B.C. Cyrus, leader of the Persians, conquered the Babylonians and welcomed the Jews back home. The Jews who returned rebuilt the Temple in 519 B.C.

5. GREEK AND ROMAN RULE (500 B.C.–A.D. 30)

The Jews had peace during Persian rule. Priests copied and rewrote earlier texts. Numbers, Genesis, Exodus, and the prophetic books were written as known today. Leviticus was written. Psalms and Proverbs were rewritten. Deuteronomy was finished. Nehemiah, Jonah, Ezra, Job, and Ruth were written. Alexander the Great conquered the Persian empire in 332 B.C. Greeks ruled the Jews until about 164 B.C. Song of Songs, Sirach, Ecclesiastes, and Wisdom were written. Books were translated into Greek.

Jews called *Maccabees* defeated the Greeks. Daniel, 1 and 2 Maccabees, and Tobit were written. By this time, all of the Old Testament was written. Romans began to rule in 63 B.C. Jesus was born around 6 B.C. and died around A.D. 30. The Gospels were written in A.D. 70–100 and the Letters of Paul in A.D. 50–60. Paul's followers wrote some letters in A.D. 65–100. The New Testament was completed by A.D. 120.

63
Roman rule begins.

6
Jesus is born.

30
Jesus dies and rises.

965–928
Solomon rules and builds Temple.

928
Kingdom divides.

587–537
Jewish exiles live in Babylon.

539
Jewish exiles allowed to return.

722
Assyrians conquer Israel.

587
Babylonians destroy Jerusalem.

164
Jews regain independence.

332
Greeks rule Jews.

THE PROPHETS AND THE EXILE 900–500 B.C.

GREEK AND ROMAN RULE 500 B.C.–A.D. 30

776
First Greek Olympics are held.

753
Rome is founded.

110
Trade opens between Far East and Middle East and Europe.

55
Julius Caesar attacks Britain.

THE PARTS OF THE BIBLE

Catholics believe that God inspired the Bible. This means that the Holy Spirit guided the writers of the Bible. Because the Bible is the inspired word of God, it should be treated with respect and care.

Jesus Christ entrusted the interpretation of God's word to the leaders of the Church. Through the Holy Spirit, the bishops and the pope lead us to a better understanding of the Bible, and Jesus Christ, the eternal Word of God, opens our minds to understand the Bible.

The Bible read by Catholics contains the books that the Church reveres as inspired by God. About A.D. 400, Saint Jerome, a brilliant priest and scholar, helped the Church decide which books would form the *canon*, or official list, of books of the Bible. He also translated the books of the Bible into Latin for the Latin-speaking Christians. (The books were originally in Greek and Hebrew.) Centuries later, the Bible was divided into chapters and verses. The first translation of the Bible into English was completed in 1384.

Not all religious denominations share the same collections of books. The Protestant Bible contains only 66 books. The Jewish Bible, or Hebrew Scriptures, contains books from the section we call the Old Testament. Here are the books of the Catholic Bible.

Old Testament

Pentateuch
(first five books of the Bible, about Israel's covenant with God)

Genesis   Numbers
Exodus   Deuteronomy
Leviticus

(more of the Israelites' story)

Joshua   Ruth
Judges

Historical Books
(Israel's religious history)

1 Samuel   Nehemiah
2 Samuel   Tobit
1 Kings   Judith
2 Kings   Esther
1 Chronicles   1 Maccabees
2 Chronicles   2 Maccabees
Ezra

Wisdom Books
(poetry and instruction)

Job   Song of Songs
Psalms   Wisdom
Proverbs   Sirach
Ecclesiastes

Prophetic Books
(God's word through the prophets)

Isaiah   Obadiah
Jeremiah   Jonah
Lamentations   Micah
Baruch   Nahum
Ezekiel   Habakkuk
Daniel   Zephaniah
Hosea   Haggai
Joel   Zechariah
Amos   Malachi

New Testament

The Gospels
(life and teachings of Jesus)

Matthew   Luke
Mark   John

Acts of the Apostles
(works of the early Church)

Letters
(letters to early Christians)

Romans   Philippians
1 Corinthians   Colossians
2 Corinthians   1 Thessalonians
Galatians   2 Thessalonians
Ephesians   1 Timothy

2 Timothy   1 Peter
Titus   2 Peter
Philemon   1 John
Hebrews   2 John
James   3 John   Jude

Book of Revelation
(apocalyptic writing)

HOW TO FIND SCRIPTURE PASSAGES

The Bible is divided into books. The books are divided into chapters. The chapters are divided into verses. For example,

Exodus 19:8–9

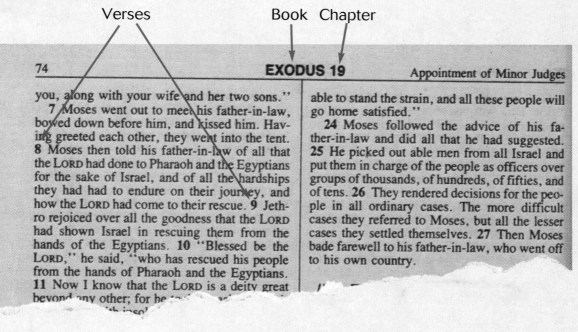

Verses

Book   Chapter

74   **EXODUS 19**   Appointment of Minor Judges

you, along with your wife and her two sons."
7 Moses went out to meet his father-in-law, bowed down before him, and kissed him. Having greeted each other, they went into the tent. 8 Moses then told his father-in-law of all that the LORD had done to Pharaoh and the Egyptians for the sake of Israel, and of all the hardships they had had to endure on their journey, and how the LORD had come to their rescue. 9 Jethro rejoiced over all the goodness that the LORD had shown Israel in rescuing them from the hands of the Egyptians. 10 "Blessed be the LORD," he said, "who has rescued his people from the hands of Pharaoh and the Egyptians. 11 Now I know that the LORD is a deity great beyond any other; for he ...

able to stand the strain, and all these people will go home satisfied."
24 Moses followed the advice of his father-in-law and did all that he had suggested. 25 He picked out able men from all Israel and put them in charge of the people as officers over groups of thousands, of hundreds, of fifties, and of tens. 26 They rendered decisions for the people in all ordinary cases. The more difficult cases they referred to Moses, but all the lesser cases they settled themselves. 27 Then Moses bade farewell to his father-in-law, who went off to his own country.

To find a Scripture passage, follow these three simple steps. Try to use the steps to find the passage *Matthew 5:1–12*.

Step One:

Find the name of the book you need on the alphabetical index page. This page displays all the books in your Bible in an alphabetical list. (The name *Matthew* can be found under the heading *New Testament*.)

Step Two:

In the same list, find the page number of the book you need. This number will be to the right of the name of the book. It will tell you the page on which the book begins. Turn to that page within your Bible.

Step Three:

Now turn the pages forward until you find the chapter you need. The chapter number is shown either next to the name of the book at the very top of the page or as a large number within paragraphs on the page. (Chapter 5 of Matthew starts just a few pages away from the first page of Matthew's Gospel.) When you find the chapter, locate the verses. These are the small numbers within the paragraphs on the page.

SCRIPTURE SEARCH GAME

Complete the chart by finding and reading the Scripture passages listed. You may find the full names for the abbreviations on the abbreviations page of your Bible.

Scripture Passage	Book	Chapter	Verses	Found in Bible on Page	Summary of Story
Lk 2:1–7					
Ex 20:1–17					
Gn 1:1–31					

THE TYPES OF WRITING IN THE BIBLE

Fill in examples where lines have been provided.

Songs: poems or hymns that are often prayers. *Example*: the Book of Psalms

Laws: instructions on how to behave. *Example*: Deuteronomy

Parables: tales that teach a moral lesson. *Example*: _____

Sagas: lengthy stories about a person or group. *Example*: Exodus

Letters: written messages from one person or group to another. *Example*: _____

Myths: ancient stories that attempt to explain life. *Example*: Adam and Eve

Prophecies: messages from God as explained through the words of prophets. *Example*: Ezekiel

The mezuza is a small covered scroll containing biblical text. It is fixed to the doorpost of Jewish homes.

Answers to "What Is Your Bible IQ?" (page ix)
1) b, 2) b, 3) b, 4) c, 5) a, 6) d, 7) a, 8) d, 9) c, 10) c, 11) d

Scoring:
Give yourself one point for each correct answer.
8–11 points: You are a Bible Brainiac!
5–7 points: You get a B in the Bible business!
3–4 points: Brush up on the Bible just a bit!
1–2 points: Don't worry. You will improve your Bible IQ this year!

We Answer God's Call

Abraham and Sarah are our ancestors in faith because they were the first to respond to God's call to holiness and fidelity. God calls each of us to be faithful to his word and to lead others in holiness.

The LORD said to Abram: "Go forth from the land of your kinsfolk and from your father's house to a land that I will show you."

Genesis 12:1

Abraham and Sarah's Journey

MESOPOTAMIA
• Haran
Mediterranean Sea
• Shechem
Dead Sea
EGYPT
• Beersheba
ARABIA

Abraham and Sarah traveled across the desert, just as these nomads are doing. The map shows their journey.

1

I Say "Yes," Lord/ Digo "Sí," Señor

Words and Music by Donna Peña
Arranged by Marty Haugen

Family Time

A choice of things to do at home

Revelation and Response

This chapter introduces the story of our ancestors in faith with the Old Testament figures Abraham and Sarah, who accepted God's plan even though they were unsure of what God had in store for them. Many of us experience challenges that make us wonder about God's plan for us and how he expects us to respond.

A family faith tree

Create a colorful family tree showing not only lineage but each person's journey of faith. Include what you know about major changes in the person's life, his or her fears about these changes, and the positive things that resulted. You may even include dates of each person's baptism, first communion, confirmation, and so on.

What is the plan?

Focus on the talents, accomplishments, and qualities of each family member. Explore what God's plan might be for each person. Brainstorm about ways in which each person's gifts could help fulfill that plan.

Keeping the faith

Family members might share an experience in which having faith helped them face a problem or challenge. The accounts could be recorded on paper or on video, CD, or audiocassette.

Robert Borsos
(confirmed 1979)
(married Amy 1990)
Job required relocation to Texas.

Amy (Pál) Borsos
(confirmed 1979)
(married Robert 1990)
Was afraid to leave parents but found wonderful new life in Texas.

Emil

Karl

Sari
(baptized 1995)
Had to switch schools and was nervous. Prayed for courage and made lots of new friends.

✝ A Prayer for the Week

God of Abraham, help us be people of faith. Grant us the faith to trust in your love for our family, and give us the courage to trust in your plan for us.
Amen.

3

Family Time

Something to Do . . .

On Sunday

Listen to the readings and the homily for stories about people whose faith helped them through major changes.

Through the Week

Share examples of people you know or heard about who are facing challenges but have faith.

Visit Our Web Site

 www.blestarewe.com

Something to Think About . . .

A Moral Guide to Fidelity

Abram put his faith in the LORD, who credited it to him as an act of righteousness.
Genesis 15:6

The story of Abraham and Sarah is about the trust between them and God. Abraham and Sarah took a great risk by relocating to an unknown land. God, too, risked his plan for salvation by choosing this couple. Through difficult times, Abraham and Sarah were faithful to God, and he was true to them.

The Church, in the Rite of Matrimony, tells us that a family should reflect God's love and fidelity. When your family faces difficult times, reflect on the reality of God's faithfulness to his promises and the importance of your own fidelity to each other.

Something to Know About . . .

Our Heritage

God promised Abraham, "I will bless you abundantly and make your descendants as countless as the stars of the sky and the sands of the seashore" (Genesis 22:17). Today, thousands of years later, followers of Christianity, Islam, and Judaism consider Abraham part of their religious heritage. Christianity has about 2 billion followers, including Catholics, Protestants, and members of the Eastern Orthodox Church (an Eastern Orthodox cathedral is shown at right). Islam is the religion of more than 1 billion people. Followers of Judaism number about 14 million people. In effect, we are all descendants of Abraham.

1 Revelation and Response

How varied are your works, O Lord!
The earth is full of your creatures.
They all look to you to give them food in due time.

Based on Psalm 104:24, 27

Share

Even though we can't touch God with our hands or see God with our eyes, he is all around us. God's presence can be found in many ways. Can you remember a time when you felt like God was with you?

Activity

Complete the following sentences with words that describe ways that God is with us. Some of the letters in the words are already filled in for you.

1. God speaks to us when we read the

   s c r i p t u r e s.

2. When we tell God our feelings and thoughts

   in p r a y e r, God responds to us.

3. We can see God's work in the beauty of

   n a t u r e.

4. Sometimes we feel closest to God in s i l e n c e, when everything gets quiet.

5. God's love is in the h a n d s that reach out to us when we share the Sign of Peace.

6. In the sacrament of Reconciliation, we celebrate

   God's f o r g i v e n e s s.

Now unscramble the boxed letters to spell the secret word.

Secret word: f a i t h

How should we respond to God?

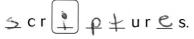

5

Hear & Believe

 ## Scripture   Abraham and Sarah

Our story of **faith** began almost 4,000 years ago with Abram, who was a descendant of Noah. Abram and his wife, Sarai, were nomadic shepherds, shepherds who moved around in search of new pastures. They had been married for a long time but had no children.

When Abram and Sarai were old and living with relatives in a land called Haran, the LORD spoke to Abram. The LORD told Abram to leave Haran and his relatives for a new land chosen by the LORD. The LORD said, "I will give you many descendants, and they will become a great nation."

Abram and Sarai did as the LORD said. Guided by the LORD, they set off for the new land. When they arrived at Shechem, a holy place in the land of Canaan in present-day Israel, the LORD spoke to Abram again. He said, "This is the land that I am going to give to your descendants." Abram built an altar for the LORD at that place.

Abram and Sarai moved on, worshiping the LORD along the way. They eventually settled in Canaan. Years passed. The LORD again spoke to Abram and said, "Look up at the sky and count the stars, if you can. You will have as many descendants as these." Abram trusted the LORD's promise.

When Abram and Sarai were very old, the LORD said to Abram, "I promise that you will have so many descendants that they will become nations. I will be your God and the God of all your descendants." He changed Abram's name to Abraham, which means "ancestor of many nations." The LORD promised that the land of Canaan would belong to Abraham's people. Then he promised that Sarai would have a son. He changed her name to Sarah, which means "princess."

The LORD asked that Abraham and his descendants honor him always. The LORD told Abraham, "Walk in my presence and be blameless."

Sarah gave birth to a son, Isaac. Sarah felt blessed to have a son in her old age. She was filled with joy and laughter.

Based on Genesis 12:1–7; 13:1–4,
12; 15:1, 5–6; 17:1–9, 15–16; 21:1–7

Models of Faith

Abraham and Sarah's trust in God and his promises showed great faith. They left for an unknown land, believing in something they could not see and knowing that God's promises would come true. They lived this definition of faith: "Faith is the assurance of things hoped for, the conviction of things not seen" (based on Hebrews 11:1). Isaac's birth was not only a gift in itself but a sign of the special relationship God had formed with Abraham and Sarah. Their descendants would become the nation of Israel.

When God asked Abraham to follow him, it was the beginning of God's loving relationship with the people he would call "my people." God was beginning a special relationship with the Hebrews, the ancestors of Jewish people. This relationship eventually embraced all people. God said to Abraham, "All the communities of the earth shall find blessing in you" (Genesis 12:3). Because of this, Abraham is the **patriarch**, or father, of the Jewish people, he is our own father in faith, and he is honored in the Islamic faith because Muslims trace their religion back to him, too. All who believe in God's mercy and love can be called children of Abraham.

Activity

The Lord told Abraham, "Walk in my presence and be blameless." Imagine that you have been asked to create a CD that captures the meaning of God's message. In the space below, write six song titles that express ways to walk in God's presence and be blameless (for example, "Pray Every Day"). Or design a CD cover, using drawings, words, or symbols that capture the meaning of God's words.

Who else in the Bible showed great faith, just as Abraham and Sarah did?

7

Mary Says Yes

All Jews descended from Abraham. In the New Testament, the Gospel writer Matthew lists the ancestors of Jesus' family, beginning with Abraham. This helps us understand how God's promise to Abraham, "All the communities of the earth shall find blessing in you," came true. In the Gospel of Luke, we read that God's promise to Abraham could not have come true without a certain woman's faith.

The angel Gabriel was sent to a town in Galilee called Nazareth, to a virgin named Mary, who was to marry Joseph. Gabriel appeared to Mary and said, "Behold, you will conceive in your womb and bear a son, and you will name him Jesus. He will be great and will be called the Son of the Most High." Gabriel then told Mary that Jesus would rule over Abraham's house and that his kingdom would never end.

Like her ancestors Abraham and Sarah, Mary trusted God. She believed that nothing was impossible for God and that what God promised her would come true. Mary said, "Behold, I am the handmaid of the Lord. May it be done to me according to your word." Mary agreed to allow God's Son to be conceived in her womb.

Based on Luke 1:26–38

Our Church Teaches

Catholics believe in **revelation**, or God's act of revealing who he is and what he wants. God makes himself known through his Son, Jesus Christ. We can know God by reading and learning the Scriptures, which teach God's word, and by living our faith according to the Tradition of the Church passed down by the apostles. We can speak with God in prayer. We can see God in creation, the sacraments, the liturgy, and the good works of our church community.

Abraham and Sarah responded to God's revelation with open hearts. They sought to know God's will, and they obeyed it completely. Saint Paul called this type of response to God "the obedience of faith" (Romans 16:26). In the same way, Mary, the mother of Jesus, trusted God's promise. When the angel told her she was going to be the mother of God's Son, Mary's faith was so strong that she answered, "May it be done to me according to your word" (Luke 1:38). Catholics are devoted to Mary and view her as a perfect model of faith.

GO TO page 360 to learn more about Mary's great faith.

Activities

1. Describe a person of faith. Choose someone you know personally or someone from the news or from history. List some qualities of this person that you admire.

   _____

   _____

   _____

2. In the New Testament we read: "What good is it, my brothers, if someone says he has faith but does not have works?" (James 2:14) Using each of the letters of the word *faith*, create new words that describe some "works" performed by faithful people (for example: *Feeding the hungry*).

   F _____

   A _____

   I _____

   T _____

   H _____

We Believe

People with faith in God welcome God's revelation. They long to understand and obey God's will completely.

Faith Words

revelation
Revelation is God's act of revealing who he is and inviting us to respond with faith.

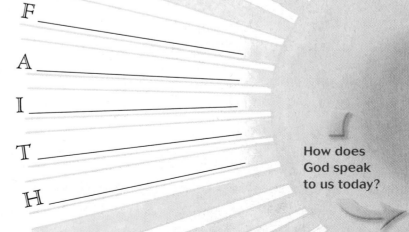

How does God speak to us today?

Respond

Complete Trust

God invites ordinary people to do his work, including us. We might react with doubt and confusion. Even Abraham, Sarah, and Mary had questions about what they were supposed to do. Yet they trusted in God completely.

Activities

1. Read the three stories. Complete the third story by writing on the lines how Rosa can respond with faith.

Abraham

Abraham believed in God's promise to make him the father of God's own people. In the beginning, he showed his devotion to God without words. He built altars to worship God at each stage of his journey to Canaan. Later, Abraham gave the LORD a gentle reminder that he was still waiting for this promise to be possible.

Abraham said, "O Lord GOD, what good will your gifts be, if I keep on being childless?" (Genesis 15:2)

God told Abraham he did not forget his promise, and Abraham believed. Then Abraham and Sarah were blessed with a baby boy.

Mary

An angel told the Blessed Virgin Mary that she would be the mother of a baby, but not just any baby—God's Son. Mary asked the angel, "How can this be, when I do not have a husband?" (Based on Luke 1:34)

But Mary accepted that she would be the mother of God's Son. Her child grew up and spread God's love throughout the world.

Rosa

Rosa and her religion class were working hard to organize a sixth-grade penance service. They chose Scripture readings, rehearsed songs, and practiced a candle-lighting ceremony.

Rosa was busy gluing letters onto a banner for the service. Being in the background was fine with Rosa. She stuttered when she was nervous, so she was happy that she didn't have a visible role in the service. Then her teacher approached her.

"Rosa," said her teacher, "you are an excellent reader. Will you do the first reading at the service?"

Rosa couldn't believe what her teacher was asking. How could Rosa stand up and read in front of everyone? Rosa thought for a moment before she responded.

_____

_____

_____

2. Our lives can take many turns. Imagine that the maze shows your life. Choose the path through the maze that would bring you closer to God. At the finish line, draw your own symbol of faith.

START

FINISH

How might we pray when we are not sure of what God wants?

11

✝ Prayer Celebration

Praying with the Faith of Abraham

Abraham's faithful offerings and prayers to God are important examples of prayer from the Old Testament. Thomas Merton, a well-known monk and writer who lived from 1915 to 1968, wrote the following prayer of trust in God. After each part, repeat:

I trust you always, though I may seem to be lost.

My Lord God,
I have no idea where I am going.
I do not see the road ahead of me.
I cannot know for certain where it will end.
Nor do I really know myself,
and the fact that I think I am following
your will does not mean that I am
actually doing so.

But I believe that the desire to please you
does in fact please you.
And I hope I have that desire in all that I am doing.
I hope that I will never do anything apart
from that desire.

And I know that if I do this
you will lead me by the right road, though I
may know nothing about it.
Therefore I will trust you always though I
may seem to be lost and in the shadow
of death.

I will not fear, for you are ever with me,
and you will never leave me to face my
perils alone. Amen.

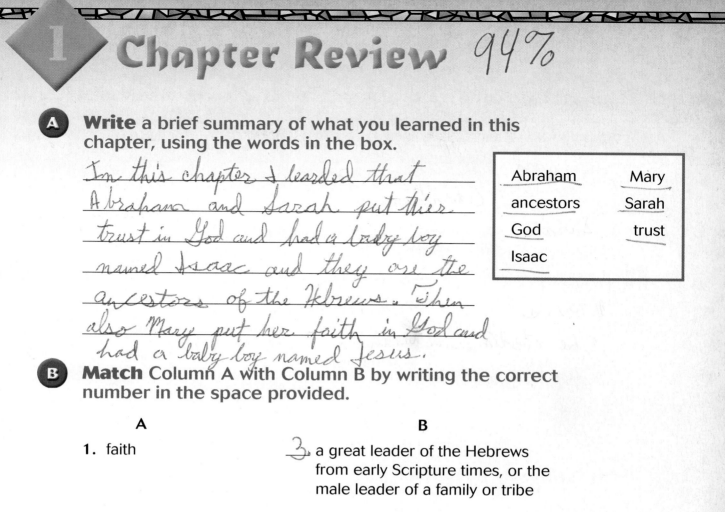

1 ◆ Chapter Review ~94%~

A **Write** a brief summary of what you learned in this chapter, using the words in the box.

In this chapter I learded that Abrahan and Sarah put thier trust in God and had a baby boy named Isaac and they are the ancestors of the Hebrews. Then also Mary put her faith in God and had a baby boy named Jesus.

Abraham	Mary
ancestors	Sarah
God	trust
Isaac	

B **Match** Column A with Column B by writing the correct number in the space provided.

A

1. faith

2. revelation

3. patriarch

B

_3_ a great leader of the Hebrews from early Scripture times, or the male leader of a family or tribe

_1_ the assurance of things hoped for, the conviction of things not seen

_2_ God's act of revealing who he is and inviting us to respond with faith

C **Write** the name of the person described by each clue.

1. My name means "princess," and I am the wife of Abraham.

   Sarah

2. I am the patriarch of the Jewish people, Christians' father in faith, and a person honored by Muslims. _Abraham_

3. I am the son of Abraham and Sarah. _Isaac_

4. I accepted the invitation to be the mother of God's Son. _Mary_

D **Complete** the statements below.

1. People with faith in God long to understand and obey God's _word **will**_

2. The patriarch _**Abraham**_ and his wife, _**Sarah**_, are models of faith because they responded to God with open hearts.

3. God began a special relationship with the _**Hebrews**_, the ancestors of the Jews.

4. "_**The obedience of faith**_" is what Saint Paul called the act of seeking God's will and then obeying it completely.

5. Catholics are devoted to _**Mary**_ and view her as a perfect model of faith.

E **Respond** to the following.

1. List three sources of God's presence in everyday life.
   **Three sources are in the church, in each other and in nature.**

2. Name three forms of God's revelation.
   **Three forms are God reveals himself to us also by reading the scriptures and by living our faith according to the Tradition of the church according to the apostles.**

3. Write a prayer that expresses your trust in God.

   _____
   _____
   _____
   _____

Number 2

E Three ways are we can see God in creation, talk to him in prayer, the sacraments, liturgy, and the good works of our church community.

Family Time

A choice of things to do at home

Sacrifice and Promise

Abraham was committed to following God's plan even when God told him to sacrifice his son Isaac. Although Abraham did not understand God's will, he had such strong faith that he was willing to do what God asked. Jesus, too, was willing to make a great sacrifice—his own life—so that we might have everlasting life.

Weekly sacrifices

Make this "Sacrifice for Others Week." Create a chart listing each family member's name next to a different day of the week. Have each person fill in something he or she will do that day to help another person or another family.

Giving thanks

Have family members write notes, make drawings, or send e-mails thanking other members for specific sacrifices they have made or promises they have kept. During the week, notice how often family members do acts of kindness or make sacrifices.

Celebrating heroes

Think of people in your family, your community, or our country who have made great sacrifices for others. Make a banner or poster that celebrates these people.

Sacrifice for Others Week			
Day	Name	Sacrifice	✓
Monday	Judith	Cook meal for neighbors.	
Tuesday	Danielle	Check on Mrs. Sisto's cat.	
Wednesday	Jennifer	Take Joe fishing.	
Thursday	Joe	Mow Grandpa's lawn.	
Friday	Paul	Drive Judith's mom to the airport.	

✝ A Prayer for the Week

Heavenly Father,
you sacrificed your Son, Jesus,
because you love us.
Keep our family strong
when our faith is tested.
Amen.

Family Time

Something to Do . . .

On Sunday

The Mass celebrates Jesus' sacrifice of his life and the promise of our salvation. Listen for the words *sacrifice* and *promise* at Mass.

Through the Week

Look for opportunities in which a small sacrifice on your part would provide pleasure to others.

Visit Our Web Site

www.blestarewe.com

Something to Think About . . .

A Moral Guide to Trials of Faith

I know now how devoted you are to God, since you did not withhold from me your own beloved son.
Genesis 22:12

It was not uncommon in Abraham's time for human sacrifice to be part of people's beliefs. In Canaan in Abraham's time, for example, people sacrificed their firstborn sons to the gods to gain favor with them. Many people have wondered if a loving God would ask a father to put his son to death. If not, what is the point of the story of Abraham and Isaac? Some scholars say that by demanding that Isaac be sacrificed, God was testing Abraham's faith. Others think Abraham believed that the God who gave him a son in his old age would never require the sacrifice of that son. What do you think?

Something to Know About . . . Our Heritage in Art

The story of Abraham and Isaac represents a profound test of a human's faith in and obedience to God. The Bible account of this story also affords a very dramatic subject for a religious painting. The Italian painter Caravaggio chose this subject matter when he created his masterpiece *The Sacrifice of Isaac* (1603).

In his paintings Caravaggio often emphasized the contrast between light and dark to heighten dramatic impact. This technique is evident in *The Sacrifice of Isaac*. This painting can now be seen in the Uffizi Gallery in Florence, Italy.

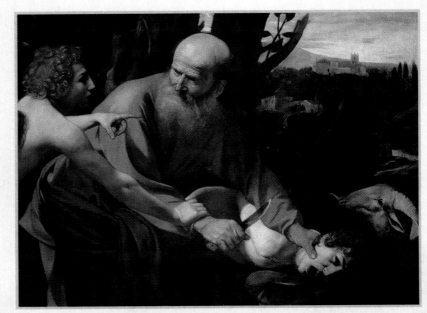

2 Sacrifice and Promise

Offer spiritual sacrifices acceptable to God through Jesus Christ.

1 Peter 2:5

Share

A dictionary definition of the word *sacrifice* is "giving up one thing for another thing thought to be more valuable." As Christians, we make sacrifices when we put God and the care of others above other things in our lives. In your own life you make sacrifices when you do good things that might help other people instead of more self-centered things. Each day, you can make "trade-offs" between things you really want and things that are better for other people or yourself.

Activity

Write the letter of each Column B item next to the Column A item for which you could trade it. Number 5 has been done for you. What word do the letters spell when you are done?

Column A

_____ **1.** Talk on the phone.

_____ **2.** Go out with your friends.

_____ **3.** Make friends with only the popular kids at school.

_____ **4.** Use the computer to play games.

__I__ **5.** Watch TV until dinner.

_____ **6.** Eat your favorite snack.

_____ **7.** Save up money to buy lots of things for yourself.

_____ **8.** Hide your belongings so that others cannot use them.

_____ **9.** Throw your clothes on the floor of your room.

Column B

C. Make friends with kids who seem lonely.

E. Clean up your room.

I. Donate some money to a good cause.

X. Help set the table for dinner.

S. Talk to God in prayer.

C. Share your belongings.

R. Use the computer for homework.

A. Go to Mass with your family.

F. Give up your favorite snack for Lent.

What great sacrifice was Abraham asked to make?

17

Hear & Believe

Worship Easter Vigil Reading

At the Easter Vigil liturgy, we celebrate the great **sacrifice** and Resurrection of Jesus. The second reading, which is from Genesis 22, is about a great sacrifice that proved Abraham's faith in God.

A reading from the Book of Genesis.

God put Abraham to the test. He called to him, "Abraham!" "Ready!" he replied. Then God said: "Take your son Isaac, your only one, whom you love, and go to the land of Moriah. There you shall offer him up as a holocaust on a height that I will point out to you."

When they came to the place of which God had told him, Abraham built an **altar** there and arranged the wood on it. Then he reached out…and took the knife to slaughter his son. But the LORD's messenger called to him from heaven, "Abraham, Abraham!" "Yes, LORD," he answered. "Do not lay your hand on the boy," said the messenger. "Do not do the least thing to him. I know now how devoted you are to God, since you did not withhold from me your own beloved son." As Abraham looked about, he spied a ram caught by its horns in the thicket. So he went and took the ram and offered it up as a holocaust in place of his son.

Again the LORD's messenger called to Abraham from heaven and said: "I swear by myself, declares the LORD, that because you acted as you did in not withholding from me your beloved son, I will bless you abundantly and make your descendants as countless as the stars of the sky and the sands of the seashore; your descendants shall take possession of the gates of their enemies, and in your descendants all the nations of the earth shall find blessing—all this because you obeyed my command."

Genesis 22:1–2, 9–13, 15–18

The word of the Lord.
Thanks be to God.

Faith in the Promise

In Abraham's time, people believed that gods controlled their fate. To stay on the gods' "good side" or to ask for special favors, they offered sacrifices of animals, food, or firstborn sons to them. But Abraham offered sacrifices to the one, true God for a different reason. A sacrifice was a way to express his feelings toward the Lord. A holocaust, or burnt offering, was offered as a loving gift to God.

Imagine how confused Abraham felt when the Lord asked him to sacrifice his own child, Isaac! This was a difficult moment for Abraham. Abraham knew that the Lord's **promise** depended upon Isaac. Isaac needed to grow up and have children of his own if God's people were to be Abraham's descendants. If Abraham tried to understand God's command without having faith, he might have refused to complete the sacrifice.

Without having faith, people could not understand how the sacrifice of Jesus' own Body was necessary for everyone to have everlasting life with God. In the Gospels, when Jesus explained this to crowds of people who followed him, they questioned him. How were they going to eat his Body and drink his Blood? Jesus answered, "Unless you eat the flesh of the Son of Man and drink his blood, you do not have life within you" (John 6:53). Jesus Christ invites us to receive his Body and Blood so we can share in everlasting life.

Faith Words

sacrifice

A sacrifice is an act of unselfish giving. It is also the act of making an offering at an altar.

altar

An altar is a raised place where sacrifices are offered. The altar used for the center of worship during the Mass is also a table.

promise

A promise is a pledge to do something.

Activity

In the New Testament, we read that we should offer ourselves as a "living sacrifice" (Romans 12:1). In this way, we fully join in Jesus' sacrifice of his Body and Blood at Mass. What does it mean to be a living sacrifice? List three ways by which you can offer yourself as a living sacrifice (for example, doing a difficult task for someone).

_____

_____

_____

Why is Jesus' sacrifice of himself so important?

The Eucharistic Sacrifice

At Mass, we celebrate a special sacrifice. We celebrate the Eucharist—the Body and Blood of Christ, which Christ offered up to God for our salvation.

"I am the bread of life," Jesus once said while he was teaching people. "Whoever eats this bread will live forever. The bread that I give is my flesh for the life of the world."

The people listened in amazement. They said to one another in disbelief, "How can this man give us his flesh to eat?"

But Jesus replied, "Unless you eat my flesh and drink my blood, you do not have life within you. Whoever eats my flesh and drinks my blood has eternal life. My flesh is true food, and my blood is true drink."

"Whoever eats my flesh and drinks my blood remains in me and I in him. Just as my Father sent me and I have life because of him, anyone who feeds on me will have life because of me. Unlike your ancestors who ate and still died, whoever eats this bread will live forever."

Some time later, before Jesus was crucified, he sat down with his apostles to eat the last meal he ever would share with them before he died. At this supper, he took some bread, blessed and broke it, and then handed it to them to eat.

"Take it; this is my body," he said.

Then he took a cup of wine, thanked his Father, and gave it to his friends to drink.

"This is my blood, which will be shed for many," he said.

Based on John 6:48–59 and Mark 14:18, 22–24

Our Church Teaches

An altar is a raised place for sacrifice and worship. Abraham built altars for God wherever God spoke to him. At Mass the changing of bread and wine into Christ's Body and Blood takes place on an altar. This altar is also a table, a place where we gather to share a meal. We gather around this table to celebrate that Jesus sacrificed himself for *us*. We celebrate what happened at the Last Supper, when Jesus shared a meal with his friends at a table. He gave them his Body and Blood in the form of bread and wine as part of a meal. Jesus invited all generations to share this meal together. We offer our own sacrifice of praise and thanksgiving to God for his blessings, especially for Jesus Christ!

Activity

At the Last Supper, Jesus said, "I will not leave you orphans; I will come to you" (John 14:18). When we receive the Body and Blood of Jesus Christ in the Eucharist, the Holy Spirit comes to us. He remains in us, and we remain in him.

Write a prayer saying "thank you" to Jesus for the gift of the Eucharist.

_____

_____

_____

_____

_____

_____

_____

_____

What promises can we make?

Giving Blood

A girl named Christina suffered from a rare and serious disease. Her only chance for recovery seemed to be a blood transfusion from her five-year-old brother, Vincent. Vincent's blood had special fighting cells that Christina needed to get better. The doctor explained the situation to Vincent and his parents.

Vincent hesitated for a second, then took a deep breath and said, "I'll give my blood if it will save Christina."

The transfusion, or transfer of blood, from Vincent to Christina began. Vincent smiled when the color started to return to Christina's cheeks. Then his smile faded and his face grew pale. He looked up at the doctor and asked with a trembling voice, "Will I start to die right away?" He had misunderstood the doctor—he thought he was going to have to give his sister all of his blood!

What was Vincent's sacrifice? What did he think he was doing?

Vincent's sacrifice was giving blood to his sister and he thought he was giving all his blood and thought he was going to die.

What does this tell you about Vincent?

This tells you that Vincent loves his sister and he was willing to give up his life for her and he is a kind person.

BLOOD DRIVE

PLEASE TURN YOUR
REGISTRATION FORM IN
BEFORE LEAVING SITE

YOU MUST HAVE YOUR
BLOOD PRESSURE TAKEN
BEFORE YOU HAVE A
BLOOD TEST.

Activities

1. God kept his promise to Abraham by sparing Isaac's life. Imagine that you are Isaac living in modern-day times. You want to send an e-mail to a friend about what happened that day in Moriah. In the e-mail below, describe what God promised your father, your feelings that day, and how God kept his promise.

To: _____

Subject: _____

2. Write a journal entry about promises you have made in your own life. At the end of your entry, write one small thing you promise to do this week for someone else.

A Promise Journal

I will be nice to people in my neighborhood.

How can we honor Jesus' sacrifice in our prayers?

Prayer Celebration

Food from Heaven

Sunday is our Sabbath, or day of rest in honor of God. We celebrate Mass. Jewish families celebrate their Sabbath from sundown on Friday to sundown on Saturday. They end the Sabbath with a ritual called "Havdalah." With a braided candle, sweet spices, and a cup of wine, they gather and pray:

Wine Blessing: Blessed are you, Lord, God of all creation; you have given us the fruit of the vine.

Spice Blessing: Blessed are you, Lord, God of all creation, Creator of the spices that bring sweetness and joy to our lives.

Candle Blessing: Blessed are you, Lord, God of all creation, Creator of the light of fire.

All: Blessed is the Lord, who separated the Sabbath day from the other days.

Based on the Jewish Havdalah prayers

The family puts the candle out with wine and wishes each other a good week.

All: Lord,
may the food we receive from heaven
give us hope and strength
to work for our own needs
and those of our brothers and sisters.

We ask this in the name of Jesus the Lord. Amen.

Prayer after communion, Mass in Time of Famine or for Those Who Suffer from Famine, Roman Missal

88

A **Write** a brief summary of what you learned in this chapter, using the words in the box.

I learned that Abraham and his son Isaac went to a mountaintop to make a holocaust in the land of Moriah. Also that if we eat of the Eucarist that we will have everlasting life and also we learned that we will have a meal and live forever in the land. We also learned about the land of Moriah. about the last meal Jesus had with his deciples.

Abraham	Eucharist
Isaac	meal
Moriah	
everlasting life	

B **Complete** the puzzle using the clues.

1. a pledge to do something

2. an act of unselfish giving, or the act of making an offering to God at an altar

3. a raised place where sacrifices are offered, the center of worship during the Mass

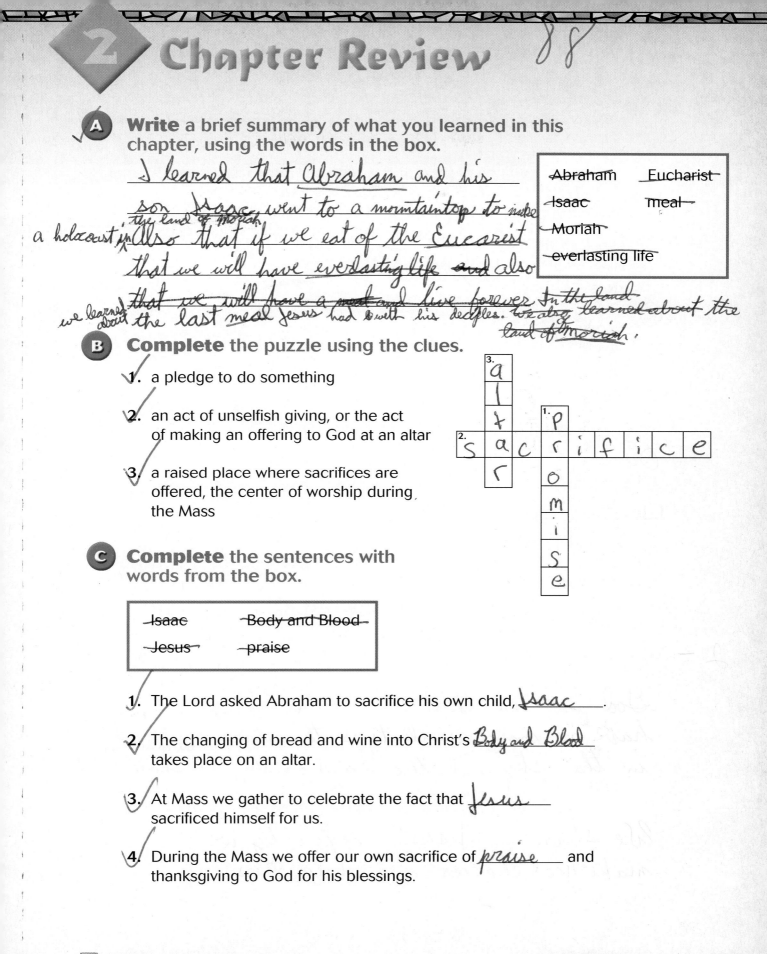

(crossword)
3. a l t a r
1. p r o m i s e
2. s a c r i f i c e

C **Complete** the sentences with words from the box.

Isaac	Body and Blood
Jesus	praise

1. The Lord asked Abraham to sacrifice his own child, *Isaac* .

2. The changing of bread and wine into Christ's *Body and Blood* takes place on an altar.

3. At Mass we gather to celebrate the fact that *Jesus* sacrificed himself for us.

4. During the Mass we offer our own sacrifice of *praise* and thanksgiving to God for his blessings.

D **Circle** the letter of the best answer.

1. Abraham took the _____ and offered it up to God as a holocaust in place of his son.
   a. lamb   c. ram
   b. dove   d. goat

2. "Unless you eat the _____ of the Son of Man and drink his blood, you do not have life within you" (John 6:53).
   a. words   c. bread
   b. flesh   d. robe

3. A _____, or burnt offering, was offered as a loving gift to God.
   a. child   c. wood
   b. animal   d. holocaust

4. Abraham built _____ for God wherever God spoke to him.
   a. altars   c. temples
   b. churches   d. statues

5. Sunday is our Sabbath, so we celebrate _____ on this day
   a. the church   c. Mass
   b. Havdalah   d. Christmas

E **Respond** to the following.

1. What did God promise Abraham for his willingness to obey God's commands and sacrifice his son?

   God promised that Abraham will have as many disendents as the stars in the sky and the sand on the sea shore

2. How do we share in Jesus' sacrifice in our daily lives?

   We share in Jesus' sacrifice by we make good chocies and help others.

Family Time

A choice of things to do at home

Covenant and Commitment

A covenant is a kind of agreement that was common in the time of the Old Testament. Covenants were sealed in many different ways. Often there was an exchange of gifts, a sacred sacrifice, a special blessing, or a ritual meal. In this chapter the children will discover some signs of the covenant between God and Israel and how this covenant was renewed with Jacob in the generations after Abraham. In many ways the same covenant has been renewed for us through Jesus.

A well of love

In the Book of Genesis, Jacob loved Rachel with a love as deep as a well. Sometimes we go for days or even weeks without telling each other how deep our love is. Write *I Love You* on a card or sew the words onto a pillow. Pass the object around when you are together at dinner.

Fidelity awards

Make a list of chores and responsibilities for each member of the family. Use stickers or stars to mark the number of times during the month each person has remembered to do his or her chore. Reward the most faithful with a chore-free week.

A covenant meal

Plan a family meal that honors a covenant your family has made, such as an agreement to care for an elderly relative. At the meal, mention the covenant in a prayer and an opening toast.

A Prayer for the Week

Lord, your covenant with Abraham's descendants fills us with wonder. You are so great, yet you promise us your faithfulness. Help us to be faithful. Thank you for your love. Amen.

Family Time

Something to Do...

On Sunday

Think about how attending Mass represents part of our covenant with God.

Through the Week

Devote an extra ten minutes to listen to, help, or just be with each member of your family.

Visit Our Web Site

www.blestarewe.com

Something to Know About...

Our Heritage

Since Bible times, Jewish family meals have often begun with blessing wine, the day, and family members. The wine is held in a special cup called a kiddush cup or blessing cup. The cup Jesus raised at the Last Supper was probably a special cup. Tradition says the apostles saved this cup and Peter used it to celebrate the Eucharist. The cup was handed down through the centuries, and its whereabouts were the subject of many legends. It became known as the Holy Grail. The only cup in existence that might be the true cup is a small agate one, shown in the photograph, located in a cathedral in Valencia, Spain.

Something to Think About...

A Moral Guide to Decision-Making

Isaac blessed Jacob, saying, "Be master of your brothers, and may your mother's sons bow down to you."
Based on Genesis 27:29

When Esau traded his birthright to Jacob for a bowl of stew, he was only thinking of his immediate needs, certainly not of his future or the future of his family. He made this irresponsible choice even though he was well aware of the responsibilities and rewards that came with his family's covenant with God. Unless we take the time to think about the results of our decisions, we can act thoughtlessly and selfishly. Families who talk through their important decisions with one another are often more successful than families who forget this important step.

3 Covenant and Commitment

May God give to you
of the dew of the heavens
And of the fertility of the earth.

Genesis 27:28

Share

In Abraham's time, agreements between people were mostly verbal, or spoken. There were no written legal contracts. Only the spoken word was required. Agreements were sealed, or made final, with symbolic rituals. In a custom we still use today, giving a blessing involved laying hands upon the head of the person being blessed. Gestures such as these still seal some of the promises or agreements we make in our everyday lives. Can you think of gestures that you have used to show that your words are truthful?

Activity

Draw a line from the gesture to the promise or thought it expresses.

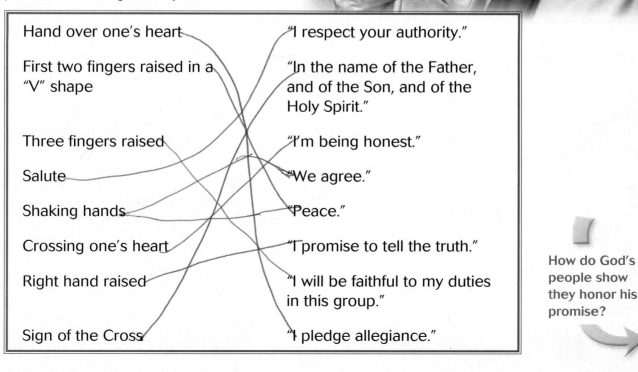

Hand over one's heart	"I respect your authority."
First two fingers raised in a "V" shape	"In the name of the Father, and of the Son, and of the Holy Spirit."
Three fingers raised	"I'm being honest."
Salute	"We agree."
Shaking hands	"Peace."
Crossing one's heart	"I promise to tell the truth."
Right hand raised	"I will be faithful to my duties in this group."
Sign of the Cross	"I pledge allegiance."

How do God's people show they honor his promise?

29

Hear & Believe

Scripture   Jacob and the Covenant

Isaac honored the **covenant** the LORD had made with his father, Abraham. But Isaac's wife, Rebecca, was unable to have children. Isaac prayed to the LORD, and Rebecca became pregnant with twin boys. Rebecca could feel the babies wrestling in her womb. She asked the LORD why the babies were fighting. The LORD told her, "Two nations are in your womb, but one will be more powerful, and the older shall serve the younger."

Esau was born first. Esau grew up to be burly and hairy, and he enjoyed being outdoors. He was Isaac's favorite. Jacob was the second son. Jacob liked simple things and would rather stay inside. Jacob was Rebecca's favorite, and she tried hard to protect him.

According to custom, Esau was entitled to Isaac's birthright, the right to become the family patriarch and receive a large inheritance when Isaac died. Esau did not care much about his birthright. He even traded it with Jacob for a bowl of stew.

One day, Isaac, who was old and ill, called for Esau so he could say a special blessing to give Esau his birthright. Isaac was blind. Rebecca remembered the LORD's words about the older boy serving the younger. To help fulfill God's promise, Rebecca helped Jacob pretend he was Esau. She dressed Jacob in Esau's clothes and hairy animal skins and sent him to see Isaac.

Isaac fell for the trick. He gave the blessing to Jacob, saying, "May God give to you
    of the dew of the heavens
And of the fertility of the earth
    abundance of grain and wine.

"Let peoples serve you,
    and nations pay you homage."

The blessing could not be taken back, even though Isaac was tricked. Esau was angry with Jacob, so Jacob went away to a safe place. He wandered to a holy place named Bethel. One night, he fell asleep with his head on a rock. He dreamed that the LORD promised him many descendants, protection, and land. These were the same promises God had made to Isaac, Jacob's father, and Abraham, Jacob's grandfather. Jacob vowed to be faithful to the LORD.

Based on Genesis 25, 27, 28:10–22

Covenant People

It was important for Jacob to receive Isaac's birthright because it meant a special blessing and the right to be the patriarch. Jacob would later have twelve sons whose children would become the Twelve Tribes, or large family groups, of Israel. Jacob's story shows how God renewed his original promise to give Abraham as many descendants as stars in the sky. Rebecca and Jacob's plot to get the birthright was dishonest, but it shows that the **fulfillment** of God's promises often happens in ordinary, unexpected ways.

In Jacob's dream at Bethel, God said to him, "I will never leave you until I have done what I promised you" (Genesis 28:15). Knowing how faithful God was, Jacob vowed to be faithful in return. Later on, Jacob would wrestle with a messenger of God, and God would change Jacob's name to Israel, which means "one who struggled." This experience changed Jacob. He was filled with wonder at the power of God.

> **Faith Words**
>
> **covenant**
> A covenant is an agreement or relationship sealed by a ritual or ceremony.
>
> **fulfillment**
> Fulfillment is the accomplishment of a promise.

Activity

The Bible has a lot to say about God's covenant with his people. Each of the following statements from the Bible teaches something about what it means to have a covenant with God. Read each statement, then write what you learn about God's covenant from it.

"Am I not protected by God? He has made an eternal covenant with me, set forth with detail and secured" (based on 2 Samuel 23:5).

_____

"I will live among you and not turn my back on you. You will be my people, and I will be your God" (based on Leviticus 26:11–12).

_____

"If you listen to my voice and keep my covenant, you will be dearer to me than all others throughout the earth" (based on Exodus 19:5).

_____

What covenant did God make with Noah?

Noah and the Covenant

The Old Testament tells this important story to explain what it means to have a covenant with God.

Long before Abraham, Isaac, and Jacob, there lived a man named Noah. He was good and decent and obeyed God. Noah and his family followed God's laws. Other people were so sinful that God had decided to send a flood that would destroy everyone.

To save Noah and his family, however, God instructed Noah to build an ark. It had to be big enough to house his family and a zoo-like variety of birds and beasts. Once the huge boat was finished and Noah and his family and all the animals had gone aboard, God unleashed a flood onto the land. Torrents of water flooded over all life and raised the ark above the mountaintops.

Once the rain ceased and the land had begun to dry out, Noah emerged from the ark.

God said to Noah, "See, I am now making a covenant with you and your descendants after you." God promised that there would never again be a flood to destroy the earth. The sign of this covenant, God told Noah, would be a rainbow.

Based on Genesis 6:5–8, 11–13; 7:21–23; 8:13, 18; 9:9–17

Whenever we see a rainbow, we can remind ourselves that God dwells with us and protects us.

Our Church Teaches

The covenant was a loving and sacred relationship between God and his people. God began this everlasting covenant with all living beings when he promised Noah that he would never again destroy the earth by flood. Noah, Abraham, Isaac, and Jacob honored the covenant by being faithful to God. We have a part in continuing this relationship. If we try to live as Christ did, honestly, simply, and lovingly, we are covenant people. The Bible says, "If you belong to Christ, then you are Abraham's descendant, heirs according to the promise" (Galatians 3:29). Jesus fulfilled the promises God made to Abraham, Isaac, and Jacob. In Jesus Christ, we have forgiveness of sin and hope of everlasting joy. Believing in Jesus, following his teachings, and participating in the Mass strengthen our **commitment** to God.

As Catholics, we have many types of covenants in our lives. Matrimony is a covenant between one man and one woman that requires them to be faithful to each other for their entire lives. Through the Holy Spirit, Confirmation strengthens our bond with the Church and our obligation to carry out its mission. We also make everyday covenants by being loyal to our friends, respecting our parents, and being honest. We try not to make promises we cannot keep. We only take oaths when necessary, and they must be truthful.

We Believe

God calls us to bear witness to our faith, in our words and through our actions.

Faith Words

commitment
A commitment is a pledge to completely accomplish a promise.

Activity

A covenant is like an agreement between two people. Both parties have duties and obligations to fulfill as part of the agreement. But God's covenant is an amazing gift. He promises to dwell with us, love us, and share with us his eternal life. List five ways that we can keep our end of the covenant.

1. ~~do not hurt others~~ act in kindness
2. ~~follow of God~~ pray
3. ~~Love one another~~ sacrifice
4. help others
5. respect others
   Love one another

How does God's love change people?

33

Saint Paul

The early Christians were often *persecuted*, or punished, sometimes even killed, for their beliefs. If Christians identified themselves publicly as Christ's followers, they put their lives at risk from those who did not believe.

Before Saint Paul was a follower of Christ, he was one of the people who hated the early Christians. His original name was Saul. Saul's mission was to persecute people who called themselves Christians.

One day, while Saul was on his way to Damascus to hunt for more Christians, a great light shone around him. Suddenly, he fell to the ground and was struck blind.

A voice said, "Saul, Saul, why are you persecuting me?"

"Who are you, sir?" Saul asked.

"I am Jesus, the one you are persecuting."

Shaken and confused, Saul asked, "What do you want me to do?" Jesus told him to go on to Damascus, where he would be told what to do. At that moment, through the power of God, Saul received the gift of faith in Jesus. Temporarily blinded, he could see the truth with his heart.

Saul was baptized. He took the name of Paul. After this experience, his mission was to teach people to know and love Jesus. After a life of preaching and imprisonment for his teachings, Paul returned the gift that Jesus gave. He gave up his life for his beliefs, dying as a martyr in Rome. Martyrs were ordinary people whose extraordinary faith enabled them to give their lives in Christ's name. The greatest sign of commitment to Jesus and the Church is dying for one's belief in Christ. Paul's story shows just how much believing in the Lord can change someone. Saint Paul's feast day is June 29.

The stories of Abraham and Sarah, Jacob, and Saint Paul show us how God's revelation can change people so much that they need new names to identify themselves. Catholics sometimes use new names to mark an important change in themselves. For Confirmation, Catholics may choose saints' names as a sign of commitment to following Christ. What is another situation in which Catholics take new names?

Activities

1. Write your full name on the lines provided. Using the letters in your name, create words that describe something special about you, and write them on the lines below.

Betsy • Carol • Roger • David • **The Name Game** • **Christine** • Carolyn • Siok-Tin

Myrtle • Mary-Jean • Regina • Elaine

Marilyn • Joyce • Irene • Olga • John

_____   _____   _____
first name   middle name   last name

_____   _____
_____   _____
_____   _____

• **Peggy** • Kathy • Nannette • **Brian** • Sara • Ray • Pat • **Janet** • Faith • Jovito • **Denise** •

2. Acts of faith are not always as dramatic as Abraham's, Jacob's, or Saint Paul's. Draw or write one thing you can do in your everyday life to show you are committed to following Jesus.

How can we pray as Isaac did?

35

✝ Prayer Celebration

God Bless You

Blessings ask God to make someone or something holy. Before their Sabbath meal, Jewish families pray blessings for the day and one another. They hold a candle-lighting ritual and a ceremony called *kiddush*, which involves blessing wine and bread. The prayers that the priest says over the gifts during Mass are similar.

Blessed are you, Lord, God of all creation,
Creator of the fruit of the vine.
You have taught us the ways of holiness through your commandments.
Blessed are you, O Lord; you make holy the Sabbath day.

Based on the Jewish kiddush blessings

Placing their hands on their children's heads, parents also bless their children. Share the following Catholic family blessing with your class today and later with your family.

Group 1: May God help you and keep you.

Group 2: May he guide you in life.

Group 1: May he bless you this evening.

Group 2: And keep you from harm.

Group 1: May God bless (make the Sign of the Cross over Group 2) you, (name the people being blessed).

Group 2: And God bless (make the Sign of the Cross over Group 1) you, too, (name the people being blessed).

Based on the Parental Blessing of Children, Canadian Catholic Conference

84

A **Circle** the gestures that indicate a promise or agreement has been made.

(Sign of the Cross)   ("thumbs up" signal)

(shaking hands)   waving a flag

(a hand over one's heart) (crossing one's heart)

crossing one's fingers   (smile)

(salute)   (right hand raised)

B **Describe** how God fulfilled his promises to Jacob and Rebecca.

God fulfilled his promises to Jacob and Rebecca by he blessed them with two boys because Rebeca was unable to have children he did this because Rebeca prayed to the lord.

C **Match** Column A with Column B by writing the correct number in the space provided.

A	B
1. covenant	_5_ a sacrament that strengthens our bond with the Church
2. fulfillment	_1_ a promise that must be truthful and only taken when necessary
3. commitment	_3_ a covenant between one man and one woman
4. Matrimony	_6_ a pledge to completely accomplish a promise
5. Confirmation	_4_ an agreement or relationship sealed by a ritual or ceremony
6. oath	_2_ the accomplishment of a promise

Complete each sentence below.

1. God promised Jacob's father, Jacob's grandfather, and Jacob _many desendents_ _protection_, and _land_.

2. Saint _Paul_ became a martyr, one who shows commitment to belief in Christ by _dying_ for it.

 List commitments that Catholics make.

Some commitments that the Catholics made make are sacraments such as Confirmation, Holy Orders, and Matrimony.

 Write a prayer that asks for God's blessing for your family by completing the sentence below.

May God bless _Me and my family by protecting me and watches watch over us_.

Circle the gesture below that you would use with the prayer above.

Laying hands on the head of a family member
(Making the Sign of the Cross)

Number the events from the story about God's covenant with Noah. The first answer is provided.

-15

_3_ _8_ God told Noah to build an ark.

_7_ God promised he would never again flood the earth.

_4_ _5_ God unleashed a flood over the land.

_1_ Many people sinned and did not follow God's laws.

_5_ _6_ The water flooded over all life on land.

_2_ God decided to send a flood to destroy everyone.

_6_ _4_ Noah came out of the ark.

Family Time

A choice of things to do at home

Piety and Prayer

Joseph was one of Jacob's sons and a patriarch, or founding father, of the People Israel. His story is one of the great adventures of all time. His jealous brothers sold him into slavery in Egypt. Through a series of miraculous events Joseph rose from being a servant to being Pharaoh's chief assistant. Throughout all the ups and downs of his life Joseph was directed by his faith in God. He trusted that God would reveal what he should do. Joseph's trust and attention to prayer were richly rewarded.

Family callings

Have family members draw outlines of themselves and fill them in with clothing, tools, or other objects that illustrate what they would like their lives to be like five or ten years from now. Talk about the work, cooperation, and trust involved in realizing your goals.

Silence, please

Joseph heard God's voice during moments of silence—in dreams and when he prayed. With computers, phones, TVs, radios, video games, and so on, most families have very little quiet time. Spend a half-hour in silence one evening this week. Then share your thoughts about what you felt.

Are you really listening?

Try to have a conversation with family members about recent family events while standing in separate rooms. Then go into the same room to continue the conversation. When you are finished, discuss the advantages of speaking to each other face to face.

A Prayer for the Week

God, help us hear your voice in our hearts and in the presence of those around us. Help us make a place for you in our busy lives.
Amen.

Family Time

Something to Do . . .

On Sunday

When the priest says, "Let us pray," speak to God quietly and listen for God speaking to you.

Through the Week

Set aside at least five minutes of quiet time each day. Write down any ideas or pleasant thoughts that come to you during these times.

Visit Our Web Site

 www.blestarewe.com

Something to Think About . . .

Supporting Each Other's Dreams

They said to one another: "We shall then see what comes of his dreams."
Genesis 37:19–20

Joseph's brothers were so worried that his dreams would interfere with their happiness that they decided to get rid of him one way or another. As it turned out, the fullfillment of Joseph's dreams saved their lives.

Envy is one of those vices that can corrode our very spirit and cause us to seek evil rather than good. Encouraging the dreams of our family members can only help everyone find happiness and fulfillment in the long run.

Something to Know About . . .

Our Heritage in Theater

Andrew Lloyd Webber and Tim Rice wrote a musical titled *Joseph and the Amazing Technicolor Dreamcoat* that recounts the Bible story of Joseph. It has fictional elements, but it also brings our attention to the plight of people who find themselves discriminated against because they are different. Joseph was a dreamer. He was less physical than his brothers and less capable of the farming and animal tending that made up the bulk of their work. But his gifts ultimately saved their lives.

4 Piety and Prayer

The Mighty One has done great things for me, and holy is his name.

Luke 1:49

Share

Finding and being a loyal friend are wonderful blessings. What do you look for in a good friend? You probably want someone with whom you can share your private feelings. You want a friend you can trust not to judge you or betray you. A good friend will also look out for your safety. Most likely, you will do the same things for your close friend, too. This is what loyal friendship is all about. In the same way, God is loyal and true to his people. God is always there when we need him to listen. God will not betray us, and he protects us always.

Activity

A local newspaper is doing a story on friendships and has chosen you and a good friend as the subjects of the article. Below, write a headline for your article, and draw two pictures about your friendship to go with the story. On the lines under each picture, write a description of what the picture shows.

PAGE 2 • THE COMMUNITY H

VOLUME 16 ISSUE 173 50¢

The COMMUNITY HERALD

How does God respond to our loyalty?

Hear & Believe

Scripture   Joseph, the Loyal Son

After Jacob left Bethel, God kept him safe. He journeyed to Haran and married a woman named Rachel. Rachel could not have children. She prayed to have a child. She finally gave birth to a son, Joseph. Jacob and his family settled in Canaan.

Jacob had eleven other sons, but his favorite son was Joseph. Joseph's eleven brothers were jealous of him, especially of a colorful tunic that Jacob had given him. They began to hate him even more when he told them about his dreams. In one dream, Joseph saw eleven stars, the sun, and the moon all bowing down to him. "Are you planning to rule us?" the brothers asked Joseph. They said to each other, "Let us kill Joseph. We can say a wild beast ate him. We shall then see what comes of his dreams!"

The brothers stripped Joseph of his tunic, threw him into a well, and left him out in the desert. Finally, they decided to sell Joseph as a slave, and passing traders took Joseph to Egypt. The brothers dipped Joseph's tunic in goat's blood and gave it to a messenger to bring to their father. "My son's tunic!" Jacob cried. "A wild beast has eaten him!"

But God protected Joseph. Joseph came to live in the home of Potiphar, an assistant of **Pharaoh**, Egypt's king. Potiphar liked Joseph and gave him the job of running his household. From then on, the LORD's blessing was upon everything in the home. But then Potiphar's wife began to flirt with Joseph. Joseph ignored her. "How could I commit so great a wrong and offend God?" he said. Potiphar's wife was insulted. To get revenge, she falsely accused Joseph of attacking her, and Joseph was thrown into jail.

Even in jail, the LORD blessed Joseph. The chief jailer put him in charge of the other prisoners. Joseph had a gift for telling other prisoners the meaning of their dreams. Pharaoh was having nightmares, so he sent for Joseph. "In one dream," Pharaoh told Joseph, "I saw seven ears of grain, growing fat and healthy. Behind them sprouted seven ears of grain, shriveled and thin. They swallowed up the seven healthy ears."

Joseph told Pharaoh, "God is telling you that seven years of plentiful food will be followed by seven years of famine." Pharaoh put Joseph in charge of storing food to prepare for the famine. When the famine came, Egypt was ready.

After two years of famine, Jacob and his other sons were running out of food. Jacob sent his sons to Egypt to buy grain, except Benjamin, the last child Rachel had before she died. Jacob's sons went to see Pharaoh's chief assistant, who was actually Joseph!

Joseph recognized his brothers, but they did not recognize him. Wanting to see his brother Benjamin, Joseph sent his brothers back to get Benjamin. The brothers feared that Jacob, still mourning over

42

Joseph, would never let them take Benjamin. But they did what Joseph asked. Joseph was so happy to see Benjamin. He told a servant to hide a silver cup in Benjamin's grain bag. Then Joseph accused the brothers of stealing it and ordered Benjamin to be jailed. The brothers panicked.

"If Benjamin is not with us when we go back home, our father will die of grief!" pleaded Judah, one of the brothers.

Joseph was touched by his brothers' concern for their father. "I am your brother Joseph," he revealed, "whom you sold into Egypt." The brothers were shocked. Joseph said he forgave his brothers because he understood God's plan for him. "It was not really you but God who had me come here, for the sake of saving lives," he said. "God has made me a father to Pharaoh, lord of his household, and ruler over Egypt."

The brothers went home and told Jacob the news, and the whole family moved to Egypt. Pharaoh treated the family well. The twelve sons of Jacob had many children and grandchildren. They all became known as the Twelve Tribes of Israel. Each tribe was named after one of Jacob's sons. The tribes waited patiently for the time they would return to Canaan.

Based on Genesis 29; 30:1, 22–24; 37; 39:1–47:12; 48:21

Faith Words

Pharaoh
Pharaoh is the title for a ruler of ancient Egypt.

fidelity
Fidelity is faithfulness and loyalty to something or someone.

piety
Piety is putting God above everything else.

An Example of Piety

Joseph brought joy to his father and reconciliation to his family. His story shows us the rewards of being loyal to God. Joseph remained faithful to God, never seeking revenge for his brothers' actions. When Joseph was tested, he did not betray God. He resisted Potiphar's wife. He was patient even when he was jailed unfairly. God rewarded him for this **fidelity** by making him a great ruler in Egypt. Even as a ruler, Joseph was humble. His only concern was how to serve God. Joseph's **piety** is an example for us.

Activity

Write about one challenge that Joseph had and how he responded. How was his response an example of piety? _____

_____

_____

How was another Joseph from the Bible an example of piety?

Saint Joseph

The Bible tells the story of another Joseph. This story is found in the New Testament and is about the man who was Jesus' foster father and Mary's husband. This Joseph had many qualities in common with Joseph in the Old Testament. Just as his Old Testament namesake, Jesus' foster father faced some extremely difficult decisions. Dreams also play an important role in his story.

Joseph was engaged to Mary when she was found to be pregnant through the Holy Spirit. Joseph was considering his difficult situation when an angel appeared to him in a dream. The angel said, "Joseph, do not be afraid to take Mary your wife into your home. For it is through the Holy Spirit that this child has been conceived in her."

When Joseph awoke he did as the angel told him.

After Jesus was born, Joseph had another dream. In it an angel told him, "Rise, take the child and his mother, flee to Egypt, and stay there until I tell you. King Herod is going to search for the child to destroy him."

Joseph immediately left for Egypt with Mary and Jesus, staying there until Herod died and was no longer a threat. In doing this he fulfilled the prophecy "Out of Egypt, I called my son."

Based on Matthew 1:18–20, 24; 2:1, 13–15

Just as Joseph in the Old Testament, Jesus' foster father obeyed God. He stood by Mary, believed the astonishing news that the child was born of God, and loved Jesus as his own. Like the Joseph before him, Mary's husband listened to God.

Our Church Teaches

As we see from the story of Joseph in the Old Testament, there will always be challenges that can keep us from God. Placed in many difficult situations, Joseph always tried to learn God's will. Separated from his own father, Joseph relied on God as his father. The story of Joseph in the New Testament teaches us similar lessons.

Sometimes we face challenges. For example, we can become distracted when we pray. Like both Josephs, we should think of God as our caring Father and try to turn our hearts back to God.

We Believe

Prayer requires keeping our hearts and minds focused on God. Because we trust God, Christians pray to God as "Father."

Activities

1. From time to time, we all are faced with tough decisions to make. Describe three ways that God helps you with these decisions.

   a. _____

   b. _____

   c. _____

2. Name moments in your life when you have needed or will need to trust God.

   How can your trust in God grow?

How did Hebrew prayers address God?

45

The Lord Helps the Lowly

Joseph's own brothers had plotted to kill him. They threw him into a ditch, and he ended up a slave. But the Bible tells us that "the LORD was with him and brought success to all he did" (Genesis 39:23). So even when Joseph became a ruler, he believed that God was responsible for all his blessings. He was a servant of God before anything else.

The Hebrews often prayed to God in hymns and songs that said they were servants of the Lord. They praised God as the protector of all humble servants. Let us sing or pray this traditional hymn, which praises God for the help he gives to faithful people who are powerless or poor.

Alleluia.
Praise the LORD, O my soul;
    I will praise the LORD all my life;
        I will sing praise to my God while
           I live.
Happy he whose help is the God
      of Jacob,
    whose hope is in the LORD,
      his God,
Who made heaven and earth,
    the sea and all that is in them;
Who keeps faith forever,
    secures justice for the oppressed,
    gives food to the hungry.

The LORD sets captives free;
    the LORD gives sight to the blind.
The LORD raises up those that were
      bowed down;
    the LORD loves the just.
The LORD protects strangers;
    the fatherless and the widow
      he sustains,
    but the way of the wicked
      he thwarts.
The LORD shall reign forever;
    your God, O Zion, through all
      generations. Alleluia.

Psalm 146:1–2, 5–10

Activities

1. Reread the lines of the hymn that are in blue. They name things that God does for people who are powerless or in need. How would you rewrite the blue lines to describe how God helps you?

The Lord _sets me free_

The Lord _gives me sight_

The Lord _loves me_

The Lord _helps me protect strangers_

The Lord _sustains me._

2. Mary, the mother of Jesus, was a Hebrew woman who may have prayed many traditional hymns such as the one you just prayed. When God asked her to be the mother of Jesus, she praised the Lord in a *canticle*, a sacred song whose words are from Scripture. Her prayer said that the Lord takes care of the poor and lifts them up.

The following song is based on Mary's prayer. Complete Verse 3 by writing two sentences, one that praises God and one that names something wonderful God has done.

Chorus:
Proclaim the greatness of God; rejoice in my God, my Savior!
Rejoice in God, my Savior!

Verse 1:
My soul is filled with joy as I sing to God my savior:
you have looked upon your servant, you have visited your people.

Chorus

Verse 2:
I am lowly as a child, but I know from this day forward
that my name will be remembered, for all will call me blessed.

Chorus

Verse 3:

I will always love God and worship him with all my soul, heart, and mind.

Chorus

Chorus: Luke 1:46–55, James Chepponis ©1989 GIA Publications, Inc.
Verses 1 and 2: Luke 1:46–55, David Haas ©1989 GIA Publications, Inc.

What were Mary's own words to God?

47

✝ Prayer Celebration

The Magnificat

Mary's canticle is called the *Magnificat*, which means "praises." The Magnificat is from Luke 1:46–55. Catholics pray it as an evening prayer.

Leader: Let us pray Mary's canticle of praise.
And Mary said:

(Kneel.)

All:
My soul proclaims the greatness of the Lord,
    my spirit rejoices in God my Savior;
for he has looked with favor on his lowly
    servant.
From this day all generations will
    call me blessed:
The Almighty has done great things for me:
    holy is his Name.
He has mercy on those who fear him
    in every generation.
He has shown the strength of his arm,
    he has scattered the proud in their
        conceit.
He has cast down the mighty from their
        thrones,
    and has lifted up the lowly.
He has filled the hungry with good things,
    and the rich he has sent away empty.
He has come to the help of his servant
        Israel,
    for he has remembered his promise of
        mercy,
the promise he made to our fathers,
    to Abraham and his children forever.

Amen.

B **Unscramble** the words and write them correctly on the lines after the sentences.

1. Early Christians were (C D E R S E E P T U), or punished, sometimes even killed, for their beliefs. _persecuted_

2. After the angel told Mary she would be the mother of God's Son, she praised God in a (N A L C T I E C), a sacred song whose words are from Scripture. _Canticle_

3. Mary's canticle is called the (A G M A C F I N T U), which means "praises." _Magnificat_ Catholics pray it as an (G N E I V N E) prayer. _evening_

4. In prayer, Christians call God (T R A F E H). _Father_

C **Circle** the letter of the best answer.

1. Joseph in the New Testament, like Joseph in the Old Testament, faced some difficult _____.

    a. wars   **b.** news   (**c.**) decisions   **d.** relatives

2. When Joseph took Mary as his wife, he showed his trust in _____.

    a. dreams   (**b.**) God   **c.** Mary   **d.** King Herod

3. If we experience _____ when we pray, we must try to turn our hearts back to God.

    (**a.**) distractions   **b.** unity   **c.** fidelity   **d.** blessings

4. Even though he was a great ruler in Egypt, Joseph's only concern was how to serve _____.

    a. his brothers   **b.** Pharaoh   **c.** Egypt   (**d.**) God

D **Write** two ways that we can know God.

We can know God ~~through~~ through prayer, and
Thanksgiving.

E **Match** Column A with Column B by writing the correct number in the space provided.

A

1. altar

2. commitment

3. covenant

4. faith

5. fidelity

6. fulfillment

7. patriarch

8. Pharaoh

9. piety

10. promise

11. revelation

12. sacrifice

B

_12_ an act of unselfish giving, or the act of making an offering to God at an altar

_4_ the assurance of things hoped for, the conviction of things not seen

_11_ God's act of revealing who he is and inviting us to respond with faith

_6_ the accomplishment of a promise

_5_ faithfulness and loyalty to something or someone

_9_ putting God above everything else

_3_ an agreement or relationship sealed by a ritual or ceremony

_2_ a pledge to completely accomplish a promise

_1_ a raised place where sacrifices are offered, the center of worship during the Mass

_10_ a pledge to do something

_7_ a great leader of the Hebrews from early Scripture times, or the male leader of a family or tribe

_8_ the title for a ruler of ancient Egypt

F **Write** the Magnificat on a separate sheet of paper.

God Saves and Delivers Us

God saved the Hebrew people from slavery in Egypt. Through the life, death, and Resurrection of Jesus Christ, we are freed from the slavery of sin to live as the new people of God.

Sing to the LORD, for he is gloriously triumphant;
horse and chariot he has cast into the sea.

Exodus 15:21

Hebrew slaves may have helped build this statue of Pharaoh Ramses II. The map shows the Hebrew people's journey out of Egypt to the promised land.

Mediterranean Sea

Sea of Galilee

Jaffa

Promised Land

Jordan R.

Gaza

CANAAN

Jerusalem

Jericho

Dead Sea

Goshen

SINAI

Memphis

Exodus

E G Y P T

Gulf of Suez

Mt. Sinai

Red Sea

Journey
to the
Promised
Land

Wade in the Water

African-American spiritual
Arranged by Diana Kodner

REFRAIN
All:

Wade ____ in ____ the wa-ter, wade ____ in ____ the wa-ter, chil-dren, wade ____ in ____ the wa-ter, God's a gon - na trou - ble ____ the wa - ter.

VERSE
Cantor:

1. See ____ that ____ host all dressed ____ in white, ____
2. See ____ that ____ band all dressed ____ in red, ____
3. Look ____ o - ver yon - der, what do I see? ____
4. If you don't be-lieve I've been ____ re - deemed, ____

All:

God's a gon - na trou - ble ____ the wa - ter;

Cantor:

The lead - er looks like the Is - ra-el - ite, ____
Looks like ____ the band that ____ Mo - ses led, ____
The Ho - ly Ghost a ____ com - in' on me, ____
Just fol - low me down to ____ Jor - dan's stream, ____

All: D.C.

God's a gon - na trou - ble ____ the wa - ter.

Arrangement © 1994, GIA Publications, Inc.

Family Time

A choice of things to do at home

Slavery and Deliverance

The story of Moses and the Exodus is a key part of the salvation story of God's people. God spoke to Moses in a burning bush and asked Moses to lead the Israelites out of slavery to their own land. Through escaping slavery in Egypt, the Israelites learned new lessons about themselves as God's special people. We can learn from their story and from our own family journeys.

Family hieroglyphics

The ancient Egyptian alphabet, called hieroglyphics, consisted of symbols that represented letters. Create an alphabet of symbols that mean something to your family. For instance, a stick figure of a girl could represent the letter *J* if there is a girl in the family named Jennifer.

Pyramid project

Investigate how pyramids were built using the Internet or an encyclopedia. Have family members cover rectangular tissue boxes in red construction paper and build their own pyramids.

New address, new life

The journey out of Egypt was hard for the Israelites. They accused Moses of freeing them only to let them die in the desert. If your family has ever moved, have each family member list the pros and cons of moving.

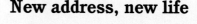

✝ **A Prayer for the Week**

Our freedom is a gift. Thank you, God, for freedom from sin. Help us love each other freely and live free from temptation. Amen.

Family Time

Something to Do . . .

On Sunday

Listen to the second reading at Mass for themes of slavery and freedom.

Through the Week

"Although I am free, I have made myself a slave to all," said Saint Paul. Be aware of ways to serve others this week.

Visit Our Web Site

www.blestarewe.com

Something to Think About . . .

A Moral Guide to Deliverance

But the Lord said, "I have witnessed the affliction of my people and have heard their cry."
Exodus 3:7

Ordinary human beings are agents for bringing God's aid to those who need it. This is clearly demonstrated in the story of Moses. Moses was viewed as almost more Egyptian than Hebrew, yet God told Moses that he had chosen Moses to free God's people, the Hebrews. Remember that Moses was an ordinary person, just as you, whom God had called to carry out an unexpected but important mission. When you notice someone is suffering and you help out, you are bringing God's relief to that person's pain.

Something to Know About . . .

Our Heritage in History

Saint Peter Claver, a Spanish Jesuit missioner, was sent to Cartagena (part of modern Colombia) in 1610. Cartagena was a port of entry for African slave trading ships. Peter soon found himself busy with all the sick and demoralized slaves who had survived the inhumane treatment on the ships. He went into the holds of the ships and gave the slaves food and water. He told them about Jesus. He told them that they were precious in God's eyes. Slave owners believed that slaves only had worth as

This is a painting of the hold of a slave ship.

property, so Saint Peter Claver's message was a subversive one. He called himself "a slave to the Negroes forever." His feast day is September 9.

5 Slavery and Deliverance

Sing to the LORD, for he is gloriously triumphant;
horse and chariot he has cast into the sea.

Exodus 15:21

Share

When you hear the word *slave*, what do you think of? You may not know this, but people can become enslaved in their hearts and spirits. Poverty, prejudice, addiction, violence, materialism, and other wrongs in society prevent people from seeking goodness and happiness. They lose their freedom to live peacefully and lovingly. How does faith in God help free people from various kinds of slavery?

Activity

Complete the sentences under each photograph.

The people in this picture have become slaves of _poverty_.
They do not have the freedom to _live happily, to have a home_.

The people in this picture have become slaves of ~~An an~~ _materialism_.
They do not have the freedom to _share, appreciate the little things in life_.

Pick one photograph and write how the people in it might be delivered, or freed, from their slavery. _____

_____

What does **Yahweh** mean?

61

Scripture   The Exodus

Before Joseph died, he told his brothers, "God will surely lead you to the land he promised to Abraham, Isaac, and Jacob." For many years, the descendants of Joseph's family prospered in Egypt. They were known as the Hebrews or Israelites.

But then a new Pharaoh told the Egyptians, "The Israelites keep growing! Let us stop them before they become powerful." He made the Hebrews slaves, forcing them to build cities and work in fields.

The Hebrew families kept growing. Pharaoh ordered, "Throw every Hebrew baby boy into the river!" Jochebed, a Hebrew woman, gave birth to a son. To keep him from being killed, she hid him. Later, she put him in a basket and placed it in the reeds on the riverbank. Pharaoh's daughter spotted the baby. She adopted him and named him Moses.

A long time passed. The Israelites cried out to God about their slavery. One day, after Moses grew up, he was leading a flock of sheep across the desert. He saw fire coming out of a bush but not burning it.

Moses heard the LORD say, "Come no closer! This is holy ground. I am the God of your father, the God of Abraham, the God of Isaac, the God of Jacob. I have seen my people suffer in Egypt. I will rescue them. I will lead them out of Egypt into a land flowing with milk and honey. Go to Pharaoh to lead my people, the Israelites, out of Egypt."

"But," Moses said, "if I tell the Israelites, 'The God of your fathers sent me to you,' and they ask, 'What is his name?' what should I say?"

God said, "I am who I am. Tell the Israelites: **Yahweh** sent me to you."

Moses went to Pharaoh and said, "The LORD, the God of Israel, has said, 'Let my people go.'"

Pharaoh answered, "Who is the LORD that I should obey his plea to let Israel go?" He made the Israelites work harder.

Because Pharaoh would not obey, plagues came upon the land. The Nile River turned into blood. Frogs, gnats, flies, animal disease, boils, hail, locusts, and three days of darkness came. Pharaoh still did not give in. Then the LORD commanded the Hebrew families to prepare a special meal and mark their doorways with lamb's blood so that the next plague would "pass over" their homes. It would be a plague of death! That night, all the firstborns in Egypt died, even Pharaoh's son. Pharaoh sent for Moses. "Leave now, you and the Israelites with you!" he cried.

The Israelites marched out of Egypt. But suddenly Pharaoh wished he had not let the Israelites go. He sent out more than 600 chariots with warriors to catch them.

Pharaoh's armies caught up with the Israelites at the Red Sea. The Israelites called out to the LORD in great fright. The LORD told Moses, "Stretch your hand out over the sea." When Moses did this, the LORD

swept the sea with a strong wind, turning the sea into dry land. The Israelites marched in, with a wall of water on their right and left. When the Egyptians chased after them, the water flowed back, drowning Pharaoh's whole army.

The Israelites sang songs thanking the LORD for leading them safely toward the **promised land**. Moses' sister, Miriam, took a tambourine in her hand, and the women followed her, dancing and praising the LORD.

Based on Genesis 50:24 and Exodus 1—15:21

God's Love Delivers Us

The story about God's freeing the Israelites from slavery and leading them out of Egypt is called the **Exodus**. Exodus is the second book of the Old Testament. The Israelites in Egypt believed in God's promises to their ancestors, so they cried out to God for help. God chose Moses to lead the Israelites to freedom and give them God's word.

At the burning bush, God revealed an important mystery he had not revealed to the patriarchs Abraham, Isaac, Jacob, and Joseph. God told Moses his sacred name: "Yahweh," which means "I am who I am." This means God is the only God, who exists forever. No one created God. God created everything and everyone. Only God has this power to create. He immediately creates our souls with the plan to reward us with everlasting life. All creation is destined for God's glory. God gives us unique personalities and talents to serve him now and in our everlasting life with him. His gift of everlasting life is the greatest deliverance of all.

Activity

Moses delivered God's people from slavery under the Egyptians. In the space below, describe one form of slavery from which Jesus frees you.

_____

_____

_____

Faith Words

Yahweh

Yahweh is the most sacred name of God, spoken to Moses. It means "I am who I am."

promised land

The promised land is Canaan, the sacred place God promised to Abraham, Isaac, Jacob, and the Israelites in Egypt.

Exodus

The Exodus is the Old Testament story of how God freed the Hebrews in Egypt.

What did Jesus say about everlasting life?

Hear & Believe

A Question About Everlasting Life

One day, there were some people in a crowd Jesus was teaching who did not believe what Jesus said about life after death. These people did not believe there was any kind of everlasting happiness after death. People at that time believed that when a man who had no children died, the man's brother had a duty to marry the widow and have children. In this way, the brother could pass down the family heritage and property. The people in the crowd decided to ask Jesus a trick question about everlasting life.

"Teacher," they said, "Moses said, 'If someone's brother dies and leaves a wife but no child, he must take up the wife and raise up descendants for his brother.' Say there were seven brothers. The first married a woman but died childless. Then the second and the third married her, and so on, but all seven died childless. Now, if all seven had been married to her, when they rose again, which one would be the woman's husband?"

"People today marry and remarry," Jesus answered, "but only the children of God can enter the kingdom of heaven. The people to whom God gives the reward of everlasting happiness are like angels. They will not need to marry in the kingdom. They will no longer die but will rise again."

Jesus explained, "Moses even let you know that the dead will rise again. When the voice in the burning bush told him, 'I am the God of Abraham, the God of Isaac, the God of Jacob,' Moses said it was the Lord. Yes, the Lord is not the God of the dead but of the living. To him all are alive."

Some of Jesus' listeners said to him in reply, "Teacher, you have answered well." And Jesus' opponents no longer dared to ask him any questions.

Based on Luke 20:27–40

Our Church Teaches

The Book of Exodus describes one of the most important saving acts of God. The Old Testament is filled with signs of God's love and faithfulness. But the New Testament tells of God's greatest act of love: sending his Son, Jesus, into the world to save all people. Jesus suffered and died for our sins. Because of Jesus, the Church can forgive any sin, no matter how great. Jesus Christ rose from the dead and ascended into heaven. We can share in the promised land of heaven. Because of Jesus Christ, people do not have to be afraid of death. Death leads to everlasting happiness if we love God and others as Jesus taught.

We Believe

Jesus Christ conquered death for us. At our baptisms he gives new life to our souls. He will also give new life to our bodies in the kingdom of heaven.

Activities

1. Jesus said that the Lord is not the God of the dead but of the living. To God, all are alive. The Church has a tradition of praying for both the living and the dead. In the space below, name one person, living or dead, for whom you wish to pray, and write a short prayer for that person.

Name: _____

Prayer: _____

_____

_____

_____

_____

2. What questions do you have about life after death?

_____

_____

_____

_____

How do God's people express their need to be free?

65

Bound by Faith

In the eighteenth and nineteenth centuries, African people were forced to come to America as slaves. African slaves were robbed of their freedom and self-esteem. They suffered in many of the same ways as the Hebrews.

To help them survive, Africans sang songs called *spirituals*. Spirituals expressed the slaves' faith in God. The slaves sang about a journey to spiritual as well as physical freedom and asked Jesus to set them free "on the inside." They called on the heroes of the Old Testament as friends who could help them in their struggles. One person began the spiritual by singing about his or her sadness or joy. A group would sing a response. The following spiritual is called "Go Down, Moses."

Solo: When Israel was in Egypt's land

Group: Let my people go!

Solo: Oppressed so hard they could not stand

All (refrain):
Let my people go!
Go down, Moses,
'way down in Egypt's land.
Tell ol' Pharaoh to
let my people go!

Solo: The Lord told Moses what to do

Group: Let my people go!

Solo: To lead the children of Israel through

Refrain

Solo: As Israel stood by the water side

Group: Let my people go!

Solo: At God's command it did divide

Refrain

Solo: When they had reached the other shore

Group: Let my people go!

Solo: They sang a song of triumph o'er

Refrain

Solo: Oh, let us all from bondage flee

Group: Let my people go!

Solo: And let us all in Christ be free

Refrain

Did You Know...

...African slaves used their songs as secret codes? The song "Steal Away to Jesus" was used to call secret meetings. Frederick Douglass, a slave liberator, used the line "I am bound for Canaan" to signal that he was going North.

Activity

The ancient Egyptian alphabet was made of pictures instead of letters. The pictures are called *hieroglyphics*. The key shows hieroglyphics for the letters in our alphabet. Use it to translate the song Miriam sang when the Hebrews crossed the Red Sea.

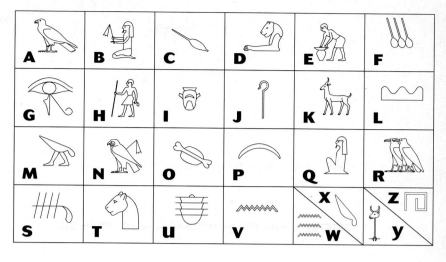

A	B	C	D	E	F
G	H	I	J	K	L
M	N	O	P	Q	R
S	T	U	V	X / W	Z / Y

M i r i a m s a n g,

"S I N G T O T H E

L O R D ! H O R S E

A N D C H A R I O T

H E H A S C A S T

I N T O T H E

S E A."

How can we praise our God, the God of Moses?

✝ Prayer Celebration

Free at Last

After crossing the Red Sea, the Israelites understood more fully the power of Yahweh. Their praises went up to God in a song. God has freed us all from sin and death by his Son, Jesus Christ. Let us stand and praise him, using the Israelites' song.

Leader: Let us sing to the Lord who is covered in wondrous glory.

All: Let us sing to the Lord who is covered in wondrous glory.

Leader: I will sing to the Lord, in glory triumphant;
horse and rider are thrown to the sea.
God of strength, of song, of salvation, God of mine,
hear these praises.

All: Let us sing to the Lord who is covered in wondrous glory.

Leader: My God is a warrior whose name is "The Lord."
Pharaoh's army is thrown to the sea.
Your right hand is magnificent in pow'r,
your right hand has crushed the enemy.

All: Let us sing to the Lord who is covered in wondrous glory.

Leader: In your mercy you led the people you redeemed.
You brought them to your sacred home.
There you will plant them on the mountain that is yours.
The Lord shall reign forever!

All: Let us sing to the Lord who is covered in wondrous glory.

Text: Exodus 15; Naimh O'Kelly-Fischer ©1992 GIA Publications, Inc., Chicago, Illinois
All rights reserved. Used with permission.

A **Respond** to the following questions.

1. What is God's greatest act of love?

   Sending his Son, Jesus, into the world to save all people

2. What did Jesus do so that we can share in the promised land of heaven?

   6 —

   Jesus rose from the dead and ascended into heven.

B **Circle** the letter of the best definition.

1. the promised land

   a. Judea

   (b.) Canaan

   c. Galilee

   d. Egypt

2. Yahweh

   a. another name for Moses

   b. the land of milk and honey

   (c.) God's most sacred name

   d. a word that means "praises"

3. Exodus

   (a.) the story of the Hebrews' escape to freedom

   b. the story of Abraham as a slave

   c. the story of Pharaoh and and his family

   d. the story of the Israelites' discovery of Egypt

4. spiritual

   a. a song about America

   b. a song about sickness

   c. a book of religious verses

   (d.) a religious song created by slaves

C **Describe** the event from Moses' life that Jesus used to teach about everlasting life.

The event is when Moses goes to the burning bush. The line that Jesus used is "He immediatly creates our souls with the plan to reward us with everlasting life."

D **Complete** the lists below to show ways that people can be enslaved spiritually and materially.

Materially enslaved:

1. always asking for things

2. always wanting more than you have

3. ~~or~~ being addicted to fasion.

4. ~~always asking for new things~~ being addicted to drugs.

Spiritually enslaved:

1. being jealous of others

2. always wanting to be like someone else

3. not caring for others

4. hurting others.

E **Praise** God in song for the gift of your freedom by completing the lyrics below.

I will sing to the Lord who is God ~~of all that~~ who frees all people.

My God shall free everybody.

I will sing to the Lord who is God of all Gods.

_____.

 F **Explain** the meaning of the statement "God's love delivers us."

The meaning of the statement "God's love delivers us" is the story of God freeing the Israelites from slavery and leading them out of Egypt. Witch is also called the Exodus.

Family Time

A choice of things to do at home

Passover and the Eucharist Celebration

This chapter recalls the Old Testament story of the Passover, when God delivered his people from the plague of death in Egypt and Pharaoh let the Israelites go. We remember that Jesus' "passover" to God gave us the freedom of salvation. We celebrate this deliverance in the liturgy and in our feasts, especially Easter.

Family identity

The Israelites were bound together as God's people. To symbolize your family's unity, have everyone dress in the same colors one day this week. Or make reduced photocopies of your family crest, cut them out, and make badges for all to wear.

Feasts around the world

What do you know about the origins of Easter customs? Rabbits and colored eggs were actually symbols of new life from pagan spring festivities long ago. List ways of celebrating Easter that are unique to your family or culture.

Remembrance meal

When Jewish families celebrate Passover, they share the Seder, a meal of symbolic foods. Plan a meal that celebrates an important event in your family's history. Choose foods that represent this event. "Toll House" cookies could commemorate your move into a new home, for example.

✝ A Prayer for the Week

Lord, you instructed the angel of death to pass over the homes of your people. Keep us safe in your love forever. Amen.

Family Time

Something to Do . . .

On Sunday

Thank God for his blessings after you receive the Eucharist.

Through the Week

Keep a journal of anything that you would consider a blessing from God. Thank God at the end of each entry.

Visit Our Web Site

 www.blestarewe.com

Something to Think About . . .

Remembering God's Goodness

God said, "This day shall be a memorial feast for you, which all your generations shall celebrate."
Based on Exodus 12:14

The Lord told his people to keep the day of their Passover holy, and so they have. One Passover song that celebrates God's goodness is the *Dayenu*, which means "That would have been enough." The Dayenu names actions God took that would have been enough for his people, then describes how God went beyond those actions and showered his people with blessings. This prayer of gratitude is a model for the way we should respond to the gift of Jesus in the Eucharist.

Something to Know About . . . Our Heritage in Art

The Last Supper was a traditional Jewish meal, but it had a whole new meaning because of Jesus' great sacrifice. The Last Supper is the subject of one of the world's most famous paintings: Leonardo da Vinci's *The Last Supper*. The masterpiece is a fresco, or wall painting, located in the church of Santa Maria delle Grazie in Milan, Italy. It miraculously survived bombings in World War II only to be threatened with deterioration from climatic conditions in the church. Fortunately, a vast restoration project has saved da Vinci's painting from destruction.

6 Passover and the Eucharist Celebration

Blessed is God forever, and blessed is his holy name.

Share

Many celebrations have unique symbols. The Jewish feast of the Exodus, called *Passover*, is held around Easter time, for seven or eight days. On the first night, Jewish families have a meal called the Seder. They share foods eaten by the Hebrews on the night that the plague of death passed over their homes. The Seder foods are symbols. Bitter herbs represent the Hebrews' bitter slavery. Lamb represents the lamb's blood on the Hebrews' doorways. Unleavened bread—bread baked without yeast—represents the hurry to flee Egypt. (There was no time for bread to rise.)

Activity

Under each symbol write the celebration or holiday it represents.

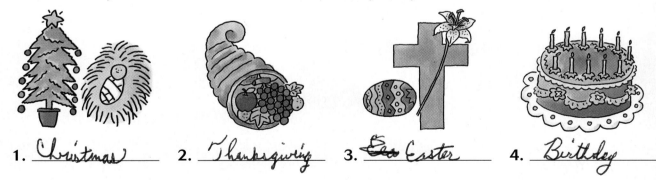

1. _Christmas_   2. _Thanksgiving_   3. _~~Eas~~ Easter_   4. _Birthday_

5. Choose one of the events above, and name items that are part of your family's celebration of it.

On Thanksgiving my family has turkey, stuffing, cranberries, and potatoes.

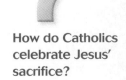

How do Catholics celebrate Jesus' sacrifice?

73

Worship   Mass of the Lord's Supper

Holy Thursday is a very important day in the Church's calendar of celebrations, the **liturgical year**. Holy Thursday honors the night on which Jesus shared the Last Supper with the Twelve Apostles. He washed their feet to teach them about serving others. Then the apostle Judas handed Jesus over to be arrested. Jesus was crucified the next day, Good Friday. His followers kept vigil outside his tomb on the following day, Holy Saturday. The period from Holy Thursday evening until the evening prayer on Easter Sunday is the *Easter Triduum*.

During the Holy Thursday Evening Mass of the Lord's Supper, we remember the Last Supper and prepare for the remembrance of Jesus' crucifixion. Priests and parishioners act out the Gospel reading about Jesus' washing of the apostles' feet. The first reading is about the final plague God brought upon Egypt: death to the firstborns. God told Moses how the Israelites should prepare for, and remember, this event.

A reading from the Book of Exodus.

The LORD said to Moses and Aaron in the land of Egypt, "Tell the whole community of Israel: On the tenth of this month every one of your families must procure for itself a lamb, one apiece for each household…You shall keep it until the fourteenth day of this month, and then, with the whole assembly of Israel present, it shall be slaughtered during the evening twilight. They shall take some of its blood and apply it to the two doorposts and the lintel of every house in which they partake of the lamb. That same night they shall eat its roasted flesh with unleavened bread and bitter herbs….

"This is how you are to eat it: with your loins girt, sandals on your feet and your staff in hand, you shall eat like those who are in flight. It is the Passover of the LORD. For on this same night I will go through Egypt, striking down every first-born of the land, both man and beast, and executing judgment on all the gods of Egypt—I, the LORD! But the blood will mark the houses where you are. Seeing the blood, I will pass over you; thus, when I strike the land of Egypt, no destructive blow will come upon you.

"This day shall be a memorial feast for you, which all your generations shall celebrate with pilgrimage to the LORD, as a perpetual institution."

Exodus 12:1, 3, 6–8, 11–14

The word of the Lord.
Thanks be to God.

The Passover of the Lord

Jesus' death and Resurrection took place during the Jewish feast of **Passover**. But Jesus gave Passover a whole new meaning. The Last Supper may have been a Passover meal. At the Last Supper, Jesus blessed the traditional bread and wine, then distributed them as his Body and Blood. He said, "Do this in memory of me" (Luke 22:19). Jesus was giving God's people a new tradition. He was about to "pass over" to new life in God through his death, Resurrection, and Ascension. His Body and Blood would enable his followers to pass over to God's kingdom, too. These gifts would keep Jesus Christ alive in the Church.

Our liturgies celebrate the great mystery that gave us the chance for happiness in God's kingdom: the Passion (suffering), death, Resurrection, and Ascension of Jesus. This is the **Paschal mystery**. We honor it at Mass in communion, songs, prayers, and readings. The seasons of the liturgical year also celebrate parts of the Paschal mystery. Easter celebrates Jesus' Resurrection. Lent is a season of sacrifice and preparation for Easter. The Triduum honors the events of Jesus' death and Resurrection. Jesus' Ascension is celebrated forty days after Easter. Our liturgies also honor people already in heaven—Mary and the saints.

GO TO page 367 for more information about the liturgical year.

Faith Words

liturgical year
The liturgical year is the Church's yearly calendar of celebrations and seasons.

Passover
Passover is the Jewish celebration of the Exodus from Egypt.

Paschal mystery
The Paschal mystery is the way that Jesus' Passion, death, Resurrection, and Ascension saved us from sin and gave us life after death.

Activity

Explain this statement: "Jesus gave Passover a whole new meaning."

_____

_____

_____

_____

_____

What events in the Bible are signs of the Paschal mystery?

The Feeding of the Five Thousand

Jesus, mourning the death of John the Baptizer, had wandered off to a deserted place. However, people soon learned where he was headed, and a vast crowd was there to meet him. When Jesus got off the boat and saw the crowd, his heart was moved with pity for them and he cured their sick.

Evening was rapidly approaching. Seeing this, Jesus' disciples urged him to dismiss the crowd so that people could go home for supper. Jesus had another idea. He told his disciples, "There is no need for them to go away; give them some food yourselves."

The disciples quickly pointed out that there were only five loaves of bread and a couple of fish. Jesus said, "Bring them here to me."

After inviting the crowd to make themselves comfortable on the grass, Jesus took the loaves and fish. He said a blessing and broke the bread. He then handed the food to his disciples, who in turn distributed it to all the people. Amazingly, all five thousand men as well as all the women and children ate until they were full. And there were even leftovers—enough to fill twelve baskets!

Based on Matthew 14:13–21

Our Church Teaches

Our Church teaches that Passover was a sign of the sacrifice of Jesus Christ. Just as a lamb was sacrificed to save the Israelites, Jesus sacrificed his life on the cross to save all people. The Church also teaches that Jesus' miracle of feeding 5,000 followers with five loaves of bread was a sign of the special food he would give the whole world: the Eucharist. We celebrate the Eucharist with confidence that we will one day be able to enjoy the glory of heaven. We are sure of this because God gave us the gifts of the Body and Blood of his Son.

Activities

1. Reread the Scripture story. Imagine that you are in the crowd gathered in the deserted place. In your own words tell the story of what happens.

   _____

   _____

   _____

   _____

   _____

   _____

The Last Supper by the Perea Master
(1400–1500)

2. Think about the similarities and differences between a Passover feast and a eucharistic celebration. Then complete the chart below.

Passover Feast and Eucharistic Celebration

Similarities	Example: They both celebrate God's love for us.
Differences	

How do you celebrate the freedom God gave you?

Children Freeing Children

Do you think a twelve-year-old can affect the decisions of world leaders? If you are Craig Kielburger, you do.

When Craig was twelve in 1995, he read about a boy in Pakistan named Iqbal Masih. Masih had been sent to work in a carpet factory when he was only four years old. He was supposed to help his parents pay off a loan. Masih worked twelve hours a day, six days a week. He could not even play or go to school. As he got older, Masih began to speak out against the child labor practices of his country. Then, at the age of twelve, he was murdered for speaking out.

This story shocked Craig. Craig discovered that millions of children around the world were forced into labor. With his friends in his native Canada, Craig formed an organization called Kids Can Free the Children. Its members were determined to get governments to do something about child labor. They handed out fliers and gave speeches. They set up displays in public places. They wrote letters to world leaders insisting that they take action immediately.

People all over the world started signing petitions urging governments to stop child labor. Because of Craig and others, some laws have been changed. New programs help poor families so that children are not forced to work. Kids Can Free the Children also collects donations to help educate poor children. Today, Kids Can Free the Children is worldwide, with members in more than twenty countries. Your parish may even have a chapter.

Adults make Kids Can Free the Children's legal and financial decisions, but only young people represent the organization to the public and decide how it is run. Youngsters in many nations are now free to celebrate their youth, all because of Craig and other young people who had the gift of freedom and wanted to share it.

Activities

1. Since the earliest times, people have used art to celebrate God and his love. Stained-glass windows are an example of this. In the outline design a stained-glass window with signs of God's love for you.

2. Jewish families end the Seder with a prayer thanking God for freeing them. Write a prayer thanking God for the freedoms we have.

How do we celebrate the Paschal mystery in prayer?

✝ Prayer Celebration

Make Us a Blessing

Did you ever listen closely to the offering prayers the priest says after the bread and wine are brought to the altar during Mass? The prayers come from blessings Jesus said at the Last Supper.

Priest: Blessed are you, Lord, God of all creation.
Through your goodness we have this bread to offer,
which earth has given and human hands have made.
It will become for us the bread of life.

Congregation: Blessed be God forever.

Priest: Blessed are you, Lord, God of all creation.
Through your goodness we have this wine to offer,
fruit of the vine and work of human hands.
It will become our spiritual drink.

Congregation: Blessed be God forever.

Roman Missal

Over foods at the Passover Seder, Jewish families say prayers such as "Blessed are you, Lord, God of all creation, because you…." Later, they may pray, "On this day of liberation, make us a blessing." Let us thank God for our own liberation and ask him to make us a blessing.

Leader: Blessed are you, Lord, God of all creation, because you have made us free to (complete the prayer).

All: Blessed be God forever.

Leader: On this day, make us a blessing by helping us to (complete the prayer).

All: Blessed be
God forever.
Amen.

*Based on prayers from
the Passover Haggadah*

A **Respond** to the following.

1. Circle three foods that are part of the Seder meal that Jewish families eat on the first night of Passover.

fish   pepper
(bitter herbs)   (unleavened bread)
spinach   (lamb)
yeast rolls   olives

2. Write the name of each Seder food from the list above and explain what it symbolizes.

Food: **Meaning:**

bitter herbs   *the bitter slavery of the Hebrews*

unleavened bread   *the hurry to leave Egypt*

lamb   *the lambs blood on the doorways.*

B **Describe** how some children in nations around the world have been "set free" by the efforts of Craig Kielburger and others like him.

Some people in different parts of the world have been set free by the efforts of Craig and the group he started are by theirs are now child labor laws that kids can not work until they are adults.

C **Define** <u>Easter Triduum</u> and <u>Holy Thursday</u>.

The Easter Triduum is the days before Jesus rose to new life and those days are Holy Thursday, Good Friday, and Holy Saturday and Easter. Holy Thursday is the day that Jesus had the Last Supper with his disiples and Jesus washed thier feet. The church celebrates this by washing the feet of 12 people to reminp us what Jesus did on Holy Thursday.

D Complete the sentences below with words from the box.

Passover	~~sin~~	~~God~~
~~cross~~	~~Last Super~~	~~Paschal mystery~~
~~Eucharist~~	~~death~~	~~liturgical year~~

1. The event of _____ was a sign of the sacrifice of Jesus Christ.

2. The _Last Supper_ may have been a Passover meal.

3. The Church's yearly calendar of celebrations and seasons is called the _liturgical year_

4. Our liturgies celebrate the ~~Paschal mystery~~ _Paschal mystery_ the way that Jesus' Passion, death, Resurrection, and Ascension saved us.

5. Like the lamb sacrificed to save the Israelites, Jesus sacrificed his life on the _cross_ to save all people.

6. Jesus' feeding many people with five loaves of bread was a sign of the food he would give the world: the _Eucharist_.

7. The same _God_ who freed the Jews from slavery in Egypt delivered us from _sin_ and _death_ through his Son.

E Identify the two events during which both of the following blessings are prayed.

1. Blessed are you, Lord, God of all creation.

   Mass, Passover, Jewish Seder.

2. Blessed be God forever.

   Mass, Passover Seder, Jewish Seder

Family Time

A choice of things to do at home

Commandment and Fulfillment

The Israelites traveling in the desert toward what would become their homeland were hungry, thirsty, and angry at Moses. Their complaints were met with miracles from God that filled their needs: food falling to the ground each morning, water bursting from a rock . . . and the Ten Commandments. Not simply a list of laws, the commandments were really gifts that filled the Israelites' needs by offering ways to love people and remain in a faithful, rewarding relationship with God.

House Rules

1. Stereos off by 10 p.m.
2. No TV-watching during dinner.
3. Put all dirty clothes in hampers.
4. Don't waste water.
5. Keep the front door locked.
6. Wipe your feet when you come in the door.
7. Wash your hands before you eat.

House rules

Post your family rules. Such rules might be enforced each day without anyone thinking about it. Have everyone contribute to the list.

Migration demonstration

Stage a migration play throughout your home to help your family understand the feelings of Israelites journeying through the desert or of ancestors emigrating to this country. Share possible fears, complaints, and hopes.

Be the best you can be

In some ways, the commandments name only the bare minimum needed to live in harmony. Jesus taught us to keep the commandments and to do much more. List ways your family can achieve true harmony.

✝ A Prayer for the Week

Lord, you formed a covenant with your servant Moses. You sent Jesus to fulfill that covenant. Help us honor your commandments and live in the fullness of your promises.
Amen.

Family Time

Something to Do . . .

On Sunday

During the first reading, listen for Yahweh's promises. During the second reading and Gospel, listen for ways God fulfilled those promises.

Through the Week

Pay attention to ways you follow the commandments, but make an effort to do things to help people, too.

Visit Our Web Site

www.blestarewe.com

Something to Think About . . .

A Moral Guide to Patience

In their thirst for water, the people grumbled against Moses, saying, "Why did you ever make us leave Egypt?"
Exodus 17:3

The Bible tells the very human story of the Hebrew people who, despite their relationship with God, had difficult times and were tempted to give up. When Yahweh did not respond to their needs quickly enough, some of them turned to other gods.

Families often want instant results. We pray, but if we don't see an immediate response, we get discouraged. But God gradually builds situations that are the best for us. Through thousands of years of human difficulties, God has kept and fulfilled his covenant.

This is a tabernacle holding the Blessed Sacrament.

Something to Know About . . .

Our Heritage in Ritual

The Israelites regularly refreshed oil lamps that burned outside the ark of the covenant, the sacred box containing the stone tablets of God's commandments. In the Temple in Jerusalem, the ritual continued in the sacred space where the ark was kept. When their Temple was destroyed, the Israelites began to worship in synagogues, where a continuously burning light called *Ner Tamid* ("eternal light") shines above the ark, now holding the Torah. The light represents God's eternal covenant.

In our churches, at least one oil lamp or candle continually shines near the tabernacle holding the Blessed Sacrament. The light signifies the purity and divinity of Christ, the Light of the World.

7 Commandment and Fulfillment

I will place my law within them, and write it upon their hearts, says the LORD.

Jeremiah 31:33

Share

You follow rules every day—in school, clubs, sports, and your home. These rules usually keep things running smoothly. Many rules help keep people and things safe. Try to think of some rules you follow each day that keep people from physical or emotional harm.

Activity

What do you remember about the rules called the Ten Commandments? In the first column, list everything you already know about this topic. In the second column, write a few questions you have about the topic. Complete the third column at the end of class.

BEACH
RULES AND REGULATIONS
NO: Disorderly Conduct
Dogs
Glass Containers
Fires - Grills
Littering
Motor Vehicles
Soliciting
Throwing missiles
or Objects
BEACH CLOSED 1 AM - 5 AM
CITY OF TREASURE ISLAND
ORDINANCE CHAPTER 20

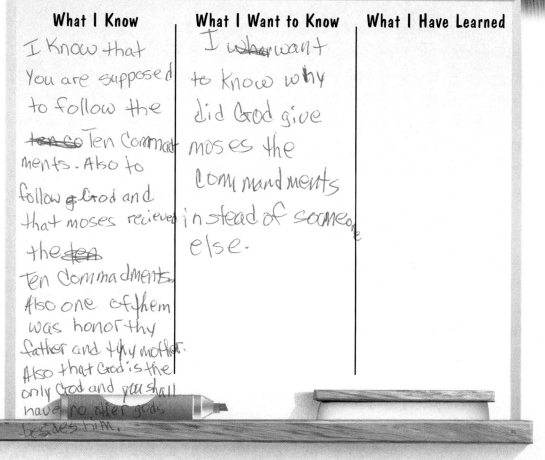

What I Know	What I Want to Know	What I Have Learned
I Know that You are supposed to follow the Ten Commandments. Also to follow God and that moses recieved the Ten Commadments. Also one of them was honor thy father and thy mother. Also that God is the only God and you shall have no other gods besides him.	I want to know why did God give moses the commandments instead of someone else.	

How are the Ten Commandments a covenant?

85

Hear & Believe

 ## Scripture — The Covenant at Sinai

After the Israelites left Egypt, God led them through the desert. The journey was rough. The Israelites complained to Moses that they were starving. In the morning, breadlike flakes covered the desert. The Israelites asked, "What is this?"

Moses told them, "This is the bread which the LORD has given you to eat." The Israelites called this food **manna**. It was white and tasted like wafers made with honey. The people also grumbled against Moses because they were thirsty. At the LORD's command, Moses struck a rock with his staff, and water flowed out for the people to drink.

About three months after they left Egypt, the Israelites came to the desert of Sinai. They camped at the foot of a mountain. Moses went up the mountain to speak to God.

The LORD said, "Tell the Israelites: You have seen for yourselves how I treated the Egyptians and brought you here safely to me. Therefore, if you listen to me and keep my covenant, you shall be dearer to me than all other people. You shall be to me a holy nation." Moses told the Israelites what the LORD said.

Then the LORD told Moses to have the people prepare to meet the LORD in three days. On the third day, there were peals of thunder and lightning, a heavy cloud over the mountain, and a loud trumpet blast. Moses led the people to the foot of the mountain. Flames and smoke rose from it. The Israelites were terrified, but Moses went up the mountain. God gave him these commandments:

"I, the LORD, am your God, who brought you out of Egypt, that place of slavery. You shall not have other gods besides me.
"You shall not take the name of the LORD, your God, in vain.
"Remember to keep holy the Sabbath day.
"Honor your father and your mother.
"You shall not kill.
"You shall not commit adultery.
"You shall not steal.
"You shall not bear false witness against your neighbor.
"You shall not covet your neighbor's wife.
"You shall not covet anything that belongs to your neighbor."

Moses told the Israelites God's commandments. They offered sacrifices to the LORD. Then Moses went up the mountain again. When Moses came down the mountain, he was carrying stone tablets upon which God had written the Ten Commandments. But the Israelites were dancing, drinking, and worshiping a golden calf made out of their melted jewelry! They thought Moses had forgotten them.

Moses angrily threw the tablets and broke them. He went back to the LORD to ask the LORD to forgive the Israelites. The LORD commanded Moses to cut two new stone tablets.

"Here is the covenant I will make," said the LORD. "Before your people's eyes I will work wonders that have never been seen in any nation on earth. People will see the power of the LORD. But you must keep my commandments. Write down these words, for with them I have made a covenant with you and Israel."

Moses wrote the commandments on the tablets. Then skillful Israelites created a gold and wood box and a special tent. Moses brought the tablets down the mountain and placed them in the box, called the **ark of the covenant**. After that, the Israelites carried the ark of the covenant in the tent wherever they traveled. It was filled with the LORD's presence.

Based on Exodus 16:1–3, 13–15, 31; 17:5–6; 19–20; 32; 34:1–4, 10–11, 27–29; 35; 40

Faith Words

manna

Manna is the breadlike food that God gave the Israelites in the desert.

ark of the covenant

The ark of the covenant was a special box that held the stone tablets of the Ten Commandments.

God's Love and Laws

The covenant was a two-way relationship. God loved his people, and he would work wonders before their eyes. The people loved God and would keep God's commandments. The Ten Commandments express the way we all want to live: without offending God or harming other people and ourselves. Our natural desire for goodness is a sign of our ability to choose between good and evil. We also have a natural need to be with other people. Other people encourage us to develop our strengths and overcome our weaknesses. They can protect us, love us, and give us joy. The need for authority is also natural. When people come together, they need rules to create goodness for everyone.

Activity

Read the Ten Commandments. Choose two of the commandments and describe ways you might keep them.

Commandment #	Ways to Keep
"Honor your father and mother"	you should do your chores when your mom or dad tells you to.
"You shall not commit adaltery"	you should not look or cheat on your wife or husband behind thier backs.

What did Jesus say about the Ten Commandments?

Jesus Teaches About the Law

Jesus had great respect for the Ten Commandments. He also had a wonderful gift for keeping his teachings simple.

One time, a man who was a Jewish scholar and religious leader tried to test Jesus. This was the question that the scholar asked: "Teacher, which commandment in the Law is the greatest?"

Jesus immediately responded with a simple answer: "You shall love the Lord, your God, with all your heart, with all your soul, and with all your mind. This is the greatest and the first commandment. The second is like it: You shall love your neighbor as yourself." And then he added, "The whole Law depends on these two commandments."

Later, Jesus told his disciples, "As for your religious leaders, who have taken the place of Moses as teachers of the Law, observe all things whatsoever they tell you, but do not follow their example. For they preach but they do not practice." Jesus said that such leaders liked to perform their good deeds in public so that everyone could see how great they were.

Jesus told his disciples, "You have but one teacher, and you are all brothers. Call no one on earth your father; you have but one Father in heaven."

Based on Matthew 22:34–40, 23:1–9

Our Church Teaches

God is the ultimate authority for our society. God revealed the Ten Commandments. By following them, we show love for God and choose good over evil. Jesus taught us how important it is to keep God's commandments, but he also said, "You shall love the Lord, your God, with all your heart, with all your soul, and with all your mind. This is the greatest and the first commandment. The second is like it: You shall love your neighbor as yourself" (Matthew 22:37–39). By sending Jesus, God sealed the covenant at Sinai.

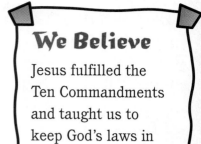

We Believe

Jesus fulfilled the Ten Commandments and taught us to keep God's laws in the spirit of love.

Activity

Look at each of the photographs. In the box next to each photograph, write the letter of the commandment that corresponds to it.

a. You shall love the Lord, your God, with all your heart, with all your soul, and with all your mind. `b`

b. Honor your father and your mother. `c`

c. Remember to keep holy the Sabbath day. `a`

How do you show that you love God and others?

Saint Teresa of Ávila

As a teenager in Spain in the 1500s, Teresa of Ávila shared many of the concerns of modern teenagers. She worried about her appearance and what boys thought of her. She liked to flirt, and the last thing she thought of was spending her life in a convent! But Teresa's strict father was worried about his daughter's behavior. He sent her to a convent when she was sixteen.

Teresa soon wanted to spend the rest of her life in service to the Lord. She became a Carmelite nun. Teresa tried to keep Jesus present within her through prayer. Teresa believed that prayer was a mental sharing between friends. She believed that prayer should be time spent alone reflecting only on God. When Teresa prayed, she felt God's presence overwhelm her. People who watched her pray said that her whole body would lift off the ground.

But there was a time in Teresa's life when praying was a struggle. She found it very hard to concentrate. She worked hard to overcome this difficulty. Teresa realized that there were others who also had trouble praying. She wanted to help them experience the beauty of prayer. So, she spent much of her life writing and teaching others how to pray. As an adult, Teresa founded a religious order called the Discalced Carmelites. Members of this order show their love for God by vowing to live a simple life of poverty, devoted to prayer. Teresa helped others discover that one finds inner peace through prayer. The Church recognized Teresa for her efforts. In 1622 she was canonized. In 1970 Saint Teresa of Ávila was named a Doctor of the Church. Her feast day is October 15.

This is a sculpture called *Ecstasy of St. Teresa* by Bernini.

Activity

Next to each commandment from the Bible write its meaning for today. Four commandments have been done for you.

Hi! Hi

BIBLE

Megan Murray

I, the LORD, am your God. You shall not have other gods besides me.

You shall not take the name of the LORD, your God, in vain.

Remember to keep holy the Sabbath day.

Honor your father and your mother.

You shall not kill.

You shall not commit adultery.

You shall not steal.

You shall not bear false witness against your neighbor.

You shall not covet your neighbor's wife.

You shall not covet anything that belongs to your neighbor.

Based on Exodus 20:2–17

MEANING FOR TODAY

You shall not have any other God or worsip any other people as a good

You shall not use the lord's name in anger

You should go to church on the sabbath day and you shall also rest on this day.

You should do what your mom and dad tell you to do.

Respect life. Take care of your health. Work to protect unborn children, the sick, and the elderly.

Avoid things that might lead to sexual sins.

Keep promises and agreements. Do not purposely keep things that you have borrowed or people have lost.

You shall not lie about your neighbor.

Keep your heart pure and thoughts focused on God. Respect people's marriage vows.

You shall not take anything that belongs to your neighbor

GO TO page 371 for more information about the Ten Commandments.

✝ Prayer Celebration

Praying with Scripture

Saint Teresa of Ávila said that she often started praying by reading Scripture and reflecting upon it. Try her method of prayer.
Silently read the following Scripture passage. (In it, Moses is speaking to the Israelites.)

> "Hear, O Israel! The LORD is our God, the LORD alone! Therefore, you shall love the LORD, your God, with all your heart, and with all your soul, and with all your strength. Take to heart these words which I enjoin on you today. Drill them into your children. Speak of them at home and abroad, whether you are busy or at rest. Bind them at your wrist as a sign and let them be as a pendant on your forehead. Write them on the doorposts of your houses and on your gates."

Deuteronomy 6:4–9

Imagine you are an Israelite. What is Moses asking you to remember? What should you do to show your love for God? The *Sh'ma*, or *Shema*, is a Jewish prayer based on the passage.

Leader: Hear, O Israel: The Lord is our God, the Lord alone! Let us all say: Blessed is God's glorious kingdom forever!

All: Blessed is God's glorious kingdom forever!

Leader: You shall love the Lord, your God, with all your heart, with all your soul, and with all your might. Keep these words in your heart. Recite them to your families. I, the Lord, am your God...

All: ... now and forever.
Amen.

Based on the Sh'ma

100%

A **Explain** how the Ten Commandments help people live in love and goodness.

The Ten Commandments help people live in love and goodness. by they tell us how we can become better people in faith and in love.

B **Write** the commandment that according to Jesus is the first and the greatest.

"You shall love the Lord your God with all your heart, with all your soul, and with all your mind."

C **Match** Column A with Column B by writing the correct number in the space provided.

A		B
1. ark of the covenant	*5*	an agreement or relationship
2. Ten Commandments	*2*	laws that guide our moral lives
3. Sinai	*4*	the breadlike food that God gave the Israelites
4. manna	*3*	the desert through which the Israelites passed
5. covenant	*1*	a special box that held the stone tablets of the Ten Commandments

D **Write** an action or behavior that you can carry out to follow each commandment listed. Examples are provided.

1. Honor your father and your mother.

   Example: help my parents with chores around the house

   Do what my parents tell me to do right away.

2. You shall not steal.

   Example: return things I have borrowed

   do not take other peoples things that don't belong to me

E **Explain** one way that Saint Teresa of Ávila showed her love for God. Then explain one way you can show your own love for God.

Saint Teresa of Ávila showed her love in God by she became a nun and also found a group of nuns called the Disalced Carmelites. I can show my own love in God by praying, also by following the Ten Commandments.

F **Complete** the following exercise, which uses Saint Teresa of Ávila's method of prayer.

1. Read the Scripture verses below. Jesus said these words to his disciples.

   I give you a new commandment: love one another. As I have loved you, so you also should love one another. This is how everyone will know that you are my disciples.

   Based on John 13:34–35

2. Think about what Jesus is telling his disciples to do. Write a brief prayer based on the Scripture verses.

   Dear Lord, please help me to follow your commandment that is to love one another. As I have loved you, so you also should love one another.

G **Write** a brief summary of what you learned in this chapter, using the words in the box.

~~Israelites~~	~~Ten Commandments~~	~~covenant~~
~~Moses~~	~~neighbor~~	~~Jesus~~

This chapter was about Moses leading the Israelites out of slavery. Also the chapter was about the Ten Commandments. Also Jesus made a covenant with the Israelites and told them to love thier neighbor

Family Time

A choice of things to do at home

Our Journey and God's Presence

We are a pilgrim people with roots in the wanderings of the nomadic Israelites. We have a "promised land" just as they did. Their promised land was Canaan, which they reached after forty years in the desert, led by God. Our promised land is a land of happiness for our souls, reached by being faithful followers of Christ throughout our lives.

Signs of God

Joshua and the Israelites had to pay careful attention to God's directions when storming the promised land. Have each family member draw a symbol of something that keeps him or her in touch with God. Swap symbols, and try to experience another person's way of hearing God's voice this week.

What is your promised land?

Share responses to the question "Have you ever had an experience that felt like a promised land?" Draw pictures of your promised lands.

You can't take it with you

Ask each person in your family, "If you *could* take something with sentimental value to heaven with you, what would it be, and why?"

✝ A Prayer for the Week

You follow us, our God, wherever we go. You keep us safe in your love forever. May we always be aware of your presence. Amen.

Family Time

Something to Do . . .

On Sunday

Think of your trip to church as a journey. You leave your home, arrive at the parking lot, enter the vestibule, sit in the pew, and so on. What is special about each place?

Through the Week

Prayer is a road map for the promised land. Pray for guidance on the way.

Visit Our Web Site

 www.blestarewe.com

Something to Think About . . .

A Moral Guide to Change

Do not fear nor be dismayed, for the LORD, your God, is with you wherever you go.
Joshua 1:9

We all take journeys. Adolescents go on to the challenge of high school. Young adults enter college and a world of new responsibility. Adults leave their parents and learn to support themselves entirely. Some leave behind total self-reliance to embrace the give-and-take of marriage. Adults also face unsettling job and career changes. In some ways, such big journeys can be unnerving, but the rewards are great. There is an element of the promised land in each of these milestones. Trust in the Lord, who goes with you on every journey, and you will glean every good thing that change has to offer.

Something to Know About . . . Our Heritage in Tradition

Joshua crossed the Jordan River, which was also the river where Jesus was baptized. Blessing nearby rivers or fountains is a custom of Eastern countries. In Africa the Nile is blessed on the Feast of the Epiphany and in commemoration of the Baptism of the Lord. Christians traditionally would dip themselves in the blessed water three times, and even animals would be herded into the water to receive its blessing.

8 Our Journey and God's Presence

 In the tender compassion of our God,
the dawn will break upon us,
to shine on those who dwell in darkness.

Based on Luke 1:78–79

Share

The natural world is filled with reminders of God's power and goodness, such as a colorful rainbow that follows a storm, a tiny, detailed snowflake, or a perfect-looking rose. What other events in the natural world remind you of God's love for people?

Activity

Inside each natural wonder below write adjectives that describe what it tells you about God.

wise
creative

strong
mighty

Loving
Kind

Beautiful
Merciful

How did God show his goodness when the Israelites reached the promised land?

Scripture   Conquest of the Promised Land

The Israelites had wandered in the desert for forty years. Moses saw that the Israelites were getting closer to the promised land, Canaan. After Moses died, the LORD told the Israelite Joshua, whom he had appointed, "Prepare to cross the Jordan River here, with all the people, into the land I will give the Israelites. Do not fear. The LORD, your God, is with you wherever you go."

Joshua secretly sent two of his men to spy on the land. The spies took shelter in a house in the city of Jericho. The house belonged to a woman named Rahab. The king of Jericho heard about the spies and sent Rahab the order "Put out the visitors who have entered your house, for they have come to spy on my land."

Instead, Rahab hid the men. She told the king's messengers, "The men you speak of came to me, but I did not know where they came from. They left at dark, and I do not know where they went. You will have to run after them right now if you want to catch them."

After the king's messengers left, Rahab said to the spies, "I know that the LORD has given your people our land. All the people here are afraid. We heard how the LORD dried up the waters of the Red Sea when you came out of Egypt. Since I am showing kindness to you, I want you to spare my family and save us from death."

She helped the spies down through the window with a rope. "Go up into the hill country," she said, "so that your pursuers may not find you. Hide there for three days. Then you may go on your way."

The men told Rahab, "Hang a red cord from this window. Gather your family. When we return," they promised, "everyone inside this house will be spared."

Early the next day, Joshua led the Israelites to the banks of the river. They camped out for three days. Then Joshua said to the people, "Tomorrow the LORD will perform wonders among you."

The next day, the LORD told Joshua, "Command the priests carrying the ark of the covenant to stop in the waters at the edge of the Jordan." When the priests entered the Jordan River, the river stopped flowing. The priests stood there until the Israelites had crossed the Jordan safely. Then they carried the ark out and the river flowed back.

The LORD said to Joshua, "Have all the soldiers circle the city, marching once around it. Do this for six days, with seven priests carrying rams' horns ahead of the ark. On the seventh day, march around the city seven times and have the priests blow the horns."

The Israelites followed the Lord's directions. As the horns blew on the seventh day, they raised a tremendous shout. The walls of the city collapsed, and the Israelites stormed the city. The Israelites conquered the city of Jericho. But they did not harm Rahab and her family.

City by city, the Israelites took the land the Lord had promised. Years later, Joshua called the people together. He reminded them of all that the Lord had done for them. "Acknowledge with your whole heart and soul that every one of the promises the Lord has made to you has been fulfilled. Therefore, love the Lord completely and sincerely, and obey his commandments."

The Israelites agreed to serve the Lord alone.

Based on Exodus 16:35; Deuteronomy 31:23; 34:1–4; Joshua 1–6; 18:1; 24

Faith Words

chosen people

In the Old Testament the chosen people were Abraham and his descendants, whom God had selected to receive his word. People who choose to follow God's will today are also chosen people.

Listening for God's Voice

The Israelites reached the promised land, but they could not move forward without God's help. Joshua led the Israelites into Canaan by listening to God's instructions. God told Joshua how the Israelites should cross the Jordan, and it worked. God told Joshua how the Israelites should get inside the city, and they did it. As a result of talking to and listening to God, Joshua and the Israelites successfully conquered and settled the promised land. Before Joshua died the Israelites promised to continue to listen to God. They wanted to continue to be God's **chosen people**. God had chosen to reveal his love and fidelity to them so many times. God *is* love and fidelity.

Activities

1. What happened to the Israelites after Moses died?

   _____

   _____

2. How did Joshua know the will of the Lord?

   _____

   _____

How do people receive God's instructions for their lives?

A Man of Prayer: Saint Juan Diego

Juan Diego was an Aztec leader in Mexico in the sixteenth century. At this time, most people in Mexico worshiped the Aztec gods and goddesses. But Juan became a Catholic when he was about fifty years old. As a new Catholic, Juan had to walk fifteen miles into Mexico City to attend Mass. One day, on this journey, his life changed forever.

It was the morning of December 9, 1531. Juan Diego was crossing a hill on his way to Mass when he suddenly heard music and saw an unusual cloud. At the top of the hill, he had a vision of Mary, the mother of Jesus. She was wearing the colors of an Aztec princess. Mary asked Juan to have the bishop build a church at the spot at which she was standing.

Juan Diego visited the bishop, who was not persuaded by Juan's story. The bishop wanted proof. So Juan Diego returned to the hill. He was amazed to find roses blooming in the frozen ground. Tucking them into his cloak, Juan rushed back to the bishop. This time, the bishop was convinced, for not only did he see the unusual roses, but when Juan opened his cloak, a miraculous, colorful image of Mary was imprinted on the inside. Both Juan and the bishop were filled with wonder.

Soon after, the church Mary requested was built and dedicated to Our Lady of Guadalupe, who, as the "Mother of the Americas," helped millions of people turn to her son. Many Mexicans converted to Christianity because of her.

And what happened to Juan Diego? After he met Mary, he devoted his life to listening to God. This man of prayer is now a saint. His feast day is celebrated on December 9.

This photograph shows the image on Juan Diego's cloak, which is kept in the Basilica of Our Lady of Guadalupe in Mexico City.

Our Church Teaches

Prayer is talking to and listening to God. We can pray in words, thoughts, gestures, or song. Our Church teaches that praying every day can help us become people who pray continually. Praying continually—during every event of our lives—will help us hear God's instructions for our lives. Our Church has certain prayers for each day of the week, for the morning, the middle of the day, and the evening. Praying as much as we can—every day—will make it easier to discover God's will. This discovery process is called **discernment**. It also happens through seeking God's will in the Scriptures and reflecting on the teachings of our Church.

We Believe

Prayer will help us with discernment. Continual prayer is especially important.

Activities

1. What do the stories of Joshua and Saint Juan Diego have in common?

   _____

   _____

   _____

   _____

   _____

Faith Words

discernment
Discernment is discovering, with God's help, God's will for our lives.

2. Draw a picture that depicts Juan Diego standing before the bishop, showing his cloak.

How do you show that you are one of God's chosen people?

Celebrating the Lord's Wonders

The Scripture story tells how God fulfilled his promise to the generations of Israelites who had faith in him. The following prayer is called "The Lord's Wonders at the Exodus." Pray it aloud, and think about how God showed his power and goodness to the Israelites.

When Israel came forth from Egypt,
    the house of Jacob from a people of alien tongue,
Judah became his sanctuary,
    Israel his domain.

The sea beheld and fled;
    Jordan turned back.
The mountains skipped like rams,
    the hills like the lambs of the flock.

Why is it, O sea, that you flee?
    O Jordan, that you turn back?
You mountains, that you skip like rams?
    You hills, like the lambs of the flock?

Before the face of the Lord, tremble, O earth,
    before the face of the God of Jacob,
Who turned the rock into pools of water,
    the flint into flowing springs.

Psalm 114

The Jewish people use a ram's horn called a shofar (shown at left) to celebrate the Jewish new year. The Israelites blew rams' horns to conquer the promised land.

Activity

What everyday events, such as seeing a rainbow, remind you of the power and goodness of the Lord? List or draw two of these events below.

Constant Prayer

Berahot are short blessing prayers that Jewish people may say throughout the day to praise the power and goodness of the Lord.
They pray them upon everyday events, such as noticing a blossoming tree.
Here are some examples you can pray.

Upon opening the eyes:

Blessed are you, Lord, God of all creation, for you open the eyes of the blind.

Upon going to breakfast:

Blessed are you, Lord, God of all creation, for you provide for all my needs.

Based on berahot blessings

Activities

1. Choose one of your answers from page 102. Write a berahot prayer for this event.

_____

_____

_____

_____

_____

2. Create a berahot prayer for an event or activity that is always a part of your class. You may work with your class to create this prayer, then pray it together during every religion class.

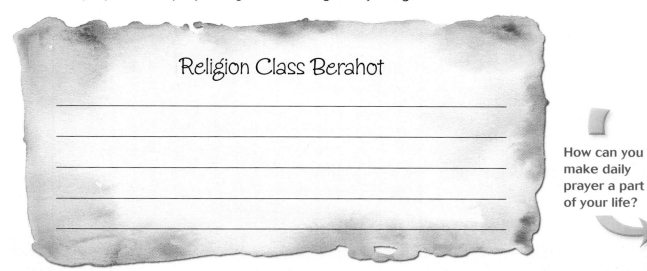

Religion Class Berahot

_____

_____

_____

_____

_____

How can you make daily prayer a part of your life?

✝ Prayer Celebration

Our Morning Prayer

Catholics have certain prayers for the morning, evening, and middle of the day. They are treasured as sources of constant prayer. The following prayer, the Canticle of Zechariah, is a morning prayer of the Church. Zechariah was the father of John the Baptizer. This was his prayer after his wife, Elizabeth, gave birth to John. Pray it in the morning, and think about how it makes you feel.

Blessed be the Lord, the God of Israel;
> he has come to his people and set them free.

He has raised up for us a mighty savior,
> born of the house of his servant David.

Through his holy prophets he promised of old
>> that he would save us from our enemies,
>> from the hands of all who hate us.

He promised to show mercy to our fathers
>> and to remember his holy covenant.

This was the oath he swore to Abraham:
>> to set us free from the hands of our enemies;

free to worship him without fear,
>> holy and righteous in his sight
>>> all the days of our life.

You, my child, shall be called the prophet of the Most High,
>> for you will go before the Lord to prepare his way,

to give his people knowledge of salvation
>> by forgiveness of their sins.

In the tender compassion of our God
>> the dawn from on high shall break upon us,

to shine on those who dwell in darkness
>>> and the shadow of death,
>> and to guide our feet on the
>>> road to peace.

Based on Luke 1:68–79

✗ 100% ✗

A **Describe** how the Israelites conquered the promised land.

The Israelites conquered the promised land by for six days the Israelites marched around the walls of jerico and on the seventh day they blew horns and the walls came crumbling down, and they attacked the city.

B **Match** Column A with Column B by writing the correct number in the space provided.

A	B
1. berahot	_1_ short blessing prayers
2. discernment	_3_ a ram's horn
3. shofar	_5_ Canaan
4. chosen people	_2_ discovering God's will
5. promised land	_4_ Abraham and his descendants

C **Respond** to the following.

1. Describe two ways that we can become people who pray continually.

We can become people of prayer by we can ask for God's help + we can pray every day, and we can go to church.

2. What is discovered during the process of discernment?

The thing that is discovered during the process of discernment is discovering with Gods help the will of our lives.

Megan Murray

List some examples of God's blessings that can be a source of prayer in each of the following places.

natural world

_____

home

_____

school

_____

Reread page 104. Why is praying the Canticle of Zechariah a good way to begin the day?

_____

_____

_____

_____

F **Circle** the letter of the best answer.

1. Where did Juan Diego live?

    a. New Mexico

    b. Mexico

    c. Mexico City

    d. Guadalupe

2. Of whom did Juan Diego have a vision?

    a. Mary

    b. God

    c. Jesus

    d. Saint Dominic Savio

3. Where did Juan Diego pray every day?

    a. at his farm

    b. at Mass

    c. at the bishop's residence

    d. near the church

4. What happened to Juan Diego?

    a. He built a church.

    b. He was made a saint.

    c. He became a bishop.

    d. He became a Christian.

WE CARE About the World

The Right to Be a Child

In countries that have civil wars, sometimes armies kidnap children and force them to fight their own people. These child soldiers have to carry heavy supplies. They fight on the front lines of battle. They are sent out to detect landmines. They act as spies, messengers, and lookouts. They may be forced to injure or kill other child soldiers. Many of the children are violently beaten. Some of the children are drugged so that they will hurt people more easily.

More than 300,000 child soldiers have been used in more than twenty-five countries around the world. A war that began in 1991 in Sierra Leone, Africa, is called "the children's war." Armies enlisted more than 10,000 children under the age of eighteen. Most of these young soldiers were kidnapped and forced to attend military training. Children have been used in wars in southern Sudan and northern Uganda, as well.

The children who survive the fighting may be disabled by their injuries. They are also robbed of their families, of fun, of innocence, and of their education. The children need to be healed and comforted, then returned to normal society. Otherwise, they will grow up to be violent and unstable.

Children living in countries where wars are taking place need to be protected. Some of the countries do not have enough money to help the children. Organizations such as Catholic Charities and Catholic Relief Services work to protect children and help them recover. Catholic missions have special recovery homes for children who were forced to fight or who were harmed by war. One school in Los Angeles, California, sells green ribbons for three dollars each and sends the money to recovery homes.

What will happen to society if armies keep forcing children to fight in wars?

Think About It

A school in Baltimore started a letter campaign to help stop this problem. The teachers and students write letters to United States government officials, asking them to support a worldwide increase in the minimum age for participation in war. One sixth-grade class writes letters to the leaders of Sudan, Uganda, and the United Nations, asking them to stop the armies from forcing children to become soldiers. Other students have written letters to the editors of newspapers to increase people's awareness.

If you were to write a letter to a newspaper or government official about child soldiers, what would it say?

Learn About It

Children are the future. Children can grow up to achieve wonderful things and to benefit society if they are treated with respect. Forcing children to participate in war continues because some people do not value children as special creations of God. Our Church teaches that children's rights will be better protected when people learn to respect every human being.

Write your letter here.

Do Something About It

How can you learn more about children in war-torn countries?

_____

_____

Write three steps your class can take to help these children.

1. _____

2. _____

3. _____

97%

Each chapter in Unit 2 taught a story about the Hebrews' journey of faith. Match each Scripture quote to the story from which it came.

2
The Exodus

4
The Passover

1 "Prepare to cross the Jordan River here, with all the people, into the land I will give the Israelites. Do not fear. The Lord, your God, is with you wherever you go."
based on Joshua 1:9, 11

2 "I am who I am. Tell the Israelites: Yahweh sent me to you."
based on Exodus 3:14

3 "Write down these words, for with them I have made a covenant with you and Israel."
based on Exodus 34:27

4 "This day shall be a memorial feast for you, which all your generations shall celebrate with pilgrimage to the LORD, as a perpetual institution."
Exodus 12:14

3
The Covenant at Sinai

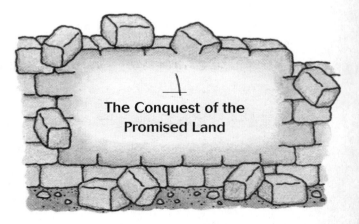

1
The Conquest of the Promised Land

Review

A **Write** the name of the person or group described by each clue.

1. God gave me the Ten Commandments to help people live in love and goodness. _Moses_

2. I listened and talked to God and successfully led the Israelites to the promised land. _~~Joshua~~ Joshua_

3. Mary appeared to me and requested that a church be built where she was standing. _~~Jesu~~ Juan Diego_

4. Because of me, the Church can forgive any sin and no person has to fear death. _Jesus_

B **Circle** the letter of the best answer.

1. The same God who delivered his people from slavery in Egypt delivered _____.

   a. the Egyptians from death
   b. us from hunger by giving us fish and bread
   (c.) us from sin and death through Jesus Christ
   d. us from slavery to material things

2. Jesus' miracle of feeding 5,000 followers with five loaves of bread was a special sign of the food he would give the whole world in _____.

   (a.) the Eucharist **b.** Easter **c.** Passover **d.** the Last Supper

3. By sending _____, God sealed the covenant at Sinai.

   ~~a.~~ Moses **(b.)** Jesus **c.** 600 chariots **d.** the Israelites

4. Our liturgies celebrate _____.

   a. novenas
   (b.) the Paschal mystery
   c. the promised land
   d. the Book of Exodus

C Match Column A with Column B by writing the correct number in the space provided.

A

1. greatest commandment
2. everlasting life
3. Easter Triduum
4. God's will
5. spirituals
6. Ten Commandments
7. Teresa of Ávila

B

2 what death leads to if we love God and others as Jesus taught

4 praying as much as we can will help us discover this

1 to love God with all your heart, soul, and mind

7 a saint and Doctor of the Church who taught people about prayer

5 songs African slaves sang to express their faith in God and desire for freedom

6 by following these, we show love for God and choose good over evil

3 the period from Holy Thursday evening until the evening prayer on Easter Sunday

D Complete each sentence with the correct word or words.

1. Jesus' death and Resurrection took place during the Jewish feast of _Passover_. Passover was a _example_ of the future sacrifice of Jesus Christ.

2. God is the ultimate _authority_ for our society.

X 3. The _Red Sea_ stopped flowing so that the Israelites could enter the promised land.

E **Match** Column A with Column B by writing the correct number in the space provided.

A

1. ark of the covenant

2. chosen people

3. discernment

4. Exodus

5. liturgical year

6. manna

7. Paschal mystery

8. Passover

9. promised land

10. Yahweh

B

_2_ Abraham and his descendants, selected by God to recieve his word

_9_ Canaan, the sacred place God promised to Abraham, Isaac, Jacob, and the Israelites in Egypt

_1_ a special box that held the stone tablets of the Ten Commandments

_3_ discovering, with God's help, God's will for our lives

_6_ the breadlike food that God gave the Israelites in the desert

_5_ the Church's yearly calendar of celebrations and seasons

_8_ the Jewish celebration of the Exodus from Egypt

_10_ the most sacred name of God, meaning "I am who I am"

_4_ the Old Testament story of how God freed the Hebrews in Egypt

_7_ the way that Jesus' Passion, death, Resurrection, and Ascension saved us from sin and gave us life after death

 **Write** the Canticle of Zechariah on a separate sheet of paper.

God Invites Us into His Kingdom

The people of Israel were called to build up a kingdom that would be a tribute to God's love. Jesus taught us about the kingdom of heaven, where God's love will be evident in justice and peace.

It is he who shall build a house for my name. And I will make his royal throne firm forever.

2 Samuel 7:13

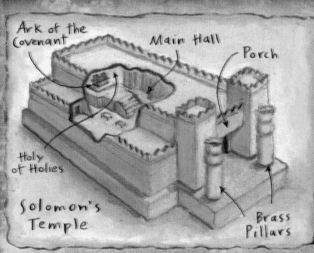

Ark of the Covenant

Main Hall

Porch

Holy of Holies

Solomon's Temple

Brass Pillars

The Israelites wanted a permanent holy place to worship God, so they built the Temple on Mount Zion in Jerusalem.

Let Us Go Rejoicing

Psalm 122, Adapted by Michael Joncas

Music by Michael Joncas

REFRAIN

Let us go re - joic - ing to the house of the Lord;

Let us go re - joic - ing to the house of the Lord.

VERSE

1. I rejoiced when I heard them say:
   "Let us go to the house of the Lord,"
   and now our feet are standing
   within your gates, O Jerusalem.
   Refrain

2. Jerusalem is a city built
   with unity and strength.
   It is there, it is there that the tribes go up,
   the tribes of the Lord.
   Refrain

3. For Israel's law is to praise God's name
   and there to give God thanks.
   There are set the judgment thrones
   for all of David's house.
   Refrain

4. Pray for the peace of Jerusalem!
   "May those who love you prosper;
   May peace ever reign within your walls,
   and wealth within your buildings!"
   Refrain

5. For love of my fam'ly and love of my friends,
   I pray that peace be yours.
   For love of the house of the Lord our God
   I pray for your good.
   Refrain

Family Time

A choice of things to do at home

Our Land and God's Kingdom

The story of Israel's first king teaches a powerful lesson about leadership. The Jewish people in the promised land were guided by the wisdom of several leaders called *judges*. But some Israelites wanted a king to represent all the tribes of Israel. The judge and prophet Samuel asked God for guidance in choosing a king. God revealed how the people could follow a king and remain loyal to God. A family can function well under different styles of leadership, as long as God is behind all its decisions.

Your kingdom is your castle

Think of your home as the kingdom of your family. Have family members draw or paint a sign expressing what this kingdom is all about. It may show a popular expression or your last name with symbols of things you value, such as a drawing of a cross. Frame and hang the sign so that all will see what is valued in the kingdom of your family.

Everyone in this family is a special sign of God's love.

Did you call me?

As a young man Samuel awoke to the sound of someone calling him. He went to the priest Eli, but Eli was not calling Samuel. This happened twice more before Eli realized God was calling Samuel. As a family, recall times when you were slow to realize what God wanted. Share how you came to understand God's desires.

Family Bible

Place a Bible in a prominent place in your home as a sign that your household is guided by God. During dinner each night this week, take turns reading aloud a Scripture passage.

✝ A Prayer for the Week

Thank you, Lord, for your kingdom. The hope of living in the kingdom of heaven keeps us going. You are our joy. Help us build your kingdom now. Amen.

Family Time

Something to Do . . .

On Sunday

Think of fellow parishioners as travelers on the journey to God's kingdom. Ask God to bless them.

Through the Week

Appreciate all the things your family "leaders" do, such as cook meals, do laundry, give rides, or take care of sick family members.

Visit Our Web Site

 www.blestarewe.com

Something to Think About . . .

Being Open to Love

If you are called, reply, "Speak, LORD, for your servant is listening."
1 Samuel 3:9

As followers of Jesus we are called to love our neighbors as we love ourselves—and even to love our enemies. It may be difficult to allow ourselves to be open to such love. But if we consider all the mercy and love God shows us, we will be less apt to withhold our love and mercy from others. We are called to share with others the mercy that God shows us. Practice being open to love and forgiveness in your home, and it will become easier in the outside world. Remember, "Charity begins at home" (based on 1 Timothy 5:4).

Something to Know About . . .

Our Heritage in Music

The Messiah is a famous oratorio composed by George Frideric Handel. "Messiah" is a name meaning "anointed one" or leader. Handel wrote the music in twenty-four days beginning in August 1741, after being asked to set to music a collection of Scripture passages. Handel felt the music was inspired. He is said to have remarked, "I did think I did see all heaven before me and the great God himself." The music is divided into three themes: Advent and the birth of Christ, Jesus' Passion and death (this includes the famous "Hallelujah Chorus"), and the Resurrection.

9 Our Land and God's Kingdom

 Do you not know that your bodies are members of Christ?

1 Corinthians 6:15

Share

God made each of us unique, but we were not meant to live alone. We are part of families, neighborhoods, cities or towns, states, and countries. In many of these communities, people are appointed to lead us.

We are also part of parish communities. What is the name of your parish? Your parish is part of a bigger community, the Catholic Church. The Catholic Church guides the Catholic parish communities all over the world through the leadership of the pope and the bishops of each diocese. We call the Church our "Mother" because it teaches us about faith and spreads and protects the truth God has revealed. We also call it the "Bride of Christ" because of Christ's sacrifice and love for the Church.

Activity

What groups or communities do you belong to? Draw yourself participating in one of these groups or communities.

What makes a good leader?

Hear & Believe

Scripture   The First Leaders of Israel

After Joshua died, judges helped the Israelites stay faithful to the covenant. Judges were leaders gifted with good judgment. A wise judge named Deborah helped the Israelites conquer a Canaanite ruler who treated them badly. The Israelites enjoyed peace for forty years.

The Israelites had an especially wise judge named Samuel. Samuel was the son of Hannah, a faithful Israelite woman. She could not have children at first. One day, she prayed hard for a son. "Lord," she promised, "if you give me a son, I will give him to you as a servant for as long as he lives." God heard Hannah's prayer, and Samuel was born. Hannah brought Samuel to the Temple to live with the priest, Eli. "This child shall be dedicated to the Lord as long as he lives," she told Eli.

Eli taught the boy about serving God. One day, something remarkable happened. As Samuel was sleeping in the Temple, he heard, "Samuel!"

Samuel woke up and ran to Eli. "Here I am. You called me."

"I did not call you," Eli said. "Go back to sleep."

Samuel went back to sleep. Again, a voice called him. He got up and went back to Eli. "Here I am," he said. "You called me."

Eli answered, "I did not call you, my son. Go back to sleep."

The voice called Samuel a third time. Samuel went to Eli again. Eli then understood that the Lord was calling Samuel. He told the boy, "Go to sleep. If you are called, reply, 'Speak, Lord, for your servant is listening.'"

After Samuel fell asleep, the Lord called again. Samuel answered, "Speak, for your servant is listening." The Lord told Samuel about events that would happen later. Samuel told Eli, and Eli knew Samuel would be a great prophet.

God watched over Samuel as he grew up. All of Israel came to know Samuel as a leader and a prophet of the Lord. When the people wanted him to choose a king to lead them, Samuel asked God for help.

One day, a man named Saul came to the city looking for lost donkeys. Saul was a descendant of Benjamin, one of Jacob's sons. The Lord told Samuel that Saul would be king. Samuel anointed Saul with oil and declared him king in the name of God. The Israelites praised God and said, "Long live the king!"

Samuel reminded them, "The Lord made you his people. Now you have the king you want, a king the Lord has given you. But you must obey the Lord."

As king of Israel, Saul bravely fought Israel's enemies and delivered Israel from its invaders. But then he disobeyed the Lord. Samuel told Saul, "Because you have rejected the Lord's command, the Lord has rejected you as king."

Based on Judges 2:16, 18; 4—5; 1 Samuel 1—15

Kingdoms on the Earth

The Israelites in the promised land sometimes failed to keep their covenant with God. Samuel and the judges helped keep the Israelites on the right path. When the Israelites decided they wanted a king, Samuel asked for God's help. Samuel knew that the king had to be someone who made decisions based on what God wanted. God chose Saul. When Saul failed to obey the LORD, he could no longer lead the people.

Just as God gave the Israelites the promised land, God promises us that we will share in his heavenly kingdom. Like the Israelites in Canaan, we experience sin and suffering in our world. The Church helps keep us on the path of Jesus. In many ways God's kingdom is present in the community of the Church, because we make God's kingdom known to the world when we spread goodness and joy by serving others. The Church also spreads the saving message of Jesus throughout the world.

Like Samuel, we are called by God to carry out the Church's mission and give witness to the kingdom through a **ministry**, or way of serving. We may care for the poor or sick, teach about Christ, help with the liturgy, pray for others, or work for the parish office. We may serve as religious brothers or sisters (members of communities who take vows of poverty, chastity, and obedience), as clergy (ordained ministers of the Church such as bishops, priests, or deacons), or as **laity** (all other people who serve in the Church). Many different ministries accomplish the Church's one mission.

Activity

God calls you to participate in the Church by using your gifts and talents to serve others. What is something you do well?

_____

How might you use this talent to serve others? Check the "Ways to Serve" box for some ideas.

_____

_____

_____

Faith Words

ministry
A ministry is a way of serving and caring for others in Christ's name.

laity
The laity are people who serve in the church community and are not clergy or religious brothers or sisters.

Ways to Serve

choosing songs or prayers for liturgies

greeting people at Mass

helping the disabled

participating in a prayer group

reading the Scriptures at Mass

singing in the choir

teaching others about faith

writing parish newsletters

What ministry did Jesus give to the apostle Peter?

The Keys to the Kingdom

Jesus established the Church to help the kingdom of God grow on earth. In the early Church the apostle Peter took on the role of leader. The Church believes that Jesus himself assigned Peter, whose name means "rock," to this role of leadership. The following story illustrates this belief.

One day, while Jesus was traveling with his disciples, he asked them, "Who do people say that the Son of Man is?"

Many replies came his way. Some said he was John the Baptizer, others said he was one of the Old Testament prophets.

"But who do you say that I am?" insisted Jesus.

Peter answered first. "You are the long-awaited Savior of Israel," he said. "You are the Son of the living God."

"Blessed are you, Peter, for only my heavenly Father could have revealed this to you.

"And so," Jesus said, "you are Peter, and upon this rock I will build my Church. This Church will not be conquered by the power of death. I shall give you the keys to the kingdom of heaven. Whatever you bind on earth shall be bound in heaven, and whatever you loose on earth shall be loosed in heaven."

Based on Matthew 16:13–19

Our Church Teaches

The Church is the beginning of God's kingdom on earth. But the true kingdom will not come until Christ comes again and God triumphs over evil forever. In the meantime the Catholic Church welcomes and brings together people of all lands, languages, backgrounds, and races. In this way the Church is a sign and cause of God's communion with all humanity. It is a symbol of the unity of the whole human race. That is why we say the Church is **catholic**, or universal. We also believe that the Church is one (united in faith, worship, and authority), holy (in communion with God), and apostolic (following the tradition and teachings of the apostles). Jesus gave the apostle Peter a special authority over the Church that continues with the pope today.

GO TO page 373 to learn more about the Church.

Activities

1. Reread the last paragraph in the Scripture story on page 120. Put Jesus' statement in your own words.

   _____

   _____

   _____

   _____

2. Imagine Jesus is standing in front of you as he was with Peter. What mission do you think Jesus would give to you?

   _____

   _____

   _____

   _____

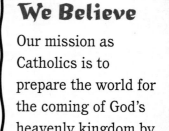

We Believe

Our mission as Catholics is to prepare the world for the coming of God's heavenly kingdom by serving others and teaching the saving message of Christ.

Faith Words

catholic
The word *catholic* means "universal." With a capital *C*, it describes the Church founded by Christ's apostles.

What are some ways we can serve others as Christ did?

Helping Hands

Dear Journal,
I met the most amazing man tonight! His name is Brother Alfred Smith. He spoke to our religious education group. He is a member of the Vincentian community, priests and brothers who live by the example of Saint Vincent de Paul. Brother Al told us that Vincent de Paul was a seventeenth-century French man. Vincent de Paul gathered priests and laity to teach poor country people about Jesus. They formed the Congregation of the Mission to assist the poor through charity and education. They now have missions all over the world.

Brother Al lives in the Germantown section of Philadelphia at Saint Vincent's parish. There are many poor and homeless families there. Brother Al said that someone had to offer them more than just a place to sleep and a warm meal. He said that Saint Vincent believed in helping the poor help themselves in the name of Christ. So, Brother Al came up with "Inn Dwelling." It's a program that provides clean, safe houses for homeless families, who can rent the homes for very little money. They can stay there for up to three years, while Brother Al and volunteers help the adults learn job skills, finish their education, and take care of their children. The families can also purchase their houses. The goal of Inn Dwelling is to help the families achieve independence.

We asked Brother Al where he gets the houses. He said that Inn Dwelling buys rundown houses at a good price, then volunteers work on them for free. The houses are done beautifully, and the volunteers get the joy of helping others get back on their feet.

I thought this was a great example of following Jesus Christ!

Activities

1. Just as Samuel, we may have trouble telling when God is calling us. But as God's children, we all have a mission. Brother Al and the volunteers carry out their mission by using their hands to create new houses for homeless people. What can you do to help others in need? In each finger of the hand, write one thing you might do to carry out your mission as a member of the Church.

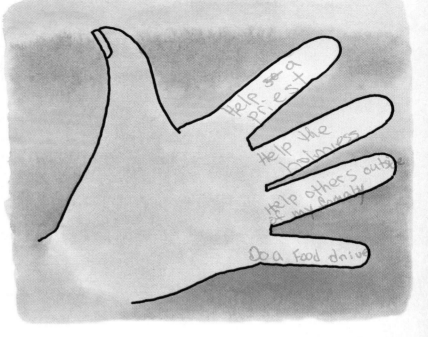

2. Complete the crossword puzzle with words you learned in this chapter.

Across

1. universal

6. _____ of God, or heaven

7. following the apostles

8. united in faith, worship, and authority

9. in communion with God

Down

1. a group of people united in some way

2. a leader with good judgment

3. to put oil on a person who has been chosen

4. a way of serving

5. people who serve in the church community

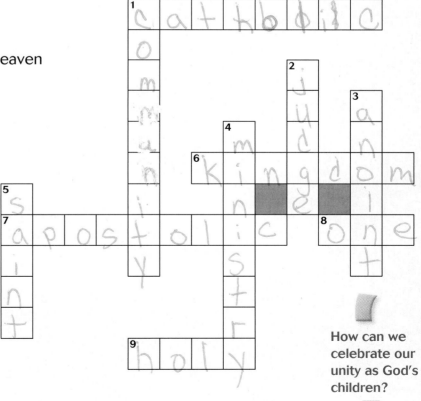

How can we celebrate our unity as God's children?

Megan

✝ Prayer Celebration

God's Creation Joined in Praise

Stand in a circle. Join hands.

Leader: Father in heaven,
from the days of Abraham and Moses
until this gathering of your Church in prayer,
you have formed a people in the image of your Son.
Bless this people with the gift of your kingdom.
May we serve you with our every desire
and show love for one another
even as you have loved us.

Alternative opening prayer for the Fourth Sunday in Ordinary Time,
Roman Missal

All: Behold, how good it is, and how pleasant, where
brothers and sisters dwell as one!

Based on Psalm 133:1

Reader A: Let all your works give you thanks, O Lord,
and let your faithful ones bless you.
Let them speak of the glory of your kingdom
and of your might.

Based on Psalm 145:10–11

Reader B: Your kingdom is a kingdom for all ages,
and your reign endures through all generations.
The Lord is faithful in all his words
and holy in all his works.

Based on Psalm 145:13

All: Save us, Lord our God, and gather us together
from the nations, so that we may proclaim your
holy name. Amen.

Based on Psalm 106:47

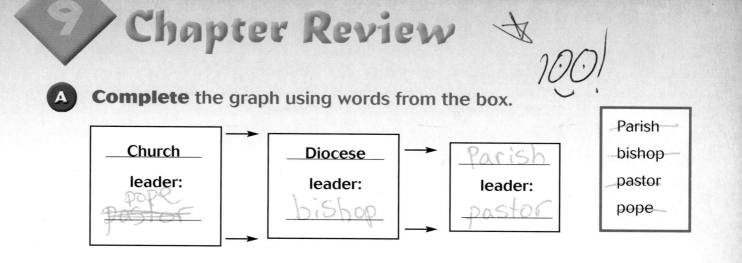

9 Chapter Review

100!

A **Complete** the graph using words from the box.

Church	→	Diocese	→	Parish
leader:		leader:		leader:
~~pastor~~ pope		bishop		pastor

Box:
Parish
bishop
pastor
pope

B **Match** Column A with Column B by writing the correct number in the space provided.

A

1. ministry
2. catholic
3. holy
4. apostolic
5. laity
6. Catholic
7. clergy
8. one

B

5 people who serve the Church and are not clergy or religious brothers and sisters

2 universal

3 in communion with God

1 a way of serving others in Christ's name

7 ordained ministers of the Church

8 united in faith, worship, and authority

6 the Church founded by Christ's apostles

4 following the teachings of the apostles

C **Respond** to the following.

1. When will the true kingdom come? The true kingdom will come not until Christ comes again and God triumphs over evil for ever.

2. What special mission was given to the Church and to Peter as the head of the Church? The special mission that was given to the Church and to Peter as the head of the Church is Peter special mission was to lead and guide the Church, the Church's special mission is to prepare the world for the coming of God's heavenly kingdom by serving others and teaching the saving message of Christ.

www.blestarewe.com

Chapter Review **125**

D **Complete** the paragraph using words from the box.

| covenant | God | heavenly kingdom |
| judges | promised land | Church |

Many of the first leaders of the Israelites were ___judges___.
They helped the Hebrew people remain faithful to their
___covenant___ with God. Samuel was an especially wise judge.
Samuel knew that a leader had to make decisions based on what
___God___ wanted. Just as God gave the Israelites the
___promised land___, God promises us that we will share in his
___heavenly kingdom___. The ___Church___ is the beginning of
God's kingdom on earth.

E **Write** a prayer of praise to God for the gift of his
kingdom on earth, the Church. Include examples of
how the Church is one, holy, catholic, and apostolic.

Dear God,
        Thank you for being so protective
of me and listening and also for makeing
the church one, holy, and catholic,
and apostoli.

F **List** some ways we can carry out the Church's mission.

We can carry out the Church's mission
by talking and listening to God. Also we
can go to mass and go to confession
and other church events

Family Time

A choice of things to do at home

The Ark and the Temple

To the Israelites, worship before the ark of the covenant in the tent was a treasured way to present oneself before God. Washing one's hands and feet before entering and continually burning lamps outside were rituals that showed respect for God's holy presence. In Canaan, the Israelites wanted a permanent holy place to keep the ark and worship God. The magnificent Temple was built, solidifying many rituals the Israelites used. Many of their rituals found new meaning in Christ and became the basis for Catholic ways of coming to the Holy Spirit through Jesus, such as Baptism.

Baptism anniversaries

Mark the dates of your baptisms on a household calendar. Celebrate your baptism anniversaries by reflecting on your mission in spreading God's love. You could even hold a family party on each person's special day.

Come to the water

Make a pilgrimage to the church or churches of your baptisms, either for a Mass or a time of quiet reflection. Light candles, and ask God to help you become what your baptism intended you to be.

Bless this home

Jewish homes are centers of religious rituals and celebrations. Every home is to be a *mikdash me'at*, or miniature sanctuary and Temple. Invite a parish priest over to bless your home, and discuss ways to make your home a sanctuary and center of God's love.

September

SUNDAY	MONDAY	TUESDAY	WEDNESDAY	THURSDAY	FRIDAY
					1
		5	6	7	8
3Shauna's Baptism Anniversary 4	LABOR DAY LABOUR DAY (CANADA)	12	13	14	
10	11			21	
17	GRANDPARENTS DAY 18	19	20		28
			27		

✝ A Prayer for the Week

Father, thank you for our sacraments and liturgies. Let them always strengthen us to live as examples of Christ and temples of the Holy Spirit. Amen.

Family Time

Something to Do . . .

On Sunday

Meditate upon the tabernacle in which the Blessed Sacrament is kept. Thank God for living among us.

Through the Week

Pay attention to daily events involving water, such as walking in the rain, washing dishes, or taking a shower. Thank God for this gift.

Visit Our Web Site

 www.blestarewe.com

Something to Think About . . .

A House vs. a True Home

God said, "I will raise up your heir after you, and I will make his kingdom firm. It is he who shall build a house for my name."
Based on 2 Samuel 7:12–13

After King David expressed his desire to build a house of worship where the ark would be kept, the Lord promised to send an heir of David who would be "as a son" to God. God said, "I will make his royal throne firm forever" (2 Samuel 7:13). This was the source of the Jewish expectation of the Messiah, which was fulfilled for us by Jesus.

God did not care as much about a concrete structure in which he would be worshiped than about the building of his kingdom on earth. Do you put too much effort in appearances? Or do you value your prayer life, values, and relationships?

Something to Know About . . . Our Heritage in Film

In *Raiders of the Lost Ark*, several people are looking for the ark that held the original stone tablets of the Ten Commandments given to Moses on Mount Sinai. Harrison Ford plays Indiana Jones, leader of the "good guys" seeking the ark. Archaeologists and fortune seekers are interested in the ark for its historical significance on one hand and its enormous worth on the other. One "bad guy" is particularly interested in the prospect of possessing an object known to have great power. Although this action-adventure flick presents an unlikely story, it does highlight the importance of the ark to present-day and ancient people.

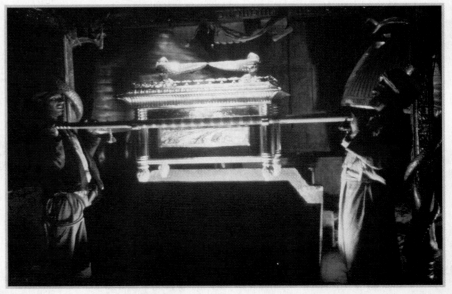

10 The Ark and the Temple

Springs of water, bless the Lord.
Give him glory and praise forever.

Easter Vigil Blessing of Water acclamation, Roman Missal

Share

Your school day usually begins with the Pledge of Allegiance. You stand, face the flag, and place your hand over your heart. Sports events usually begin with the singing of our national anthem. These are rituals, or ceremonial practices. They remind us of and honor our unity and freedom as Americans.

In the Church, rituals help us honor and prepare for God's presence. Special actions and objects remind us of Jesus Christ and prepare us for God's life in us.

Activity

The words below relate to things that remind us of Jesus Christ and prepare us for God's life in us. Find the words in the flame and circle them. You may find them across, up, down, diagonally, or backwards.

anoint
bless
candle
crucifix
genuflect
holy water
oil
palms
rosary
Sign of the Cross
Stations of the Cross

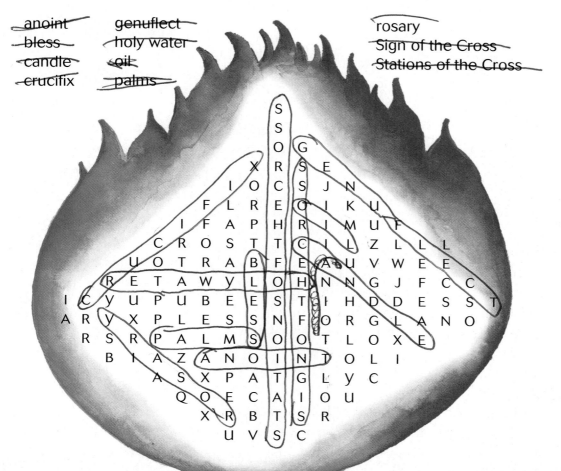

Why is water a special symbol for God's people?

129

Worship The Blessing of Water

In the Old Testament, water is a sign of God's power. The first Creation story from Genesis says God's spirit moved over the oceans. Genesis also describes the Great Flood, sent to destroy evil on earth. In the Exodus, God parted the Red Sea to help the Israelites escape Egypt, and he gave them water in the desert. God also calmed the Jordan River so the Israelites could cross over to the promised land.

In the **sacrament** of Baptism, through water blessed with the Holy Spirit, we are cleansed of original sin and given new life in Christ. During the Easter Vigil, a priest blesses water that is to be used to baptize people who have been preparing to become Catholics. In the blessing, the priest celebrates Old Testament events as signs of the saving power of the water of Baptism. He sings,

"Father, you give us grace through sacramental signs, which tell us of the wonders of your unseen power.

"In Baptism we use your gift of water, which you have made a rich symbol of the grace you give us in this sacrament.

"At the very dawn of Creation your Spirit breathed on the waters, making them the wellspring of all holiness.

"The waters of the Great Flood you made a sign of the waters of Baptism that make an end of sin and a new beginning of goodness.

"Through the waters of the Red Sea you led Israel out of slavery, to be an image of God's holy people, set free from sin by Baptism.

"In the waters of the Jordan your Son was baptized by John and anointed with the Spirit.

"Your Son willed that water and blood should flow from his side as he hung upon the cross.

"After his Resurrection he told his disciples: 'Go out and teach all nations, baptizing them in the name of the Father, and of the Son, and of the Holy Spirit.'

"Father, look now with love upon your Church, and unseal for it the fountain of Baptism.

"By the power of the Holy Spirit give to this water the grace of your Son, so that in the sacrament of Baptism all those whom you have created in your likeness may be cleansed from sin and rise to a new birth of innocence through water and the Holy Spirit."

The priest plunges the blessed Easter candle into the water once or three times as he says,

"We ask you, Father, with your Son, to send the Holy Spirit upon the waters of this font."

Based on the Blessing of Water for the Easter Vigil, Rite of Christian Initiation

Signs of God

The Israelites in the Old Testament saw God work wonders through water. They saw water's power to bring purity and goodness. In order to be pure in God's presence, they washed their hands and feet before worshiping God in the tent that held the ark of the covenant. Many Jewish people still practice ritual washings for special occasions. Through such rituals, the Israelites and their modern descendants have celebrated God's goodness throughout their history.

The Israelites felt God's presence when they were near the ark of the covenant. To honor God, they continually burned oil lamps outside it. When the Israelites settled in Canaan, they needed a permanent holy place to keep the ark and worship God together. Israel's first two kings, Saul and David, wanted to build a magnificent place to gather for worship. The **Temple** was finally built on Mount Zion, a hill in Jerusalem, during King Solomon's rule. The ark was kept in the Temple in a sacred space called the Holy of Holies. A continual light shone there, too. It reminded worshipers of the eternal covenant with God.

Activity

Look at the diagrams. How are the Temple and a Catholic church alike? How are Catholic and Hebrew, or Jewish ways of worshiping God, similar?

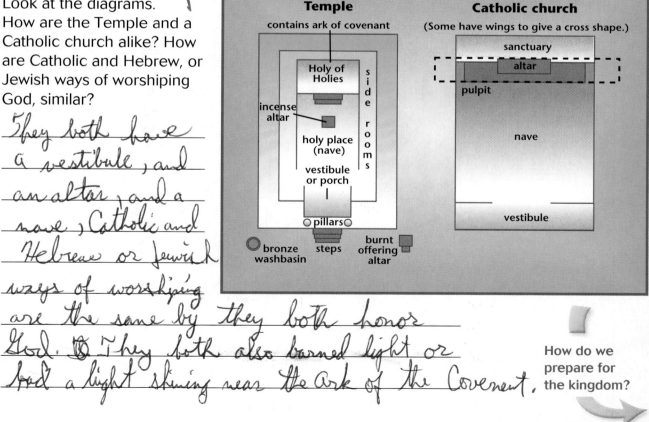

They both have a vestibule, and an altar, and a nave, Catholic and Hebrew or Jewish ways of worshiping are the same by they both honor God. They both also burned light or had a light shining near the ark of the Covenant.

How do we prepare for the kingdom?

131

Hear & Believe

A Place of God's Presence

Solomon was the Israelite king who built the first Temple. He brought in workers from all over Israel and imported cedar wood from Lebanon. He hired architects and artists from other countries and had much of the Temple covered with gold.

When the beautiful Temple was completed, Solomon ordered the priests to bring the ark of the covenant into it. The king and the people offered sacrifices at the Temple.

Solomon stood before the Temple and all of Israel. He prayed, "Can it be that God dwells with people on earth? If the heavens cannot hold back God's presence, how much less this Temple that I built!"

Then Solomon blessed the people. "Blessed be the LORD who has given peace to the people of Israel. May God be with us."

Later, the LORD said to Solomon, "I have heard your prayer. I will cause my Name to dwell in the Temple and make it holy."

Based on 1 Kings 5–6

Our Church Teaches

Jesus was the fulfillment of God's covenant with the Israelites. Early Christians adapted some of the rituals used by the Israelites to celebrate the presence of God. For example, Baptism and blessing ourselves with holy water may have grown out of Jewish ritual washings. However, Jewish rituals received new meaning from Jesus Christ. Through Jesus Christ, God could truly be present within us. Baptism and the other sacraments fill us with God's very life and presence, or grace. They are more than symbolic. They help us participate in God's kingdom on earth as well as prepare us for everlasting life with God.

Holy water, however, is a **sacramental**, something that reminds us of Jesus Christ and prepares us for God's life in us. The sacramentals of the Church change us spiritually. But they do not give grace the way sacraments do.

Catholics, like the Israelites, go to a holy place to worship and be close to God. But we also attend church to be filled with Christ. In our churches, blessed candles (which are also sacramentals) are placed upon the altar. At least one lamp continually shines near the tabernacle holding the Blessed Sacrament, Christ's Body. The light reminds us that Christ is there and that he is the eternal Light of the World.

Activity

Imagine that objects could speak in much the same way they do in cartoons. What would the following objects tell you about themselves?

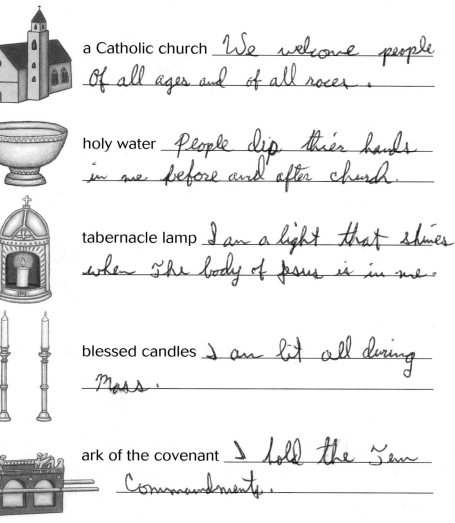

a Catholic church *We welcome people Of all ages and of all races.*

holy water *People dip their hands in me before and after church.*

tabernacle lamp *I am a light that shines when The body of Jesus is in me.*

blessed candles *I am lit all during Mass.*

ark of the covenant *I hold the Ten Commandments.*

We Believe

In Christ, symbols of creation, human life, and the Old Testament become sacramental signs. The sacraments anticipate the coming kingdom of God.

Faith Words

sacramental
A sacramental is a symbolic prayer, blessing, object, or action instituted by the Church that can lead us to a fuller participation in the grace of the sacraments.

What sacramentals are used in the sacrament of Holy Orders?

Respond

A Sacrament at the Service of Communion

Hector, Tat, and Cleo are in the cafeteria, discussing the weekend.

Hector: My uncle Rodrigo was ordained a priest on Saturday.

Cleo: What was that like? I've never seen an ordination.

Hector: Well, when men receive Holy Orders, they promise to lead and minister to Jesus' followers in the Church as bishops, priests, and deacons.

Tat: How do they promise?

Hector: First, the bishop asks if they truly want to be priests. My uncle and the other men said, "I do." They promised to follow the bishop's guidance. A bishop has the full responsibility of Holy Orders. He is in charge of a group of church communities. He has to lead and teach them, like the Twelve Apostles did with the first Christian communities. The pope guides the bishops and leads the whole Church. He is like Saint Peter, the apostle Jesus appointed to lead the first Christian communities.

Cleo: Did your uncle and the others just stand there?

Hector: Well, when they were blessed the first time, they were kneeling. Then they lay on the floor while everyone sang the Litany of the Saints, asking saints to pray for the new priests and the community.

Tat: Why were they on the floor?

Hector: My uncle says it shows their surrender to God. It can also remind them that they are servants of God and his people. They became priests when the bishop laid his hands on their heads and prayed over them. Then, they received the vestments they will wear for Mass. Their hands were also anointed with oil called *chrism*.

Cleo: Did they all get to celebrate Mass?

Hector: Yes. After the Mass, they laid their hands on us for a special blessing.

Holy Orders is a *sacrament at the service of communion*. Ordained men are dedicated to *service* to the people of the Church, who are in *communion*, or united, with Christ and one another.

page 359 to learn more about the pope and page 363 to learn more about the sacraments at the service of communion.

Activities

1. Using the clues, unscramble the words in capital letters.

MHICRS ~~Crism~~ Chrism

Clue: oil used to anoint

TRENCSAAMLA sacramental

Clue: something symbolic that reminds us of Christ's presence

EEMTLP Temple

Clue: the Israelites' center of worship

MASTCRANE sacrament

Clue: a sacred sign and cause of grace

OHYL DRORSE Holy Orders

Clue: the sacrament at the service of communion by which priests are ordained

2. In Old Testament times, people filled clay jars with water for their ritual washings. In each jar below, write something for which you are sorry—a failure you would like to wash away.

How do sacramentals bring us closer to Jesus?

Prayer Celebration

Keep Me Close to You, O Lord

Look at the objects pictured on this page. They are sacramentals. The Sign of the Cross is the sacramental that Catholics use to begin their prayers. Together, begin your prayer with it.

Now slowly gaze upon each sacramental. As you look at each object, silently ask yourself:

• When do people use the sacramental pictured?

• What events or people in the life of Jesus Christ does this remind me of?

When you have answered those questions, silently pray,

Lord Jesus, may this sacramental bring me close to you.

Now look upon the crucifix in the center. Silently gaze at it. Try to think about the many ways Jesus was suffering there on the cross, physically and emotionally.

Thank Jesus for his sacrifice, and ask forgiveness for the things you wrote in the clay jars on page 135.

Make the Sign of the Cross again.

Holy Water

OUR LA...

A Circle the words below that name an action or an *86* object in the Church that reminds us of Jesus Christ and prepares us for God's life in us.

rosary
anoint
pew
Sign of the Cross
candle
palms
holy water
Stations of the Cross

catholic
bless
genuflect
kneel
oil
holy cards
crucifix
ceremony

B Match Column A with Column B by writing the correct number in the space provided.

A	B
1. sacramental	_2_ the sacrament by which men are ordained to minister as bishops, priests, or deacons
2. Holy Orders	_5_ the Jewish place of worship in Jerusalem
3. Baptism	_4_ a sacred sign and cause of grace instituted by Christ to continue his saving action
4. sacrament	_3_ a sacrament that cleanses us of original sin and gives us new life
5. Temple	_6_ a sacred space that contained the ark of the covenant
6. Holy of Holies	_1_ a symbolic prayer, blessing, object, or action instituted by the Church

C Circle the rituals that the early Christians adapted from the Israelites to celebrate the presence of God.

blessing with water   going to a holy place to worship

praying with rosary beads   continually burning a lamp

making the Sign of the Cross

D **Follow** the steps below to compose a prayer.

1. Begin your prayer by making the Sign of the Cross.

2. Write the names of two sacramentals that could help you pray.

   Eucarist ✗   _Baptism_ ✗

3. Silently pray, "Lord Jesus, may these sacramentals bring me close to you."

4. Silently pray a prayer of thanksgiving.

5. End your prayer by making the Sign of the Cross.

E **Number** the events from the sacrament of Holy Orders. The first answer is provided.

_4_ The men lie on the floor during the Litany of the Saints.

_2_ The men promise to follow the bishop's guidance.

_1_ The bishop asks if the men truly want to be priests.

_8_ The men celebrate Mass.

_6_ The men receive the vestments they will wear to celebrate Mass.

_3_ The men kneel down to be blessed.

_5_ The bishop lays his hands on the men's heads and prays over them.

_7_ The men's hands are anointed with oil.

F **Draw** a line to match each Bible event with the idea it represents. The events are explained in the blessing of water for Baptism. _2 wrong_

Event	Idea
breath of Spirit on waters in Creation	being freed from sin by baptismal water
Great Flood	holiness of baptismal water
parting of the Red Sea	removal of sin by baptismal water

Family Time

A choice of things to do at home

David's Sin and the Story of the Fall

The happiness of many people can be lost by just one person's choosing personal satisfaction over virtue. The Bible story about David and what he did to marry Bathsheba is a prime example. Even though David was forgiven, he could not undo the consequences of his actions. The story of the Fall of Man in Genesis also explains the disobedience of humans and its consequences. But Jesus Christ brought salvation from sin, and God is always there to help us resist temptation.

Valuable tears

A tradition holds that Jewish women's tears were collected in jars and later used for special rituals. Have each family member write a one-line prayer for forgiveness on a teardrop-shaped piece of paper, fold it, and drop it into a glass jar. Imagine these prayers are tears poured out to Jesus.

Forgiveness chest

Write stories about forgiving each other, and place them inside a shoebox decorated with religious symbols. Label it "The Forgiveness Chest." Invite family members to read the stories when they have trouble showing mercy.

This is a Jewish teardrop holder.

The Spirit inside you

Draw and cut out symbols of each other's personality traits or talents, such as a clown for the family jokester or a paintbrush for the family artist. Discuss how these traits are gifts of the Holy Spirit.

✝ A Prayer for the Week

Thank you for giving us our strengths. Forgive us for sometimes acting out of weakness. Give us humility to ask forgiveness and to forgive. Amen.

Family Time

Something to Do . . .

On Sunday

Pay attention to teachings about forgiveness or mercy during Mass.

Through the Week

David's was a sin of envy toward Uriah, and Adam and Eve's a sin of envy toward God. If you feel envious of anyone, remember all the things for which you are grateful instead.

Visit Our Web Site

www.blestarewe.com

Something to Think About . . .

Remembering Legacies

*By the sweat of your face
shall you get bread to eat,
Until you return to the ground,
from which you were taken.*
Genesis 3:19

The expression "by the sweat of your brow" came from God's chastisement of Adam for eating the forbidden fruit. The legacy of the first human sin was a life of labor for all humans. Families often have stories about something that happened and its effects on future generations. What major events from the past do you think have affected your family? Try to recall events that have had positive effects on your family. How has God been with your family throughout generations?

Something to Know About . . .

Our Heritage in Legend

The flaw in Camelot in the story of King Arthur was the same as the flaw that brought down David's kingship. The musical *Camelot* tells this story in great detail. Arthur's father had Lady Igraine's husband killed in battle so he could marry the widow. Then Lancelot and Guinevere betrayed Arthur and destroyed the virtue of Camelot. Similarly, David's pursuit of another man's wife damaged his capacity for leading Israel.

11 David's Sin and the Story of the Fall

The Lord is kind and faithful to those
who keep the covenant and the laws.

Based on Psalm 25:10

Share

Making decisions is not always easy. God gave us free will, the freedom to decide how we are going to act. Think of a time when you had to choose what you knew was right over something that seemed easier to do. Since the beginning of time, people have had to make such choices. Sometimes our choices have uncomfortable consequences for us or for others. Sometimes it is hard to admit we have made a mistake.

Activity

Have you ever been in a situation when you knew the right choice was going to be difficult? What did you do? Draw yourself doing what you decided, then answer the questions.

Describe the situation that led you to have to make the choice.

_____

_____

What were the consequences of your choice?

_____

_____

Did you make the right choice? Why or why not?

_____

What happens when people do not choose goodness?

Scripture   King David and the Sin of Humanity

God was unhappy with Saul's leadership. God told Samuel to anoint a shepherd boy named David to be the new king of the Israelites. David was the youngest son of Jesse, a man from Bethlehem. The Holy Spirit rushed upon David. God blessed David as he grew.

Saul was sad that he had lost favor with the LORD. He said to his servant, "Find a talented harpist to cheer me up."

"The youngest son of Jesse is a good musician," said the servant. "He is also a good soldier. Besides, the LORD is with him."

David was brought to Saul. Saul's spirits were lifted in David's company. David was a loyal friend and soldier to Saul. Saul soon realized that God had chosen David to be the next king of Israel.

When David became king, he was a powerful leader. The LORD was with him, and he ruled honorably and fairly for many years. He made Jerusalem the capital of Israel.

But there was a beautiful married woman, Bathsheba, whom David coveted. David sent her husband, Uriah, into battle, and Uriah was killed. David and Bathsheba married and had a son. The baby died soon after it was born. God was not pleased with David's actions.

David asked for forgiveness. "I have sinned against the LORD," he said. The LORD forgave David. A new baby, called Solomon, was born.

David's sin might remind us of the story of Adam and Eve, written around David's time. It explains the human weakness for disobeying God.

Out of the soil, God created the first humans, Adam and Eve, to enjoy the beauty of the earth. God gave them a peaceful garden so that they could experience God's love every day. God also made them partners in charge of caring for the other things God had created. In return, God told Adam and Eve to not eat fruit from a certain tree in the garden, the tree of knowledge of good and evil, or they would die.

One day, a serpent tempted Eve to eat the fruit of the tree. The creature said that the fruit would make Adam and Eve smarter. Adam and Eve knew God forbade it, but they tried the fruit. Their choice made God very angry. When he asked what they had done, they were ashamed.

God said, "The humans have become like us, knowing what is good and bad!" God said to Adam, "By the sweat of your face shall you get bread to eat, until you return to the ground from which you were taken. For you are dirt, and to dirt you shall return."

God banished Adam and Eve from the happiness of the garden. The original sin of the first humans would hurt all generations after them.

Based on 1 Samuel 16; 2 Samuel 1–12; Genesis 2:4–3:23

True Freedom

The Israelites had trouble obeying God's laws and finding true happiness. Even God's anointed, Saul and David, were not free from temptation and its consequences. As we see from David's story, envy is a serious sin that is the source of many other sins. David's envy resulted in Uriah's death and damaged David's relationship with God and the kingdom. The story about Adam and Eve is sometimes called "the fall of humans." It helps explain the origin and effects of sin. The author tried to help people understand how sin affects everyone and why humans struggle. Just as Adam, Eve, and David, people sometimes use their free will to make choices that separate them from happiness and love. But David's story shows God's great ability to forgive.

Activity

From the Bible, we learn about the mystery of evil and God's power to overcome it. The story about Adam and Eve teaches us that evil came into the world because the first humans used their free will to make a sinful choice. The story about David also teaches us that sinful choices have bad consequences, but it shows that God is always ready to forgive us. Below, write a made-up story about a person who made a sinful choice but was able to find forgiveness.

_____

_____

_____

_____

_____

_____

How do we decide what is right?

143

Hear & Believe

The Parable of the Lost Son

Once, while Jesus was teaching, all the tax collectors and sinners began gathering around to listen to what he was saying. Seeing this, some people in the crowd began to complain, "This man welcomes sinners and eats with them."

"I tell you," Jesus corrected them, "there will be rejoicing among the angels of God over one sinner who repents."

Jesus began telling parables, or stories, to explain how much God loves those who repent of their sins. He said, "A man had two sons. One day, the younger son demanded his share of his father's estate. The father agreed, dividing the estate between his two sons. Packing up his belongings, the younger son departed for a distant land. There, he spent his money on whatever he desired and was soon penniless.

"When he ran out of money, he had to take a job tending pigs. He grew so hungry that he even craved the pigs' food. Finally, he came to his senses. He decided to go back to his father and say to him, 'Father, I have sinned against heaven and against you; I no longer deserve to be called your son.'

"So, the younger son walked home. His father saw him in the distance and ran out to greet him. The father embraced him, listened to his words, and ordered a great feast to celebrate his homecoming. This angered the older son, who told his father, 'All these years I have served and obeyed you, and not once have you given me the smallest feast. But when this son who has wasted all your money comes home, you throw a huge party.'

"But the father said to his dutiful son, 'My son, you are here with me always; everything I have is yours. But now we must celebrate and rejoice, because your brother was dead and has come to life again; he was lost and has been found.'"

Based on Luke 15:1–2, 10–32

144

Our Church Teaches

A good, moral act is more than something that turns out all right in the end. It is something that we start, continue, and finish with good intentions toward ourselves, others, and God. Along with free will, each of us has a **conscience**, an ability to know what is right and what is wrong. We must examine our conscience often to correctly identify what God wants. This means thinking about our choices, whether they reflect God's love, and what their results might be. If our conscience tells us that something is absolutely wrong, we must not do it. If we are sure something is right and good, we should do that. But our conscience may not always be correct, and this may not be our fault. So, God gives us **guidance** to help us develop our conscience. We are obligated to listen to the guidance of the Church, the Scriptures, and parents or other adults, and to be open to the guidance of the Holy Spirit.

The sacraments give us grace, which also helps us make good decisions. **Sacramental grace** is the unique gift of God's love that we receive in each sacrament. Through grace, we can learn to be less concerned with material goods, more holy, and more prayerful. Grace strengthens us to avoid sin. But God's love is always with us, even when we sin. We accept that love in the sacrament of Penance, or Reconciliation. Remember, the priest has made a solemn vow with God to keep our sins secret. When we repent and accept God's love in Reconciliation, God forgives us, frees us from our sins, and gives us grace so we can truly be free.

Activity

Below, draw a symbol for sin and a symbol for God's forgiveness.

How can we tell the difference between a good choice and a sinful choice?

The Tale of the Tape

One Friday, Carlos's teacher, Mrs. Meyer, showed a video about the book his class was reading for English.

"Don't forget—Tuesday is your test," she said. "There will be a bonus question based on the movie we just watched. I hope you were paying attention."

Now I am, thought Carlos. *If only she had told us before—I would have stayed awake and taken notes!* Carlos hadn't read the book, and his grades in English weren't great. Any bonus points would help.

"May I borrow the tape to watch at home?" asked Carlos.

"I'm sorry, Carlos, but it wouldn't be fair to the rest of the class," Mrs. Meyer said.

The bell rang, and the class was dismissed. As Carlos walked by the teacher's desk, he slipped the tape into his backpack. He would return it to the teacher before she knew it was missing.

That weekend, he watched the tape several times, almost memorizing it. He was sure he would be able to answer the bonus question and get the extra points.

On Monday morning, Mrs. Meyer made an announcement. "I had planned on showing the tape again today, but I can't seem to find it. Does anyone know where it might be?"

The students looked at each other. Carlos, of course, knew where it was: on his desk at home. He forgot to bring it back to school!

"Well," said Mrs. Meyer, "I have no choice but to base the test only on the book. If you read the book, you won't have any problem doing well."

Carlos panicked. The class groaned.

"This doesn't seem fair," said Theresa.

"It wasn't fair of the person who took the tape to place his or her own needs above those of the class," said Mrs. Meyer.

"Come on, whoever you are, give the tape back!" Ronnie shouted.

What would Jesus say about this?

What will happen if I keep the tape?

What would my parents think?

Activities

1. Help Carlos decide the right thing to do. Fill in answers to the questions in his mind. Then discuss what you would do if you were Carlos.

2. Think back to the situation you drew on page 141. How did you feel after your decision was made? Choose the words below that describe the way you felt. Write them inside the cardboard box where you think they belong.

relieved	happy	nervous	faithful	loved
guilty	proud	unsure	afraid	alone
lonely	ashamed	confident	free	sad

3. Prayer and the sacraments strengthen us to avoid sin. During the sacrament of Penance, we say a prayer called the Act of Contrition, or Prayer of Sorrow. In this prayer, we express our sadness about sinning and our desire to do better. We also pray that God will have mercy. Write your own act of contrition.

Dear God,

How do we ask God for forgiveness during the liturgy?

147

✝ Prayer Celebration

Cast Away Your Sins

During Rosh Hashanah, Jewish people reflect upon the past year. They remember sins they have committed. They perform symbolic gestures to show they are sorry, such as throwing pieces of bread into flowing water to cast away mistakes. Ten days later, on Yom Kippur (the "Day of Atonement"), the Jewish community repents and asks forgiveness for sins. They gather to chant a prayer called Al Cheyt, meaning "for the sins." They lightly hit their chests and list their sins, praying for forgiveness for the whole community.

During the Mass, Catholics perform the Penitential Rite. The priest asks us to call to mind our sins. Then we pray the Confiteor, a prayer of sorrow for ourselves and for our community. A Catholic tradition is to hit our chests lightly as a sign of regret while praying this prayer. Think about your day. Did you purposely do or say something that hurt someone else? If you had the chance, would you act differently?

The Confiteor

All: I confess to almighty God,
and to you, my brothers and sisters,
that I have sinned through my own fault
(gently strike your chest)
in my thoughts and in my words,
in what I have done,
and in what I have failed to do;
and I ask blessed Mary, ever virgin,
all the angels and saints,
and you, my brothers and sisters,
to pray for me to the Lord our God.

Roman Missal

11 Chapter Review

A **Write** a brief summary of what you learned in this chapter, using the words in the box.

conscience	guidance	Reconciliation	free will

_____

_____

_____

_____

B **Identify** the person who is speaking in each sentence.

1. God chose me to be king after Saul. I disobeyed God by coveting the wife of another man. _____

2. The king sent my husband, Uriah, into battle. When he was killed, the king married me. _____

3. I was born after my father, King David, asked God's forgiveness.

   _____

4. God said to me, "By hard work will you get food to eat, until you return to the ground from which you came." _____

5. A serpent tempted me to eat the fruit of the tree of knowledge.

   _____

C **Compose** a prayer of sorrow that you could pray when you have done something displeasing to God.

_____

_____

_____

_____

D **Circle** the letter of the best answer.

1. _____ is the unique gift of God's love that we receive in the sacraments.

   a. Conscience

   b. Sacramental grace

   c. Knowledge

   d. Guidance

2. The Church, the Scriptures, our parents and other adults, and the Holy Spirit can give us _____ to help us make good choices.

   a. guidance

   b. permission

   c. free will

   d. happiness

3. A _____ is an ability to know what is right and what is wrong.

   a. free will

   b. strength

   c. conscience

   d. consequence

4. The story about Adam and Eve helps explain _____.

   a. envy as a serious sin

   b. the importance of prayer

   c. the origin and effects of sin

   d. the abundance of the natural world

E **Respond** to the following situation.

Imagine that you have an opportunity to do something exciting. The problem is that you're not sure if it's the right, or moral, thing to do. Describe how you will decide what to do.

_____

_____

_____

_____

_____

_____

Family Time

A choice of things to do at home

Psalms of Praise and Works of Wonder

Music gives us a different way to experience prayer. The tone of the music can bring joy, consolation, or hope to prayer. Poetry too conveys messages of faith in more emotional ways than normal speech. Psalms are prayers, poems, and songs all wrapped up into one. They are a powerful part of the Church's prayer life, with a rich Old Testament history.

A psalm of thanksgiving

Write a poem of thanksgiving, having each family member contribute a line about something for which he or she wishes to thank God. Using magazines or family photos, decorate the poem with pictures of the people or things mentioned.

Make your own music

Have family members try to sing psalm phrases to their own melodies. See how the mood seems to change with each person's voice.

Prayer gear

At morning worship in some congregations, Jewish people wear a *tallit*, or prayer shawl, while they pray, to show that prayer time is special and sacred. Choose a holy item—the Bible, a crucifix, rosaries—that people in your family can keep close by during prayer time.

✝ A Prayer for the Week

We praise you, Lord, for your wonderful ways. You have given us many gifts, and we especially thank you for the gifts of music and poetry. Amen.

Family Time

www.blestarewe.com

Something to Do . . .

On Sunday

During the responsorial psalm, try to experience the calm that Saul felt when David sang and played the harp.

Through the Week

Try to speak in ways that bring love and calm to others, just as David's music did for Saul.

Visit Our Web Site

 www.blestarewe.com

Something to Think About . . .

God's Amazing Creations

*The heavens declare the glory of God,
and the firmament proclaims his handiwork.*

Psalm 19:2

We still believe the heavens are telling of the glory of God, and we are still humbled and awed by God's creation. The Psalms are unique in that they speak to us today in much the same way they did to the Hebrews centuries before Christ's birth. The meaning of the language of these very old prayers has not become lost to us, nor do they suffer any distortion of rhythm that might have been caused by their translation from Hebrew. The Psalms help us renew our wonder for creation and bring it into our homes, where each person may be viewed as a remarkable, wonderful creation of God.

Something to Know About . . .

Our Heritage in Poetry

Gerard Manley Hopkins was a Jesuit priest who lived in the nineteenth century. He was the brilliant son of a wealthy English couple, whom he shocked by becoming Catholic and then a priest. He had a unique way of expressing his thoughts and a deep appreciation for God in nature. He ended the poem "Pied Beauty" by reminding the reader to praise God. Hopkins lived only forty-five years and was not published until thirty years after his death.

12 Psalms of Praise and Works of Wonder

You are God: we praise you;
You are the Lord: we acclaim you;
You are the eternal Father:
All creation worships you.

Te Deum, Roman Missal

Share

How do you feel when someone compliments you?
We all feel special when we are noticed for
something good. We like it when people see
what we have done and say, "Wow!"

What makes you say "Wow!" about God? a sunrise
or sunset? a forest? the mountains? another person?
Everything around you shows that God is great and
loves you. The world is full of things that remind us
of God and make us say, "Wow!"

Activity

Fill in the following song of praise for God,
using the clues for parts of speech to help you.

Every day I will _____ you, and
            (verb)

I will bless your _____ forever and ever.
                (noun)

I will _____ the fame of your goodness and sing
        (verb)

_____ of your _____.
    (adverb)   (noun)

The Lord is _____ to all his people, and holy
              (adjective)

in all his _____.
              (noun)

May my _____ speak of the praise of the
              (noun)

Lord, and may all_____ bless his
                    (noun)

_____ name.
    (adjective)

Based on Psalm 145

When do we
sing songs of
praise for God?

153

Hear & Believe

✝ Scripture   David's Songs

King David had great faith in the LORD. He liked to use his musical talent to praise and thank God. David had to defend Israel in battle many times. After one victory, he sang the following song to thank God for God's protection, power, and faithfulness.

"O LORD, my rock, my fortress, my deliverer,
    my God, my rock of refuge!
'Praised be the LORD,' I exclaim,
    and I am safe from my enemies.
In my distress I called upon the LORD
    and cried out to my God;
From his temple he heard my voice,
    and my cry reached his ears.
The LORD thundered from heaven;
    the Most High gave forth his voice.
He sent arrows to put my enemy to flight;
    he flashed lightning and routed them.
He rescued me from my mighty enemy."

Later, when David was too old to rule over Israel, God chose Solomon, the son of David and Bathsheba, to be the next king. David knew Solomon would fulfill his dream of building a magnificent temple in Jerusalem in which to worship God and keep the ark of the covenant.

"Bless the LORD your God!" David told the people when God had chosen Solomon. David reminded Solomon to honor the LORD's covenant and to be faithful always. David said, "O LORD, God of our fathers Abraham, Isaac, and Israel, direct the hearts of your people toward you. Give my son Solomon a wholehearted desire to keep your commandments."

Solomon was anointed king. David soon ended his forty-year rule over Israel. He died a faithful follower of the LORD.

*Based on 2 Samuel 22:1–2, 4, 7, 14–15, 18; 1 Kings 1–2;
1 Chronicles 28:1–21, 29:18–28*

Singing Praise

David gained Saul's favor by singing songs of praise for the Lord. For centuries David was believed to have been the author of the **Psalms** from the Book of Psalms in the Old Testament, but several people may actually have written them from David's time until about 400 B.C. The Book of Psalms is a collection of 150 religious songs and prayers. The song of David you just read is found in the Book of Psalms as Psalm 18.

The name *psalm* comes from the Greek word *psalterion*, which was a stringed musical instrument. Often, a psalm's purpose was to express praise, thanksgiving, or sorrow. We believe that the Psalms were composed for use during religious ceremonies. The singing was often accompanied by stringed or wind instruments.

Psalms tell of God's great actions and people's response to God. The words and themes of the Psalms are still fitting today. They may be prayed alone or with a congregation.

— ✻ know

Faith Words

Psalms

Psalms are religious songs and prayers from the Old Testament. Many psalms express praise for God and are believed to have been written by David.

Activity

David sang a song to thank God for a victory. Recall a happy time or victory in the lives of the Israelites. Write a poem or song lyrics celebrating how God helped the Israelites.

_____

_____

_____

_____

_____

_____

_____

_____

_____

_____

What do the psalms mean to us today?

Hear & Believe

Psalm 23: The Lord, Shepherd and Host

For centuries, Psalm 23 from the Book of Psalms has comforted people. This psalm offers simple words of trust in God to carry us through difficult times. Tradition holds that David, the shepherd who became king, wrote Psalm 23. Since it was written, millions of people have memorized it. We believe that even Jesus himself knew it well.

For centuries, the Church has been praying this psalm during liturgies, especially at funerals. Musicians both ancient and modern have composed melodies for the inspirational words of Psalm 23. Here is a hymn based on Psalm 23 that we might sing during a liturgy today.

Psalm 23: My Shepherd Is the Lord

Joseph Gelineau

REFRAIN:

My shep-herd is the Lord, noth-ing in-deed shall I want.

VERSES:

1. The Lord is my shepherd; there is nothing I shall want. Fresh and green are the pastures where he gives me repose. Near restful waters he leads me, to revive my drooping spirit.

2. He guides me along the right path; he is true to his name. If I should walk in the valley of darkness no evil would I fear. You are there with your crook and your staff; with these you give me comfort.

3. You have prepared a banquet for me in the sight of my foes. My head you have anointed with oil, my cup is overflowing.

Our Church Teaches

Many psalms begin and end with the exclamation "*Hallelujah!*" This word—which means "Praise the Lord!"—is a combination of a Hebrew word for praise (*hallelu*) and the beginning of the word *Yahweh*. Today, we say, "Alleluia!" when we want to express our joy and praise for God. Another important part of our prayers is also a word from the Hebrew tradition of prayer—the word **amen**, which means "I believe," or "So it is."

The Catholic Church has adapted many psalms for our liturgical celebrations. In the Liturgy of the Word, we pray a responsorial psalm. A leader sings or reads a psalm, and the congregation sings or reads a response after each verse. During the Mass, we may also sing several songs that are based on psalms. Psalms are simple and loving ways for us to express how much we adore God. Modern liturgical songwriters show **reverence** to God with songs that contain words from the Psalms.

Activity

As you have learned, many psalms contain certain expressions, such as *Hallelujah!* and *Amen*. Expressions often found in psalms are listed in the box. Write a prayer that uses at least five of the expressions.

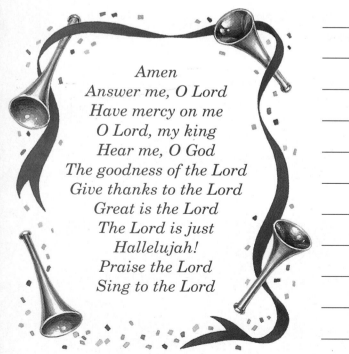

Amen
Answer me, O Lord
Have mercy on me
O Lord, my king
Hear me, O God
The goodness of the Lord
Give thanks to the Lord
Great is the Lord
The Lord is just
Hallelujah!
Praise the Lord
Sing to the Lord

What are some ways that God is worthy of praise?

Respond

"Little Less Than the Angels"

Read the verses from Psalm 8 below. What does the psalm writer say about people's place in the universe? How do humans measure up to the rest of creation?

Psalm 8	**My Psalm**

O Lord, our Lord,
  how glorious is your name over all the earth!
When I behold your heavens, the work of
   your fingers,
  the moon and the stars that you
    set in place—
What are people that you should be mindful
   of them?
You have made them little less than
   the angels
  and crowned them with glory and honor.
You have given them rule over the works
   of your hands, putting all things under
  their feet:
All sheep and oxen,
  yes, and the beasts of the field,
The birds of the air, the fishes of the sea.
O Lord, our Lord,
  how glorious is your name over all the earth!	

Based on Psalm 8:2, 4–9

Activities

1. In the second column, rewrite Psalm 8 in your own words, or write your own psalm, using Psalm 8 as a model. Address God with reverence and identify the blessings God has given you.

2. You have been asked to film some of the events that are described in the psalm below. The film is called "A Very Special Delivery." It is about the Hebrews' journey to the promised land. In the frames, draw any scenes you would like to film to show God's powerful acts for Israel.

Praise of God, Israel's Deliverer

Come and see the works of God,
  his tremendous deeds among the people.
He has changed the sea into dry land;
  through the river they passed on foot;
  therefore let us rejoice in him.
He rules by his might forever;
  his eyes watch the nations;
  rebels may not exalt themselves.
You let men ride over our heads;
  we went through fire and water,
  but you have led us
    out to refreshment.

Based on Psalm 66:5–7, 12

How might we rejoice over examples of God's goodness?

159

✝ Prayer Celebration

Rejoice!

This is a church song, based on Psalm 122, that we might sing at Mass. The actual music and lyrics are on page 114.

Group 1: I rejoiced when I heard them say: "Let us go to the house of the Lord."

Group 2: And now our feet are standing within your gates, O Jerusalem.

All: Let us go rejoicing to the house of the Lord.

Group 1: Jerusalem is a city built with unity and strength,

Group 2: It is there, it is there that the tribes go up, the tribes of the Lord.

All: Let us go rejoicing to the house of the Lord.

Group 1: For Israel's law is to praise God's name and there to give God thanks.

Group 2: There are set the judgment thrones for all of David's house.

All: Let us go rejoicing to the house of the Lord.

Group 1: Pray for the peace of Jerusalem! "May those who love you prosper;

Group 2: May peace ever reign within your walls, and wealth within your buildings!"

All: Let us go rejoicing to the house of the Lord.

Text: Psalm 122; Michael Joncas, © 1987, GIA Publications, Inc.; refrain trans. © 1969, ICEL Music: Michael Joncas, © 1987, GIA Publications, Inc.

A **Write** a brief summary of what you learned about the Book of Psalms in this chapter.

I learned that a Psalm is a religious
song or prayer from the Old Testament.
I also learned that at mass we sing
psalms to praise, and thank God and ~~we also~~ they are also
used for sorrow

B **Compose** a prayer that praises God and gives examples of his goodness. The first sentence is provided.

Words of praise to God

God, you made all things beautiful:

Examples of God's goodness

children, laughter, and blue skies.

O Lord you love all things. ~~children~~ people, land, plants, animals, sea,
Lord you are kind   you love us even if we do bad things
God you are good   you listen to your prayers,

C **Circle** the letter of the best answer.

1. Many psalms begin and end with the exclamation ___a.___.

   a. Hallelujah!   b. Amen!
   c. So it is!   d. Rejoice!

2. *Amen* is a word that means ___c.___.

   a. "praise God"   b. "Alleluia"
   c. "I believe"   d. "time to end"

3. The Catholic Church has adapted many psalms for our ___d.___ celebrations.

   a. Old Testament   b. anniversary
   c. Christmas   d. liturgical

4. Psalms are simple and loving ways for us to show how much we ___b.___ God.

   a. bless   b. adore
   c. pray to   d. enjoy

D **Respond** to the following.

1. Read the verses of Psalm 146 that appear in blue in your book on page 46. What do the verses say about God that remind us of his goodness? Rewrite the verses in blue in your own words.

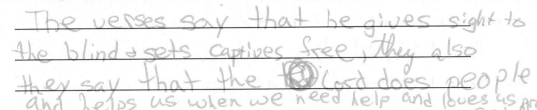

The verses say that he gives sight to the blind & sets captives free, they also they say that the Lord does people good and helps us when we need help and loves us protects us and the thwarts the wicked,

2. If you could illustrate the verses, what would you draw? Draw two illustrations that go with the verses.

E **Read** the song based on Psalm 122 on page 160 in your book. People entering the holy city of Jerusalem sang this song. How does the song praise God?

This Psalm praises God by the person that sang this Psalm were praising God for listening & talking to them like when they say "I rejoiced when I heard them say let us go to the house of the Lord."

WE CARE *About Parish and Community*

Serving the People Who Served Us

The U.S. armed forces risk their lives to protect our country. Former members of the armed forces are called veterans. Many veterans served in wars in foreign areas, such as Korea, Vietnam, the Persian Gulf, Bosnia, and Kosovo, or in World War I or II.

Many veterans received serious injuries while serving our country and need hospital care all year long. The U.S. Department of Veterans Affairs (VA) operates about 170 hospitals for veterans. There is at least one in each state. There are also many VA clinics and nursing homes. About 100,000 veterans are treated each day. Some of these veterans do not get many visitors, and they may feel very alone. Some of them also do not have much money. Veterans' hospitals need volunteers to cheer up the veterans and bring them the things they need.

Every February, the United States observes America's National Salute to Hospitalized Veterans week. People send the veterans valentines and special gifts. Veterans also need our kindness all year long. It is important to show them that we have not forgotten the sacrifices they have made for our freedom. The sixth-grade students in a Catholic school in Clifton, New Jersey, understand this. They bring handmade cards and basic necessities, such as brushes and ·socks, to the local veterans' hospital.

Finding out how to help the veterans in your community is not difficult. Visit the Web site www.va.gov.

In what ways have the armed forces promoted our freedom?

Think About It

Many veterans had to suffer in terrible conditions outdoors. They may have bravely saved others' lives or had to watch fellow soldiers die in battle. The government honors the veterans' courage, but it is important for ordinary citizens to show their admiration, too.

Learn About It

People who are suffering exist in every community. When people who were ill or hurt came to Jesus for help, he immediately helped them any way he could. When we visit people who are ill, such as veterans in hospitals, we carry on Jesus' work.

Visiting the sick is one of the corporal works of mercy. Mercy is the compassion we show for people who are suffering. The corporal works of mercy are deeds that relieve the physical suffering of others as Jesus taught. They also include feeding the hungry, giving drink to the thirsty, clothing the naked, and sheltering the homeless.

Do Something About It

In what ways does your parish or school help people who are ill?

_____

_____

_____

_____

Think of something your class can do to help veterans or other people in hospitals, and draw a picture of your idea.

If you were a veteran, how would you like the American people to show their appreciation for you?

_____

_____

_____

If you were a veteran in a hospital, what kinds of things would brighten your day?

_____

_____

_____

_____

The church banners below show the titles of the
chapters in Unit 3, but the second part of each title is
misplaced. Correct the banners by drawing a line from
the top half of each banner to its correct bottom half.
Then write the main topic of each chapter on the lines.

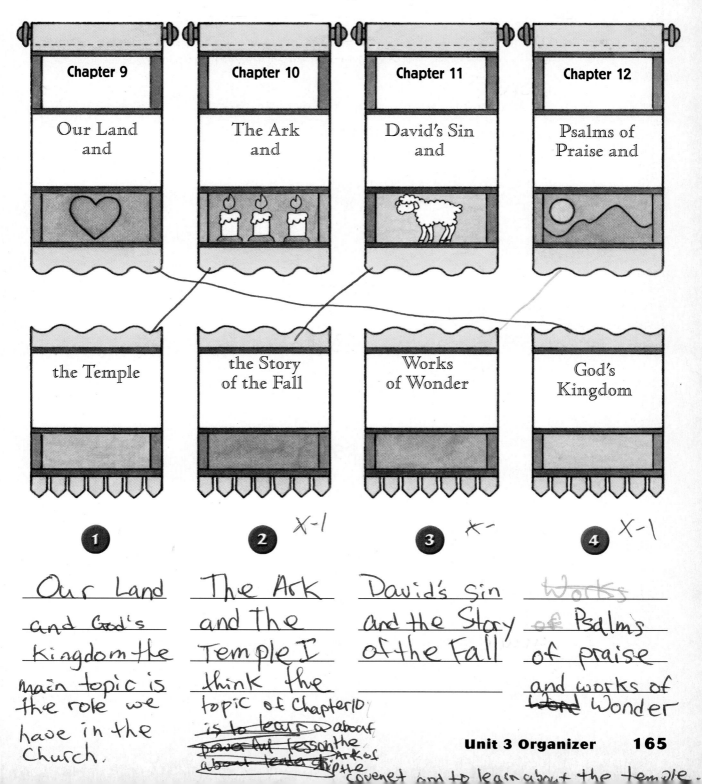

Chapter 9	Chapter 10	Chapter 11	Chapter 12
Our Land and	The Ark and	David's Sin and	Psalms of Praise and

| the Temple | the Story of the Fall | Works of Wonder | God's Kingdom |

1

2 x-1

3 x-

4 x-1

1. Our Land and God's Kingdom the main topic is the role we have in the Church.

2. The Ark and The Temple I think the topic of chapter 10 is to learn about powerful lesson about tender ship the Ark of the covenet and to learn about the temple.

3. David's Sin and the Story of the Fall

4. Works of Psalms of praise and works of Word Wonder

A **Complete** the sentences with words from the box. One word is used twice.

~~pope~~	~~bishops~~	~~psalms~~	~~Temple~~
~~grace~~	~~free will~~	~~Baptism~~	~~forgive~~
~~power~~	~~kingdom~~	~~sins~~	~~songs~~

1. The ___pope___ leads the whole Church. The Church is made up of parish communities that are part of dioceses, which are led by ___bishops___.

2. According to tradition, many of the ___songs___ and prayers from the Book of Psalms were written by David, the shepherd who became king and the father of Solomon.

3. Just as God gave the Israelites the promised land, God promises us a share in his ___Kingdom___.

✗ 4. In the stories of Creation, the Great Flood, and the Exodus, water is a sign of God's ___grace power___

5. The sacrament of ___Baptism___ may have grown out of Jewish ritual washings.

6. When we repent, God forgives our ___sins___.

7. The Church has adapted many ___Psalms___ for its liturgical celebrations.

8. The story of King David shows that God is always ready to ___forgive___ us.

9. King Solomon built the ___Temple___.

10. God gave us ___free will___ for choosing between right and wrong.

11. The ___grace___ we receive in the sacraments strengthens us to avoid sin.

✗ 12. Jesus gave Saint Peter a special authority over the Church that continues with the ___power pope___ today.

B **Circle** the letter of the best answer.

1. The Church is called _____ because it teaches us about faith and protects the truths God has revealed.

   a. Father   **b.** Mother   **c.** holy   **d.** Catholic

2. Another name for the Church is the "_____ of Christ" because of Christ's sacrifice and love for the Church.

   a. Devotion   **b.** Family   **c.** Gift   **d.** Bride

3. The _____ is the beginning of God's kingdom on earth.

   a. Old Testament   **b.** New Testament

   c. Church   **d.** Eucharist

4. When men receive _____, they promise to lead and minister to Jesus' followers in the Church as bishops, priests, and deacons.

   a. Holy Orders   **b.** sacramental grace

   c. gifts of the Holy Spirit   **d.** Christ's Body

5. We develop our _____ by listening to the guidance of the Church, the Scriptures, parents or other adults, and the Holy Spirit.

   a. dignity   **b.** conscience   **c.** holiness   **d.** grace

C **Describe** the Catholic Church using each word in the box.

one	holy	catholic	apostolic

The Catholic Curch is one by we are one united in faith, worship & athority, we are all catholic, we are holy by going to Mass, and we are apostolic by following the aposels

D Match Column A with Column B by writing the correct number in the space provided.

A

1. amen
2. catholic
3. conscience
4. guidance
5. laity
6. ministry
7. psalms
8. reverence
9. sacrament
10. sacramental
11. sacramental grace
12. Temple

B

__9__ a sacred sign and cause of grace instituted by Christ

__10__ a symbolic prayer, blessing, object, or action instituted by the Church

__6__ a way of serving

__2__ a word meaning "universal" and describing the Church founded by Christ's apostles

__3__ an ability to know what is right and what is wrong

__4__ help in making the right choices

__8__ honor and respect

__5__ people who serve the church community and are not clergy or religious brothers or sisters

__7__ religious songs and prayers from the Old Testament

__12__ the Jewish place of worship in Jerusalem that contained the ark of the covenant

__11__ the unique gift of God's love that we receive in each sacrament

__1__ a word meaning "I believe" or "So it is"

God Reminds Us to Do His Will

The faith of the Israelites was tested through exile and persecution. We are called to remember our faith, even in a world that challenges our Christian values.

> For the LORD of hosts will have his day against all that is proud and arrogant, all that is high, and it will be brought low.
>
> Isaiah 2:12

Exile of the Israelites

Haran
Nineveh
ASSYRIA
BABYLONIA
Damascus
Babylon
Mediterranean Sea
Samaria
Jerusalem
ARABIA
EGYPT

Exile from Israel to Assyria →
Exile from Judah to Babylon →

Forced into exile, the Israelites carried their possessions on their backs, as they traveled to Assyria and Babylon. The map shows their journeys.

We Are Climbing Jacob's Ladder

African-American spiritual

1. We   are   climb - ing   Ja - cob's   lad - der,
2. Ev - 'ry   round   goes   high - er,   high - er,
3. Sin - ner,   do   you   love   my   Je - sus?
4. If   you   love   him,   why   not   serve him?
5. We   are   climb - ing   high - er,   high - er,

We   are   climb - ing   Ja - cob's   lad - der,
Ev - 'ry   round   goes   high - er,   high - er,
Sin - ner,   do   you   love   my   Je - sus?
If   you   love   him,   why   not   serve him?
We   are   climb - ing   high - er,   high - er,

We   are   climb - ing   Ja - cob's   lad - der,
Ev - 'ry   round   goes   high - er,   high - er,
Sin - ner,   do   you   love   my   Je - sus?
If   you   love   him,   why   not   serve him?
We   are   climb - ing   high - er,   high - er,

Sol - diers   of   the   cross. _____

Family Time

A choice of things to do at home

Disobedience and Guidance

This chapter explores what happens when people feel that they no longer need God, concentrating on the period of King Solomon's rule of Israel. The nation enjoyed a time of renown and riches when Solomon ruled. Good fortune began to cloud the people's ability to focus on God. Prophets stepped in and tried to remind the Israelites of their covenant with God. Who plays the role of prophet in your family's life of faith?

There's an old saying . . .

Solomon gained fame for his wise sayings, or proverbs. Work together on a poster listing some proverbs that are popular in your home. Contact grandparents or great-grandparents for their input.

Be a mentor

Look for mentoring opportunities for your family. Adults might join an organization of mentors for disadvantaged youngsters. Children might mentor younger siblings.

Play the prophet

Family members could role-play the parts of the prophets Elijah, Micah, and Isaiah (see pages 174 and 175 of this chapter). The players should emphasize the main message of the prophet they portray.

✝ A Prayer for the Week

Lord, we know that your ancient prophets expressed your will. Let us always find the guidance we need in our own lives. Give us the wisdom to guide others.
Amen.

Family Time

Something to Do . . .

On Sunday

At the Sunday liturgy, listen for wise sayings in the readings that can provide guidance for particular areas of your life.

Through the Week

Share examples of how people in your lives have provided you with guidance.

Visit Our Web Site

www.blestarewe.com

Something to Know About . . .

Our Heritage in Language

Many everyday sayings come from the Bible or from Catholic tradition. Have you ever said that someone "got off Scot free"? This used to refer to being exempt from a tax to support the clergy, paid with a coin called a *sceat*. Do you call important days "red letter days"? This referred to saints' feast days and holidays, traditionally printed in red on calendars. The word *tawdry* is a corruption of the name of Saint Audrey, at whose annual festivals showy, low-quality jewelry once could be seen. When you say, "Leopards never change their spots," you echo the feelings of Jeremiah about the sinfulness of Jerusalem (Jeremiah 13:23).

Something to Think About . . .

Hearing the Prophets

Early and often did the LORD send his messengers to them, for he had compassion on his people.
2 Chronicles 36:15

Have you ever wondered whether you would have heeded the prophets of old if you had lived when they did? Prophets are the messengers of the Lord. Their messages are often rejected because they go against the beliefs or habits of a culture. People are often reluctant to do what prophets tell them to do. Think of people in your own life who acted as messengers of God. How did you respond to their message? If you ignored their message, examine your reasons for doing so. Think of people in the world today who may be prophets. What messages are they sending us?

The Filbert nut is named after Saint Philibert because it is ripe by his feast day.

13 Disobedience and Guidance

When you look for me, you will find me.
Yes, when you seek me with all your heart.

Jeremiah 29:13

Share

Sometimes when things are going well for us, we forget to thank God. We might even forget about God altogether. We can be so caught up in the good things that are happening and the fun we are having that we forget to take time out for God. It sometimes takes another person to remind us to pray, to worship, and to do good things for other people.

Activity

Place a check mark next to each person who reminds you to stay faithful to God.

❏ parent

❏ grandparent

❏ coach

❏ friend

❏ brother or sister

❏ priest

❏ religious sister

❏ teacher

❏ neighbor

❏ mentor

❏ other: _____

How did God remind his people to be faithful?

Hear & Believe

 ## Scripture   The Rule of King Solomon

After Solomon became king of Israel, he told God, "You have shown great favor to my father David, and you have allowed me to follow in his footsteps as king. Give me wisdom and knowledge to lead this people."

God replied, "You have not asked for riches, treasures, or glory. Instead, you have asked for wisdom and knowledge to rule my people. So, I will give you wisdom and knowledge. I will also give you riches, treasures, and glory." The LORD kept his promise. He blessed Solomon, giving him a glorious reign no other king of Israel had enjoyed.

Other kings came to hear the wisdom God had put in Solomon's heart. Solomon had many wise sayings, called *proverbs*. People brought treasures to Solomon. His nation soon had thousands of horses, chariots, gold and silver items, and garments. Israel became a rich and powerful nation. Solomon decided to build a great temple in Jerusalem to honor the LORD. When it was finished, priests carried the ark of the covenant into the Temple. The community of Israel gathered in the Temple. They sang and offered sacrifices to the LORD. But Solomon turned to other gods when he was old.

Solomon ruled Israel for forty years. When he died, his son Rehoboam became king. Rehoboam ignored advice from elders who had helped Solomon rule. Seeing that the king would not listen to them, some Israelites revolted. The kingdom divided into Judah in the south and Israel in the north. Many of the people, spoiled by their riches, began to forget their covenant with the LORD. They did not keep God's laws. They worshiped false gods. Rich people mistreated the poor.

The LORD was displeased. The LORD sent people to remind the Jews of Israel and Judah of their covenant with him. One **prophet**, Elijah, called the people together and said, "The God who answers with fire is God." The people prepared a sacrifice. Then Elijah asked the LORD to bring his people back to their senses. Suddenly, the LORD's fire came and consumed the sacrifice. The people fell to the ground and said, "The LORD is God!" But they did not change.

The LORD sent the prophet Hosea, who told the people that their behavior was similar to that of an unfaithful wife. He said that even though they had broken their covenant with the LORD, the LORD still loved them and waited for their return as a loving husband would.

The prophet Micah urged the people to act justly and love others. He saw that if the people did not change their ways they would be scattered among their enemies.

Finally, the prophet Isaiah warned, "This land is full of treasures and idols. Get behind the rocks and hide from the terror of the LORD. For the LORD will have his day against all that is proud and arrogant. All that is high will be brought low."

Based on 1 Chronicles 29:25; 2 Chronicles 1:1–15, 5, 9:23–31, 10:3–19, 36:14–16; Hosea 3–4; 1 Kings 11:4, 15:22–24, 18:21–39; Isaiah 2:6–19; Micah 2–6

Guidance from the Lord

When the Israelites were suffering, it was easier for them to remain faithful to God. They needed God's help, so they prayed and worshiped him. After they settled into the kingdom, they enjoyed great wealth under Solomon's rule. Many of them stopped praying and worshiping. Once they stopped praying and worshiping, they were open to distractions from God. They eventually began to worship other gods altogether, and the wealthy mistreated the poor.

God was not about to let his people abandon him, however. God intended to save them from their sinful ways. The Old Testament prophets, such as Hosea and Micah, served God's plan by preaching to the people that God would forgive them, free them from sin, and welcome them back into God's covenant relationship. Through the prophets, God helped the people begin to hope for **salvation**.

Faith Words

prophet

A prophet is a person sent by God to speak out against accepted behavior that does not follow God's will.

salvation

Salvation is freedom from the pain of sin.

Activity

Imagine that the prophet Elijah, Hosea, Micah, or Isaiah were alive today. What sinful ways in our world would this prophet speak out against? Write newspaper headlines that describe the prophet speaking about such issues.

How are we guided back to God today?

Hear & Believe

A Special Gift

When he was still a great king, and long before he began to worship other gods, Solomon enjoyed many gifts from God. God's greatest gift to Solomon was wisdom. The following story illustrates Solomon's special gift of wisdom.

Two women who lived in the same house each gave birth to a son around the same time. But when one woman's baby died, she stole the other woman's baby and put her dead son in his place. Both mothers claimed that the living infant was their own.

To resolve the matter, the women argued their cases before King Solomon. Solomon listened to them, then said to his attendant, "Bring a sword and cut the child in half. Give half to one woman and half to the other."

"Yes, go ahead and divide the child," said one of the two women. "Then it will be neither mine nor hers!"

But the other cried out, "Please, give her the baby—don't kill it!"

Hearing her cry, the wise king said, "Give the child to that woman. She truly is the mother."

When all of Israel heard the judgment the king had given, they were in awe. They saw that his gift of wisdom had come from God.

Based on 1 Kings 3:16–28

Unfortunately, King Solomon lost his gift of wisdom when he became obsessed with his own power and wealth and chose to stop being faithful to God. This led to the downfall of Solomon's kingdom.

Our Church Teaches

God made the world good and created people to be faithful to him. Respect for the laws God intended for humanity is a basis for making moral choices. But the Bible tells us that the sin of the first humans, Adam and Eve, brought disobedience of God into the world. Sin and death resulted for everyone, and all humans now disobey God's law at times. But Jesus Christ came to save us. Jesus Christ gave us the gift of Baptism, which washes away **original sin**, the sin of the first man and woman that was passed on to all human beings.

Jesus' obedience to God brought new life to the world. Jesus is the "new Adam" and the son of Mary, the "new Eve." *Christ* means "anointed one." God anointed Jesus Christ with the Holy Spirit and made him our priest, our king, and the prophet who would always guide us back to God. We can find his guidance in the Scriptures, in the Eucharist, in the sacraments, in forgiveness, in faithful Christians, and in prayer.

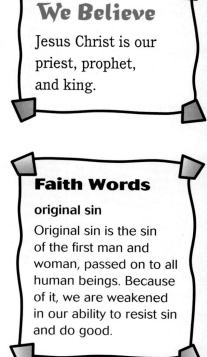

We Believe

Jesus Christ is our priest, prophet, and king.

Faith Words

original sin
Original sin is the sin of the first man and woman, passed on to all human beings. Because of it, we are weakened in our ability to resist sin and do good.

Activities

1. King Solomon lost his gift of wisdom when he stopped being faithful to God. Name a gift that becomes stronger as we become more faithful. _____

   Silently pray that God will help you develop this gift.

2. The people of Israel sometimes turned their backs on God, and disaster followed. The prophets called them to turn back. Then God sent Jesus Christ, who guides all people back to God.

   Below, write ways that people your age might turn their backs on God. Then write a proverb, or wise saying, that could turn them back to God. An example has been done for you.

Backs Turned	Turn Back
Not praying	*Seven days without prayer makes one weak.*
_____	_____
_____	_____
_____	_____

How can we act as modern-day prophets?

Respond

Prophets Today

Modern-day prophets continue to speak out against the injustices of our world. Sometimes a group of people work together to fight injustice. Café 458 in Atlanta, Georgia, is the result of many individuals who speak out on behalf of the homeless. Run by a staff of unpaid volunteers, the café is more of a restaurant than a soup kitchen. Waiters and waitresses take orders and serve food just as in regular restaurants. The only difference is that the meal does not cost anything. Instead, the diner must agree to work on one goal for self-improvement. Restaurant workers help the person identify ways to reach this personal goal. Through the efforts of the café's workers, many homeless people have gained the dignity and self-respect that society denies them.

Activities

1. Do you know of a person or group of people who has spoken out against accepted unfair behavior? Complete the form to nominate the person or group for a Modern Prophet Award.

Modern Prophet Award Nomination

Name of Nominee: _____

Unfair Behavior Spoken Out Against: _____

Way Nominee Tried to Change the Behavior: _____

_____

2. What do you do when you see a person being mistreated? Do you speak out, or do you make believe you do not see what is happening? Write a diary entry about a time when you observed unfair treatment and describe how you reacted.

_____

_____

_____

_____

_____

_____

_____

_____

What kind of prayer can keep us focused on God?

Prayer Celebration

Litanies

A litany is a prayer in which we call upon Jesus, God, Mary or other saints, or holy people and repeat a response. The repetition gives the prayer rhythm and helps people concentrate on the prayer. Praying litanies helps us focus on God. Litanies are popular in several religions. At a Jewish Day of Atonement service, worshipers may pray this litany.

Leader: Our Father, our King, we have sinned before you.

Our Father, our King, grant us a year of happiness.

Our Father, our King, pardon all our sins.

Response: Our Father, our King.

Our Father, our King.

Our Father, our King.

Based on the Jewish "Our Father, Our King" litany

Our Church has litanies for different liturgical celebrations. The Litany of the Most Holy Name of Jesus is one example. As the leader prays each line about Jesus, relax and pray the response with your eyes closed. Focus on the idea that Jesus is in the center of your being. Whenever you are distracted, return to Jesus by focusing on the repetition.

Leader: Jesus, Son of the living God:

Jesus, our God:

Jesus, king of glory:

Jesus, father of the poor:

Jesus, our way and our life:

Jesus, most powerful:

Jesus, king of patriarchs:

Jesus, God of peace:

All: Have mercy on us.

Have mercy on us.

Have mercy on us.

Have mercy on us.

Have mercy on us.

Have mercy on us.

Have mercy on us.

Have mercy on us.

Based on the Litany of the Most Holy Name of Jesus

Think about the presence of Jesus around and within you. Slowly and quietly pray the Lord's Prayer.

A Name a person who acts as a role model for you because his or her words or actions help you remember to pray, to worship, and to do God's will. Tell how the person brings you back to God.

Name: _____

Words or actions:

_____

_____

B Respond to the following.

1. Why did the Israelites forget their covenant with God?

_____

_____

2. How did the Israelites act when they had abandoned God?

_____

_____

3. Whom did God send to remind the Israelites of their covenant with God?

_____

_____

C Match Column A with Column B by writing the correct number in the space provided.

A	B
1. I told the Israelites that their behavior was similar to that of an unfaithful wife.	___ Micah
2. I advised them that "the God who answers with fire is God."	___ Isaiah
3. I urged them to act justly and to love others.	___ Hosea
4. I warned them that "all that is high will be brought low."	___ Elijah

Complete the sentences below with words from the box.

Scriptures	Eucharist	wisdom	forgiveness	prayer
God	faithful	Baptism	original sin	salvation

1. Solomon's greatest gift from God for being faithful was

   _____.

2. Jesus Christ is the prophet who leads us back to _____.

3. We find Jesus Christ's guidance in the _____, in the

   _____, in _____, and in _____.

4. God made the world good and created people to be

   _____ to him.

5. Jesus Christ gave us the gift of _____.

6. Because of _____, we are weakened in our ability to
   resist evil and to do good.

7. Freedom from the pain of sin is called _____.

E **Explain** the role of a prophet, and name two ways you can act like a prophet.

_____

_____

F **Create** a litany that will help you focus on God. Later, pray your litany at home. A first line is provided below.

a line about God   **the response to repeat**

O Lord, God of Peace   _____

_____   _____

_____   _____

Family Time

A choice of things to do at home

Exile and Remembrance

As time went by, the chosen people lost sight of their covenant and turned away from God. Then they were forced into exile, and they thought that God had abandoned them. They found that God was still there for them, however, when he sent prophets to guide them back to him. God is always there for us, even though we sometimes turn away from him.

Exile

Your family or ancestors may have left their homeland to come to America. Your family could explore the feelings of pain, loss, and hope that such a change would bring.

Family covenants

Draw names from a paper lunch bag. Have each family member make a covenant with the person whose name he or she picked. At the end of the week, review how well family members have fulfilled their commitments.

Comfort and consolation

Think of a friend, relative, or other person in your community who has suffered a loss. Find ways for your family to offer comfort and consolation to that person.

✚ A Prayer for the Week

God, our Father, we will all be wanderers until we go to our final home with you. In the meantime, help us feel at home wherever we are in this world.

Amen.

183

Family Time

Something to Do . . .

On Sunday

For the Sign of Peace, make an effort to grasp people's hands warmly, look them in the eyes, and smile.

Through the Week

Light a special candle each night to symbolize your covenant with God and one another.

Visit Our Web Site

www.blestarewe.com

Something to Think About . . .

Accepting Loss

I myself will gather the remnant of my flock from all the lands to which I have driven them and bring them back to their meadow; there they shall increase and multiply, says the LORD.
Based on Jeremiah 23:3–4

God does not want us to suffer the pain of separation and loss. Through his prophet Jeremiah the Lord tells us that he will gather all of us together and care for us so that we may be happy and fruitful again. God's message is one of consolation and hope. When we face loss in our lives, it is very difficult to cope with the pain of that loss. We need to accept the consolation of the Lord and of family and friends who care for us.

Something to Know About . . . Our Heritage in Liturgy

Synagogues are Jewish places of worship. Synagogue prayer and study may have begun while the Israelites were in exile in Babylon. Prayers and traditions in the synagogue and the home came to replace rituals and sacrifices that had been held in the Temple.

Many elements of Christian prayer and worship have their origins in Judaism. Although Latin was the language of Christianity for much of its history, a few Hebrew words are part of the Christian liturgy (*amen*, *hosanna*, and *alleluia*). Christian and Jewish services also share many of the same prayers and acclamations.

14 Exile and Remembrance

Lord, your Son gave his life to gather your scattered children into one family.

Based on the prayer over the gifts, Mass for Refugees and Exiles, Roman Missal

Share

Besides being in unfamiliar surroundings, there are many situations that can make us feel "lost." These can include not fitting in with a group, not knowing how to act, and being uncomfortable in a new environment. But no matter how lost we feel, God is always with us.

Activity

Each photograph shows a person who feels lost. Write what the person might be looking for and what might have caused the person to become lost.

How does God help those who are lost?

Worship   Celebration of the Lord's Passion

The chosen people had forgotten their covenant with God. When the Lord sent prophets to remind them to keep the commandments, they rejected the prophets. In 722 B.C. Assyria invaded Israel, the northern kingdom. The Assyrians captured some Israelites and took them to Assyria. Forced into **exile**, the Israelites felt lost. But God sent more prophets to guide the people. One of them was Second Isaiah, a disciple of the prophet Isaiah.

In church on Good Friday, we gather to remember the Lord's Passion, or suffering, and recall his death on the cross. We also *venerate*, or honor, the cross, often by bowing, kissing it, or genuflecting. The first reading is from Isaiah 52—53, a prophecy of Second Isaiah. Second Isaiah explains that the suffering and death of a **messiah** will save the Israelites from their sins. His prophecy gave the Israelites hope and was fulfilled by Jesus Christ.

A reading from the Book of the Prophet Isaiah.

We had all gone astray like sheep,
    each following his own way;
But the LORD laid upon him
        the guilt of us all.
Though he was harshly treated, he submitted
    and opened not his mouth;
Like a lamb led to the slaughter
    or a sheep before the shearers,
    he was silent and opened
        not his mouth.
Oppressed and condemned,
    he was taken away,
and who would have
        thought any more of
            his destiny?
A grave was assigned him
        among the wicked
    and a burial place
        with evildoers,
Though he had done
        no wrong
    nor spoken any
        falsehood.

If he gives his life as an offering for sin,
    he shall see his descendants in a long life,
    and the will of the LORD shall be accomplished through him.
Because of his affliction
    he shall see the light in fullness of days;
Through his suffering, my servant shall justify many,
    and their guilt he shall bear.

Isaiah 53:6–11

The word of the Lord.
Thanks be to God.

Saving Grace

The people in exile knew they could not rise above their failures on their own. They needed the Lord's help. Even before Second Isaiah, prophets had told the people that their loving God would send a messiah who would overcome their sins and weaknesses.

The prophets Ezekiel and Micah also told the people that their exile would end with the coming of a messiah. Ezekiel told the people that God would look after them as a shepherd looks after his sheep. The Lord had told him, "I will appoint one shepherd over them to pasture them" (Ezekiel 34:23). Micah said, "From you, Bethlehem, shall come forth one who is to be ruler in Israel. He shall shepherd his flock. He shall be peace" (based on Micah 5:1–4). The prophet Jeremiah told God's people: "Behold, the days are coming, says the Lord, when I will raise up a righteous descendant of David. As king he shall reign and govern wisely. He shall do what is just and right in the land. In his days Judah shall be saved" (based on Jeremiah 23:5–6).

Activity

The prophets described the Messiah, Jesus Christ, by likening him to figures from their everyday life, such as a shepherd or a king. Pretend that you have a prophecy to share about the Messiah. Write your prophecy on the scroll, describing Jesus Christ and what he will do for his people, using figures from everyday life.

How did Jesus describe himself?

187

The Good Shepherd

Like the prophets, Jesus used figures from everyday life to describe who he was. Once, while Jesus was in Jerusalem talking to some people who doubted he was the Son of God, he said:

"I am the good shepherd. A good shepherd lays down his life for the sheep. A hired man who is not a shepherd and whose sheep are not his own will see a wolf coming and leave the sheep and run away. The wolf will catch and scatter the sheep. This is because the man works for pay and has no concern for the sheep.

"But I am the good shepherd, and I know my sheep and my sheep know me, just as the Father knows me and I know the Father. I will lay down my life for the sheep. I have other sheep that do not belong to this fold. I must lead them also. They will hear my voice, and there will be one flock and one shepherd. This is why the Father loves me—because I lay down my life in order to take it up again."

But some of the doubtful people did not understand what Jesus meant. "How long are you going to keep us in suspense?" they said to Jesus. "If you are the Messiah, tell us plainly."

Jesus answered, "I told you and you do not believe. I have even shown you through all the good works I do in my Father's name. But you do not believe, because you are not among my sheep. My sheep hear my voice. I know them, and they follow me. I give them eternal life, and they shall never perish. No one can take them away from me."

Based on John 10:11–17, 19, 24–28

Our Church Teaches

Jesus Christ is the Messiah described by the prophets. He was the shepherd God sent to gather the lost sheep of Israel and of all nations. Christ is always there to bring us back from our own "exile"—our separation from God because of sin. We are in exile from heaven during our life on earth. In the sacraments, especially in the celebration of the liturgy, we meet Christ and receive grace to continue our journey to our heavenly home. All of the members of the Church—those here on earth and those already in heaven—form one Body of Christ. The example of those in heaven encourages us. We celebrate their memory throughout the liturgical year. We join them in praise and thanksgiving for God's goodness.

Activity

Reread Jesus' speech about the good shepherd. Try to figure out what the everyday figures that Jesus uses, such as the wolf, might symbolize. Then complete the following chart. One answer has been provided.

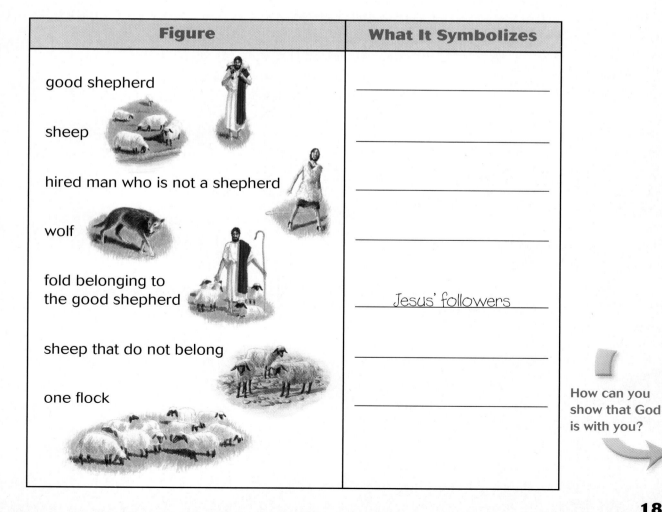

Figure	What It Symbolizes
good shepherd	_____
sheep	_____
hired man who is not a shepherd	_____
wolf	_____
fold belonging to the good shepherd	_Jesus' followers_
sheep that do not belong	_____
one flock	_____

How can you show that God is with you?

A Modern-Day Exile

In certain countries, speaking out against government policies is illegal. People who speak up can be arrested, imprisoned, or even sent into exile. This is the case in Cuba.

In Cuba in 1995, Rafael Solano created a newspaper called the *Havana Press*. This newspaper printed stories that had not been approved by the government. Soon after starting the *Havana Press*, Solano was arrested. He was accused of distributing anti-government propaganda and was told to shut down the paper. But Solano continued to publish his paper and question unfair government practices. Once again the Cuban police arrested Solano. They threatened him with imprisonment and suggested that he leave the country. Solano refused and was eventually released.

A few days later, men armed with knives visited the offices of the *Havana Press*. They claimed that Solano owed them money and demanded to see him. Luckily Solano was not at the office at the time. A week later the police arrested Solano again. Officials told Solano's family that he would never return home.

When Solano was released, the authorities suggested that Solano spend three months in Spain before his trial. Solano believed that he could continue his writing in Spain and then bring his work back to Cuba. But when the authorities gave Solano his passport, he discovered that it had been stamped for final exit. That meant he would not be able to reenter the country once he left. Solano had a difficult decision to make. If he stayed in Cuba, he would go on trial and most likely be imprisoned. If he went to Spain, he could never return to his homeland. Solano decided to leave. Today, Solano lives in exile in Spain.

Activities

1. What would you do if you were faced with Rafael's decision?

_____

_____

Can you think of a way to help people like Rafael?

_____

_____

2. Before the promised land became a rich kingdom, the Hebrew people treasured their prayers, sacrifices, and the Ten Commandments. But the success of the kingdom led to new treasures—gold and silver jewelry, fine clothing, horses, and chariots. Soon the people began to worship idols—the false gods of other religions. Discuss how our society may be similar.

3. Read through the list of "treasures" below. Add your own treasures to the list where indicated. Then rank the treasures in the order of their importance to you, beginning with the number 1 for the most important.

___ A friend who will help you through difficult times

___ A lot of money

___ Good health

___ A loving family

___ Designer clothing

___ Expensive jewelry

___ A report card full of A's

___ The latest CDs

___ Other: _____

___ Other: _____

Review your rankings. Do you treasure things more than you treasure people and God? If so, how can you overcome this?

_____

_____

_____

_____

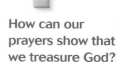

How can our prayers show that we treasure God?

Prayer Celebration

Great Hope in Spite of Loss

The *kaddish* is a Jewish prayer that is prayed by people in mourning. But it is not a sad prayer. Instead, it expresses great hope and praise for God. Pray the following form of the kaddish with your own gesture—your arms raised, your hands open, and your palms facing upward—to show that you are placing your hope in our powerful Lord.

Mourner: Magnified and sanctified be God's great Name in the world, which God created according to his will. May God establish his kingdom in your lifetime and in your days, and in the lifetime of all the house of Israel, speedily and at a near time. All say, "Amen!"

All: Amen! Let his great Name be blessed forever and ever.

Mourner: Blessed, praised and glorified, exalted, extolled and honored, adored and lauded, be the Name of the Holy One, blessed be God, beyond, yes, beyond all blessings and hymns, praises, and songs, which are uttered in the world. And all say, "Amen!"

All: Amen!

Mourner: May there be abundant peace from heaven, and life for us and for Israel. And all say, "Amen!"

All: Amen!

Mourner: May God who makes peace in his high places make peace for us and for all Israel. And all say, "Amen!"

All: Amen! May the Lord bless you. Amen!

Based on the kaddish

Chapter Review

A **Respond** to the following.

1. Describe a situation in which a young person might feel sad and alone. How could God bring that person comfort?

   _____

   _____

2. Define *exile* and *messiah*.

   _____

   _____

B **Write** the name of the person described by each clue.

1. I am the prophet who told the people that God would look after them as a shepherd looks after his sheep. _____

2. I am the prophet who told the people that the ruler of Israel would come forth from Bethlehem. _____

3. I am the prophet who compared his people to sheep who had gone astray. _____

4. I am the prophet who said that the Lord would raise up a descendant of David who would reign as king and do what is right and just. _____

5. I am the Messiah described by the prophets. _____

C **Explain** why Jesus is like a shepherd and why we are like his sheep.

   _____

   _____

   _____

Give an example of someone in exile today, and explain how the person could be helped. You might give an example from your own experience or that of a family member, or from a news story you heard recently.

_____

_____

_____

_____

_____

 Complete the sentences below with words from the box.

hope	exile	sin	kaddish
praise	Jewish	Messiah	

1. The _____ is a _____ prayer of mourning.

2. It expresses great _____ and _____ for God.

3. Christ is the _____ who brings us back from our own

    _____, our separation from God because of _____.

F **Reread** the prayer at the top of page 185 in your book. Think about its meaning. How does this prayer reflect the main idea of Chapter 14?

_____

_____

_____

_____

_____

Family Time

A choice of things to do at home

Hope and Faithfulness

When the people of Judah lived in exile, the prophet Ezekiel helped them realize that, even though they might temporarily turn away from God, God would always be ready to welcome them back. We have this same relationship with God and are called to share it with others.

For the greater good

Look for a neighborhood or community volunteer opportunity in which your family can participate. Check your local newspaper or contact local organizations.

Welcome back!

Imagine that a family member has turned away from your family. Discuss what your family could say and do to encourage that person to return to the fold.

A journal of hopes

Start a journal in which family members record some hopes or aspirations. Review the journal at regular intervals. Plan together ways to make those hopes realities.

✝ A Prayer for the Week

Help us appreciate your gift of faith, Lord. Keep us strong in our faith, and let there always be hope in our lives.
Amen.

195

Family Time

Something to Do...

On Sunday

Listen for messages of faith and hope during the readings and the homily.

Through the Week

On the weekend, share examples of how family members, just as Ruth in this chapter, have been faithful and supportive of one another during the week.

Visit Our Web Site

www.blestarewe.com

Something to Think About...

Overcoming Discouragement

I will put my spirit in you that you may live, and I will settle you upon your land; thus you shall know that I am the LORD. I have promised, and I will do it, says the LORD.
Ezekiel 37:14

When we are discouraged, we are like the scattered dry bones from Ezekiel's "Vision of the Dry Bones" discussed in this chapter of your child's book. Our discouragement drags us down, and we need to turn to God to fill us with optimism and to help us go forward. Sometimes it is difficult to even ask for help, but the Lord, in his goodness, is there for us. God's love is always available. We may have to live through hard times, but we should maintain the hope that better times will come.

Something to Know About...

Our Heritage in Literature

T. S. Eliot, who converted to Anglo-Catholicism in 1927, was one of the most renowned literary figures of the twentieth century. Born in the United States in 1888, Eliot gained fame while living in England. He was a prolific writer of poetry, essays, and plays. Eliot's devotion to religion had a profound impact on his work. In his famous poem "The Waste Land," Eliot used the imagery of the dry bones from Ezekiel 37:1–14, which is discussed in this chapter. Eliot is also well-known for a

collection of poems that became the inspiration for the popular musical *Cats*. He received the Nobel Prize for Literature in 1948. He died in London in 1965.

15 Hope and Faithfulness

Do not ask me to leave you!
For wherever you go, I will go.

Based on Ruth 1:16

Share

Do you have friends, cousins, grandparents, or other relatives who live far away? When you are not able to see them very often, you probably begin to miss them. You look forward to visits with them with great expectation.

Activity

Try to remember the last time you saw a friend or a relative whom you missed very much. Then complete the story by writing in the information and circling the bold words that describe that experience.

I remember the last time I saw my **friend cousin grandmother**

grandfather aunt uncle other: _____, whose

name is _____.

_____ is special to me

because _____

_____.

I missed _____ because

he she has shown God's love for me by _____

_____.

When we first saw each other, we _____

_____.

It was a very happy time. Now it has been _____

months years since the last time I saw _____.

I am looking forward to the next visit with lots of hope!

How did God give hope to the Jews in exile?

197

Scripture   Vision of the Dry Bones

The Babylonians conquered Judah, the southern kingdom, and exiled its citizens around 587 B.C. The Babylonians destroyed the Temple. Without their Temple in Jerusalem, the people had to find other ways to feel God's presence. Prophets helped the people learn that God did not just exist in Jerusalem and in the Temple. God was with them wherever they went. The prophet Ezekiel taught the exiles how to have faith again. He told them:

The hand of the LORD came upon me, and he set me in the center of the plain, which was now filled with bones. Then he said to me, "Prophesy over these bones and say to them, 'Dry bones, hear the word of the LORD! Thus says the Lord GOD: I will bring spirit into you so that you may come to life. I will put sinews upon you, make flesh grow over you, cover you with skin, and put spirit in you so that you may come to life and know that I am the LORD.'" I prophesied as I had been told, and I heard a noise. It was a rattling as the bones came together, bone joining bone. I saw the sinews and the flesh come upon them and the skin cover them, but there was no spirit in them. Then the LORD said to me, "Prophesy to the spirit and say, 'Thus says the Lord GOD: Come, O spirit, and breathe into these so that they may come to life.'" I prophesied as he told me, and the spirit came into them; they came alive and stood upright, a vast army. Then he said, "These bones are the whole house of Israel. They have been saying, 'Our bones are dried up, our hope is lost, and we are cut off.' Therefore, prophesy and say to them, 'Thus says the Lord GOD: I will put my spirit in you so that you may live, and I will settle you upon your land. I have promised, and I will do it, says the LORD.'"

Based on Ezekiel 37:1, 4–12, 14

Together Again

Ezekiel's "Vision of the Dry Bones" gave people hope that God would bring them back to their kingdom. The plain scattered with bones represents the Jews scattered across foreign lands during the Exile. The coming together of the bones represents the coming together of God's people after the Exile. Ezekiel said that God told him to prophesy over the bones so that God's spirit would bring life to them. Then the bones became live people, united as an army. This represents God's bringing the exiles home and into a faithful relationship again. Ezekiel's vision came true.

In 539 B.C. Cyrus, leader of the Persians, conquered the Babylonians. He said that the exiles could return home. The Jews who returned had high hopes. They rebuilt the Temple in 519 B.C. They also prayed and studied God's word in synagogues, smaller meeting places. Jerusalem again became the center of worship and government. New prophets led the people in worshiping God. People honored God's covenant with feasts and celebrations.

The Sabbath was an important occasion for the people then, as it is for us and for Jewish people today. Honoring the Sabbath means celebrating God's creation of the earth. The Sabbath recalls the seventh day in the Bible story of Creation, when God rested. The Sabbath is also a memorial of Israel's freedom from Egypt. During the Exodus God commanded the Israelites to honor the Sabbath always. Keeping the Sabbath is a way of honoring God's covenant with his chosen people.

Activities

1. Because God had a covenant with his people, he would not allow them to remain in exile for long. After the Exile, the people honored their covenant with God by observing the Sabbath, praying, and worshiping God. List three ways to honor your covenant with God.

   _____

   _____

   _____

2. Ezekiel's "Vision of the Dry Bones" captured the exiles' interest and gave them hope that they would return to their kingdom. Reread what Ezekiel said. Draw the part of Ezekiel's vision that seems the most interesting to you.

What do we, as Christians, hope for?

Hear & Believe

Hope on the Sabbath

It was Sunday, and Alicia needed to talk to someone. She had a lot of things on her mind. She was getting bad grades in math. Her teacher had accused her of disturbing the class on Friday. Her best friend, Max, was mad at her about something she had said.

In addition, Alicia's grandmother, who was called Nona, had been taken to the hospital with a heart condition a few days earlier. Not only was Alicia worried about her grandmother, but she was also feeling lonely. Nona had always spent time with Alicia, but now she wasn't around. Alicia's mom had been spending most of her free time at the hospital visiting Nona. Alicia's father also wasn't home as often, now that he was working two jobs to pay college tuition for Alicia's older sister, Olivia. And Olivia always wore headphones and locked herself in her bedroom.

Whom could Alicia turn to? Normally when her family went to Sunday Mass together, Alicia noticed that Nona spent extra time before and after Mass silently talking to God. When Alicia asked her about this once, Nona had said, "God always makes time for us if we make time for him."

So, this Sunday, before Mass began, Alicia spent extra time praying. She asked God to heal Nona, reflected on how her behavior could have been better that week, and resolved to apologize to Max. At the end of Mass, she asked her sister to wait for her while she kneeled before the tabernacle and talked to God about her worries and problems. At the end of her prayers, a sense of hope came over Alicia. She felt that God had really listened to her. Maybe her grandmother was on to something.

Our Church Teaches

We must honor the Sabbath by attending Mass each Sunday. We must also attend Mass on holy days, confess our sins in Reconciliation at least once a year, receive the Eucharist at least during the Easter season, observe the Church's days of fast and abstinence, and contribute to the Church to provide for its material needs. These are the **precepts** of the Church. They are our obligations as Catholics. Above all, we must do good and avoid evil, showing respect for the value of human life.

As Christians, we have hope, too. Our hope is for the everlasting happiness that God promises us. Hope is our trust in God to help us achieve everlasting life. Hope is one of the **theological virtues**, three spiritual qualities that come from God and help us become more holy. The other two virtues are faith and charity. Through faith, we believe in God, in everything God has revealed, and in all that the Church teaches us to believe. Charity is the love we show for others and for God. The theological virtues are signs of Christ's example and of the Holy Spirit living within us. In this way, the theological virtues connect us with the Trinity. **Moral virtues** help us avoid sin, which separates us from God. Temperance is a moral virtue. It means not doing too much of any one thing, including eating too much, driving too fast, or abusing alcohol. Temperance helps prevent danger or sin. For example, speeding and drunk driving can kill or hurt people, and endangerment of human life is a serious sin.

GO TO page 368 to learn more about the virtues.

Activity

Charity is the love we show for God and others. It is made up of many ingredients. Write your own recipe for charity (for example, a cup of courage, a teaspoon of patience, and so on).

CHARITY

We Believe

Sin separates us from God and makes us people in exile. Just as the exiled Jews, we come closer to God by making good moral decisions and following the teachings of our faith. Faith is necessary for salvation.

Faith Words

precepts
Precepts are teachings about our obligations.

theological virtues
The theological virtues, faith, hope, and charity, come from God and help us become more holy. They connect us with the Trinity.

moral virtues
The moral virtues, temperance, prudence, justice, and fortitude, help us avoid sin.

How can you be an example of faith, hope, and charity?

Respond

Faith and Charity

The Book of Ruth in the Old Testament tells this special story about faith and charity.

A Jewish woman named Naomi moved from Bethlehem, in Judah, to Moab with her husband and two sons. But soon after leaving Bethlehem, Naomi's husband died. Naomi's sons married Moabite women, Orpah and Ruth. For ten years the widow and her family lived peacefully.

Suddenly, both of Naomi's sons died. Now she was in a foreign land without her husband or her sons. And her native people, the Jews, were far away. Naomi decided it was time to return to Bethlehem. Both of her daughters-in-law decided to go with her.

On the road to Bethlehem, Naomi turned to Orpah and Ruth. "Go back to your mothers' houses!" Naomi told them. "May the Lord grant each of you a husband and a home in which you will find rest."

Orpah kissed her mother-in-law goodbye and returned to her homeland. But Ruth said, "Do not ask me to leave you! For wherever you go, I will go. Your people shall be my people. Your God shall be my God."

Naomi and Ruth continued their journey and arrived in Bethlehem during the harvest. They were desperately poor and needed food to eat. Ruth went into someone's fields and picked up grain left behind by the harvesters. For many hours she gathered food for Naomi and herself.

Then the owner of the fields, Boaz, approached Ruth. "I have heard what you have done for your mother-in-law," he said. "You have left the land of your birth and have come to a foreign land. May the Lord reward you for what you have done!" Over time, Boaz came to love Ruth. He knew that she was a good woman who lived a life of faith and charity. Boaz and Ruth married. They became the great-grandparents of David, the king.

Based on the Book of Ruth

Activities

1. Complete each sentence with a theological virtue.

   Ruth's decisions to stay with Naomi and to gather food for her are examples of _____.

   When Ruth said, "Your God will be my God," she showed that she had _____ in Naomi's beliefs.

2. Ruth put Naomi's needs above her own. Think about ways you can follow Ruth's example of charity. Complete the diagram below.

My Needs:

_____

_____

_____

_____

_____

Other People's Needs:

_____

_____

_____

_____

_____

What I Can Do to Meet Others' Needs:

_____

_____

_____

_____

_____

3. The end of the Exile showed the Jewish people once again that God was faithful and loving. The Hebrew word to describe the love and kindness of God is *Hesed*. Make a list of things people can do to be kind and loving, using the letters of the word *Hesed*.

H _____

E _____

S _____

E _____

D _____

What are you hopeful about?

✝ Prayer Celebration

Act of Hope

O my God,
relying on your infinite goodness and promises,
I hope to obtain pardon of my sins,
the help of your grace,
and life everlasting,
through the merits of Jesus Christ,
my Lord and Redeemer.

What other hopes do you have for your relationship with God?
Silently ask God to help fulfill your hopes.

15 Chapter Review

A **Match** Column A with Column B by writing the correct number in the space provided.

A

1. Sabbath

2. Ezekiel

3. Cyrus

4. Jews

5. Babylonians

B

___ This day recalls the seventh day in the story of Creation, when God rested.

___ These people rebuilt the Temple and honored God's covenant with feasts and celebrations.

___ This prophet's "Vision of the Dry Bones" gave the exiles hope that God would bring them back together again.

___ This Persian leader allowed the exiles to return home.

___ These people conquered Judah, sent its citizens into exile, and destroyed the Temple.

B **Complete** the sentences about the story of Ruth with words from the box.

family	faith	Naomi	homeland
Ruth	Orpah	charity	

1. _____ lived with her two daughters-in-law, _____ and _____, in Judah.

2. Ruth chose to leave her _____ and her _____ in order to care for Naomi.

3. Ruth's love for God and Naomi is an example of the theological virtue of _____.

4. Ruth's belief in the God of Naomi is an example of the theological virtue of _____.

Respond to the following.

1. What are the precepts of the Church?

_____

_____

_____

2. Name the theological virtues, and describe what they do.

_____

_____

_____

3. Name the moral virtues, and describe what they do.

_____

_____

 Write a brief summary of the Christian hope that is expressed in the Act of Hope found on page 204 in your book.

_____

_____

E **Respond** to the following.

1. Write the name of someone you love very much.

_____

2. Imagine not being able to be with this person for a very long time for some reason. How would that feel?

_____

_____

3. Now imagine getting to hug and be with that person again. How would that feel?

_____

Family Time

A choice of things to do at home

Trust and Prayer

God invites us into a relationship of trust and caring. We sustain that relationship through faith and prayer. The Old Testament story of Esther shows us that we can overcome even extraordinary challenges if we put our faith in God and pray for the strength to carry out his plan for us.

What's in a word?

Together, make a mobile that displays some words that exemplify the main ideas of this chapter. Display the mobile in a prominent place in your home.

Supplication
Trust
Persistence
Hope
Faith
Courage

Faith in action

Work together on a plan to help your family or a family member achieve a goal. Pray as a family for the guidance and strength needed to fulfill that goal.

It's a matter of trust

Discuss qualities that make a person trustworthy. Focus on a relative or friend whom everyone trusts. Have family members discuss why they trust that person.

✝ A Prayer for the Week

You hold us up, Lord. You come to our aid when we grow weary. Give us the strength to trust in you always. Amen.

Family Time

Something to Do . . .

On Sunday

As the General Intercessions are said, pray that you will be a courageous and trustworthy member of your community.

Through the Week

Each day, say a prayer of gratitude for the person you trust the most.

Visit Our Web Site

 www.blestarewe.com

Something to Know About . . .

Our Heritage

The Jewish holiday Purim commemorates the deliverance of the Jews in Persia from the massacre decreed by Haman. Although Purim is not a Catholic festival, the story behind it teaches us great lessons about prayer and courage. On Purim many Jews go to the synagogue, where the Scroll of Esther is read. A traditional meal is also important in the celebration of Purim. Stories, costumes, and skits are often part of the celebration. *Hamantasch*, a prune or poppy-seed pastry, is served. The pastry is shaped like the three-cornered hat that Haman supposedly wore.

Something to Think About . . .

Conquering Fears

O God, more powerful than all, hear the voice of those in despair. Save us from the power of the wicked, and deliver me from my fear.

Esther C:30

Before asking the king to save the Jews in Persia, Esther prayed for courage and guidance. She also asked God to deliver her from fear. We all know the feeling of fear. We may be afraid because of an illness. We may fear going to a new school or job. We may hesitate to try out for a sports team or for a part in the school play. We simply may be afraid to fail. Overcoming our fears often has positive results such as making new friends or developing our God-given talents. Following Esther's example of prayer can help us overcome our fears.

16 Trust and Prayer

 Father, how wonderful your care for us!

Easter Proclamation (Exultet), Roman Missal

Share

Think about the people who take care of you, such as parents or grandparents. Although you may not stop to think about it, every day these people take care of your needs and wants in several ways. What kinds of things do they provide for you daily?

Activity

Needs are things that you require to live a healthy life. Wants are things that make your life more pleasurable. Complete the chart by writing in the needs and wants that people meet for you during each part of the day. Think about how the people's actions are examples of God's love.

	Needs	**Wants**
Morning		
Afternoon		
Evening		

How does God take care of us?

Scripture A Prayer for Her People

Esther was a beautiful young Jewish woman who lived about 500 years before the birth of Christ. She was adopted by a relative, Mordecai, after her parents died. Mordecai, a Jew, lived in exile in Persia (present-day Iran), where he was appointed to the royal court after saving the king's life.

Soon after Esther went to live with Mordecai, the king decreed that all the young women in his empire move to the royal palace. He planned to choose one of them to be the new queen. Esther then moved to the palace. When the king met Esther, he was struck by her kindness and her great beauty. He made her the queen.

At this time, a man named Haman was the highest official in the royal court. Haman was greedy for fame and power. All the king's servants had to bow down in his presence. Mordecai refused. As a Jew, he would not honor a man in the way he would the Lord. Haman was angry about this. He vowed to destroy all the Jews in Persia. He wrote a royal order stating, "All Jews, young and old, including women and children, should be killed in one day."

When Mordecai learned of Haman's plan, he requested that Queen Esther ask the king to save the Jews from death. To plead for the lives of her people, Esther would have to tell the king that she was a Jew. Knowing that this could lead to death, Esther prayed to the Lord for guidance and courage.

"My LORD, our King, you alone are God. Help me, who am alone and have no help but you, for I am taking my life in my hand. Give me courage, King of all. Put in my mouth persuasive words in the presence of the lion and turn his heart to hatred for our enemy. Save us by your power . . . O LORD."

Then Queen Esther went to the king and enjoyed a great banquet with him. While dining, Esther told the king that she was a Jew. She told him of Haman's plan. She said, "If I have found favor with you, O king, I ask that my life be spared and I beg that you spare the lives of my people. My people and I have been delivered to destruction, slaughter, and extinction."

The king was enraged about Haman's plan. He ordered that Haman be punished. He appointed Mordecai to fill Haman's position in court.

Based on Esther A; 2—8

Faith Words

supplication

Supplication is humbly and earnestly asking for help.

persistence

Persistence is the act of continually pursuing something in spite of obstacles.

Faith and Prayer

Esther had great faith in the goodness and power of God. In her time of need, she prayed a prayer of **supplication** to the Lord. She humbly and earnestly asked God for help. She asked God to give her the courage to face the king and the wisdom to convince the king to spare her people. Esther's prayer arose from her faith that God could really answer her. She trusted that God would meet the needs of his people. Esther's petition, or solemn prayer of request, was granted.

When we pray, we raise our minds and hearts to God and request good things from him. Just as the people who take care of our needs every day, God meets our needs. Our prayers may require **persistence**, continually praying with complete trust. God answers our prayers if we have faith in his power and goodness.

Activity

In five words or less, write a prayer of supplication that you can pray at any time, such as "Give me courage, Lord" (Queen Esther's prayer).

How should we pray if we are in need?

The Trials of Job

In the Old Testament, there's a special story that illustrates persistence and complete trust in God. It is found in the Book of Job.

Job was a holy man who honored God above all else. Job was blessed with good health, good fortune, and a good family. But all of a sudden, everything changed. Job lost his fortune, witnessed the deaths of his children, and suffered from sores all over his body. As each terrible thing happened, Job refused to believe that God had abandoned him.

Soon friends came by to tell Job that God must have been punishing him for past sins. They urged him to repent. Job replied, "Repent for what? I am innocent of any sin."

Finally, Job questioned God. He demanded that God explain the reasons for his tragic situation. He accused God of breaking the covenant with him. To the amazement of Job's friends, God actually answered Job. God spoke in a mighty voice, explaining that he was the almighty Creator and asking for Job's trust.

God's words satisfied Job, and the suffering man placed his trust in his Creator. Job praised God, saying, "I was born with nothing, and I shall die with nothing. The Lord gave, and the Lord has taken away; blessed be the name of the Lord!"

Based on the Book of Job

Job prayed because he believed firmly in God. He knew that God really heard him.

Our Church Teaches

Prayer arises from faith. We pray because we believe that God really hears us. Our Church teaches that it is necessary to pray frequently and with patience.

We Believe

Prayer requires faith and persistence. The sources of prayer are the word of God, the liturgy, and the virtues of faith, hope, and charity.

Activities

1. Think of someone you know, or someone you have read or heard about, who demonstrates trustful prayer. Tell a story from this person's life that illustrates his or her ability to trust God in the face of trial.

_____

_____

_____

_____

_____

_____

_____

_____

_____

2. Now give an example of trustful prayer from Jesus' life.

_____

_____

_____

_____

_____

What did Jesus teach us about prayer?

The Parable of the Persistent Widow

Jesus told a parable about the necessity of praying without becoming weary. He said, "There was a judge in a certain town who neither feared God nor respected any human being. And a widow in that town used to come to him and say, 'Grant a just decision for me against my opponent.' For a long time the judge was unwilling, but eventually he thought, 'While it is true that I neither fear God nor respect any human being, because this widow keeps bothering me I shall make a just decision for her.'" The Lord said, "Pay attention to what the dishonest judge says. Will not God then help his chosen ones who call out to him day and night? Will he be slow to answer them? I tell you, he will see to it that justice is done for them speedily."

Based on Luke 18:1–8

Activity

Think about the parable. Imagine you are the widow. Think about how you feel when the judge denies your request. Then think about how you feel when your request is finally granted. Reflect on the message Jesus wants to send you through this story.

What is that message? _____

_____

Name needs that you or other people have. _____

_____

Write a short prayer asking God to fulfill those needs. _____

_____

In the future, come back to this page as often as you can and say your prayer with faith that it will be answered.

"That Would Have Been Enough!"

A Jewish custom is to praise God before asking God for something. The *Dayenu* is a Hebrew song that praises God. *Dayenu* means "That would have been enough!" The song celebrates how God delivered the Israelites every time they needed help and then went even further than just meeting each need. It is sung during Passover. Here is a version you can pray.

Leader: Had he brought us out of Egypt, and not fed us in the desert, brought us out of Egypt we'd be satisfied.

Response: That would have been enough!

Leader: Had he fed us with manna, and not then ordained the Sabbath, fed us with the manna we'd be satisfied.

Response: That would have been enough!

Leader: Had he ordained the Sabbath, and not brought us to Mount Sinai, ordained the Sabbath we'd be satisfied.

Response: That would have been enough!

Leader: Had he brought us to Mount Sinai, and not given us the Torah, brought us to Mount Sinai we'd be satisfied.

Response: That would have been enough!

Leader: Had he given us the Torah, and not led us into Israel, given us the Torah we'd be satisfied.

Response: That would have been enough!

Based on the Dayenu

Activity

Think about the ways that God has shown his presence in your class this year. Write some verses for your own class Dayenu.

_____

_____

_____

_____

How is Jesus' Resurrection an answer to our prayers?

✝ Prayer Celebration

Praise for the Resurrection

The Easter Proclamation, or Exultet, also celebrates God's glorious acts. It is sung during the Easter Vigil. It is filled with praises and rejoicings about the Resurrection of Jesus Christ.

Rejoice, heavenly powers! Sing, choirs of angels!
    Exult, all creation around God's throne!
    Jesus Christ, our King, is risen!
    Sound the trumpet of salvation!

Rejoice, O Mother Church! Exult in glory!
    The risen Savior shines upon you!
    Let this place resound with joy,
    echoing the mighty song of all God's people!

This is the night when first you saved our fathers:
    you freed the people of Israel from their slavery
    and led them dry-shod through the sea.

This is the night when Christians everywhere,
    washed clean of sin
    and freed from all defilement,
    are restored to grace and grow together
      in holiness.

Father, how wonderful your care for us!
    How boundless your merciful love!
    To ransom a slave
    you gave away your Son.

O happy fault, O necessary sin of Adam,
    which gained for us so great a Redeemer!

Excerpted from the Long Form of the Easter Proclamation,
Roman Missal

A **Respond** to the following.

1. What is the meaning of *supplication*?

   _____

2. When Esther prayed a prayer of supplication, what did she ask God to help her with?

   _____

   _____

3. Ask God for help. Write your own prayer of supplication.

   _____

B **Compare** the different ways that people have met your needs.

1. Describe some ways that people took care of you when you were a baby.

   _____

   _____

2. Describe some ways that people took care of you as a young child. _____

   _____

   _____

3. Describe some ways that people take care of you today.

   _____

   _____

C **Compose** a short prayer that asks God to help meet one of your needs.

   _____

   _____

D **Complete** the sentences using words from the box. Each word will be used more than once.

faith	persistence

1. Esther prayed because she had _____ that God could really answer her.

2. Despite the bad things that happened to him, Job continued to pray with _____.

3. Job prayed even during bad times because he had _____ that God really heard him.

4. Prayer begins with _____.

5. Our Church teaches that our prayers may require _____, or continually praying with complete _____.

E **List** three things for which the Exultet on page 216 in your book praises God.

_____

_____

_____

F **Define** persistence.

_____

_____

G **Write** answers to the following questions.

1. What did the woman in the parable about the persistent widow need the judge to do?

_____

2. What lesson about prayer and asking God for help did Jesus want to teach us in this parable?

_____

WE CARE *About Family and Friends*

Welcoming and Belonging

Halfway through her sixth-grade year, Monica began to feel that she no longer belonged. Monica couldn't keep up with the latest trends because her family just didn't have the money. Some of the girls in Monica's class started to form cliques. They excluded Monica. They criticized her appearance and made fun of her large family. Some of the kids also started to bother her about always having to babysit her younger siblings. One time, as a joke, some students collected change for "Monica's Poor Family" and dropped it on Monica's desk with a nasty note.

No one at home or at school seemed to care about Monica's feelings. But then things began to improve. First, her mother's employer started a free after-school day-care program for children of working mothers. Then, Monica's school started a "pupil peace program." Everyone was encouraged to respect everybody else and to think about how it feels to be teased. Any time a student defended someone who was being teased, the teacher gave the student a raffle ticket called a "peace ticket." Pairs of sixth graders known as "peace monitors" walked around the playground, encouraging other students to treat each other respectfully. They gave peace tickets to those who stopped making fun of other students. Every week, halves of the peace tickets were collected, and a prize was raffled off.

How do you think these changes affected Monica?

Think About It

Think about Monica's home situation and school situation.

What are some of the feelings you might have if you were Monica?

_____

_____

List three things you might tell Monica to make her feel better about herself.

1. _____

2. _____

3. _____

Why was it wrong to tease Monica about her family?

_____

_____

Learn About It

God created us all. Every one of us is created in God's image. Sometimes it is easy to forget this. We base our opinions of people on silly things, such as their possessions, their popularity, their wealth, or their background. We don't see how wonderful people are in God's eyes.

Jesus taught us that respect for each other is the most basic moral rule. Remember that Jesus befriended people who were the most outcast by society—beggars, lepers, tax collectors, and sinners. He tried to help them. He welcomed them and made them feel that they belonged.

Our Church also teaches that institutions should help and protect families.

Do Something About It

Write three ways you can show respect for classmates who may feel that they do not belong.

75511

1. _____

2. _____

3. _____

PEACE TICKET

75511

Using the key words below and your own words, write a summary of what you learned in this unit. You do not have to use all the key words.

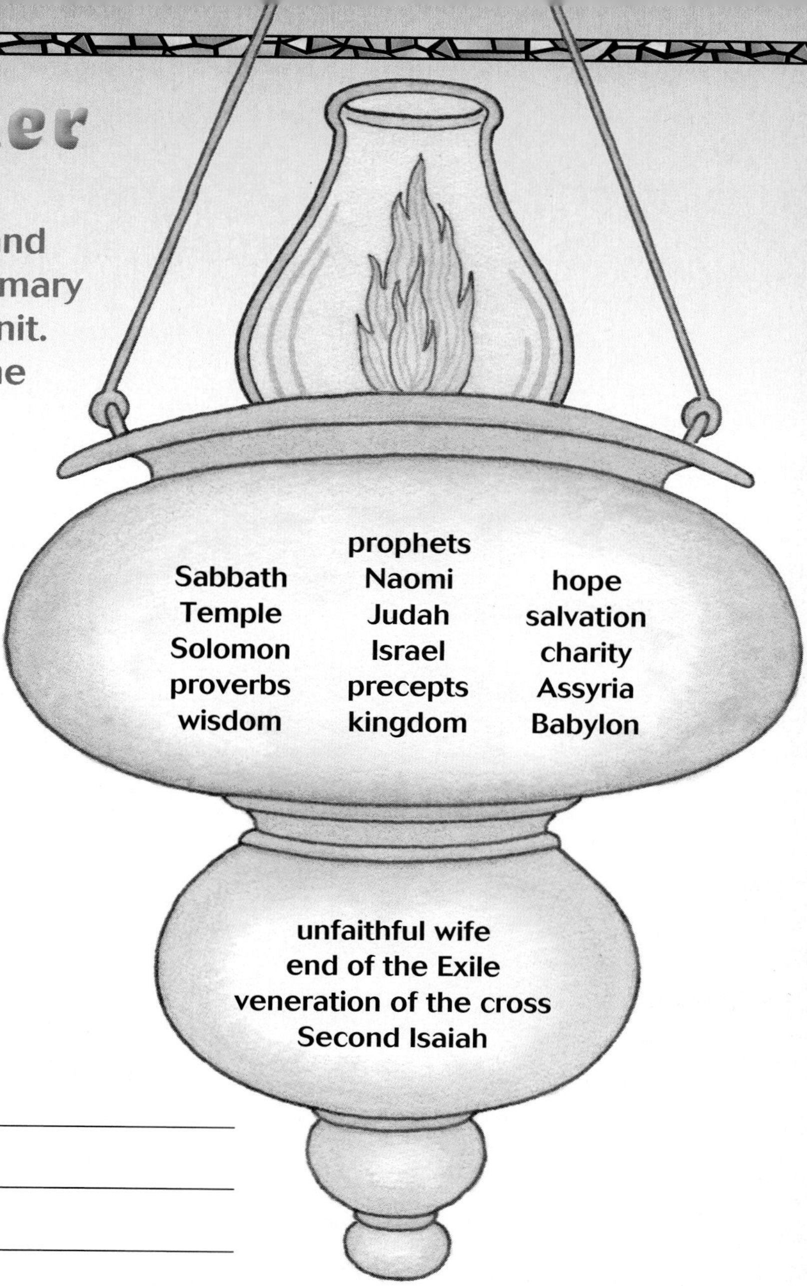

prophets

Sabbath   Naomi   hope
Temple   Judah   salvation
Solomon   Israel   charity
proverbs   precepts   Assyria
wisdom   kingdom   Babylon

unfaithful wife
end of the Exile
veneration of the cross
Second Isaiah

_____

_____

_____

_____

_____

_____

_____

_____

_____

_____

_____

_____

A **Complete** each sentence with the correct word or words.

1. Solomon had many wise sayings, called _____.

2. _____ is our priest, our king, and the prophet who guides us back to God.

3. Even though we _____, God's love for us is everlasting.

4. Prayer requires _____ and persistence.

5. Two precepts of the _____ are that we attend

   Mass each _____ and that we confess our

   sins in _____ at least once a year.

B **Write** the correct name from the box on the line next to each description.

Job	Jesus
Second Isaiah	Micah
Elijah	Ezekiel
Solomon	

1. Even though he lost his health, his fortune, and his family, he placed his trust in God. _____

2. He once described himself as a good shepherd who lays down his life for his sheep. _____

3. His greatest gift from God was wisdom. _____

4. He showed the Israelites the power of God through a sacrifice. _____

5. He said that the Israelites should act justly and love others. _____

6. His vision about dry bones gave the exiles hope. _____

7. He said that the suffering and death of a messiah would save the Israelites from their sins. _____

Review

C **Match** Column A with Column B by writing the correct number in the space provided.

A

1. Christ
2. Esther
3. litany
4. charity
5. Assyrians
6. Ruth
7. petition
8. Exultet
9. Baptism
10. venerate
11. kaddish

B

—— to honor

—— a solemn prayer of request

—— invaded Israel in 722 B.C. and forced its people into exile

—— a Jewish prayer prayed by people in mourning

—— a prayer in which we call upon Jesus, God, Mary or other saints, or holy people and repeat a response

—— washes away original sin

—— the love we show for others and for God

—— an Easter Vigil song about the Resurrection of Jesus Christ

—— a Jewish woman who saved her people through prayer

—— a word that means "anointed one"

—— a Moabite woman who showed great charity toward her Hebrew mother-in-law

D **Match** Column A with Column B by writing the correct number in the space provided.

A	B

A

1. exile

2. messiah

3. moral virtues

4. original sin

5. persistence

6. precepts

7. prophet

8. salvation

9. supplication

10. theological virtues

B

____ a person chosen to save people from a particular fate

____ a person sent by God to speak out against accepted behavior that does not follow God's will

____ faith, hope, and charity

____ freedom from the pain of sin

____ humbly and earnestly asking for help

____ teachings about our obligations

____ temperance, prudence, justice, and fortitude

____ the act of continually pursuing something

____ the sin of the first man and woman that was passed on to all human beings

____ the forced removal of people from their homeland to another land, or a person who has experienced such removal

E **Explain** how Jesus, the new Adam, is different from the first Adam.

_____

_____

_____

_____

God Promises Us Everlasting Life

John called people to a baptism of repentance. Through our baptism, we are called to turn our attention always toward the kingdom of God and to be its witnesses by the way we live.

I am baptizing you with water, for repentance, but the one who is coming after me is mightier than I.

Matthew 3:11

The Jordan River is the traditional place where John baptized Christ. Early Christians first drew pictures of baptismal scenes in the catacombs of ancient Rome.

Creator of the Stars of Night

Words: Latin 9th c.
Arranged by Carol Browning

CONDITOR ALME SIDERUM, Chant Mode IV

1. Cre - a - tor of the stars of night, your peo - ple's ev - er - last - ing light, O Christ, Re - deem - er of us all, we pray you hear us when we call.
2. In sor - row that the an - cient curse should doom to death a u - ni - verse, you came, O Sav - ior, to set free your own in glo - rious lib - er - ty.
3. When this old world drew on toward night, you came; but not in splen - dor bright, not as a mon - arch, but the child of Mar - y, blame - less moth - er mild.
4. At your great Name, O Je - sus, now all knees must bend, all hearts must bow: all things on earth with one ac - cord, like those in heav'n, shall call you Lord.
5. Come in your ho - ly might, we pray, re - deem us for e - ter - nal day; de - fend us while we dwell be - low from all as - saults of our dread foe.
6. To God Cre - a - tor, God the Son, and God the Spir - it, Three in One, praise, hon - or, might, and glo - ry be from age to age e - ter - nal - ly.

Arrangement © 2003, GIA Publications, Inc.; Tr. *The Hymnal 1982*, © 1985, The Church Pension Fund.

Family Time

A choice of things to do at home

A New Life and a Coming Messiah

Some years after their return from exile, the Jewish people were ruled by nations that tried to prevent them from practicing their faith. The Temple was filled with statues of pagan gods. A group of Jewish warriors led a revolt and reclaimed the Temple. Out of the struggles of God's people grew the hope that God would send a messiah and reward his faithful ones with peace after death.

Indoor garden

Create a peaceful space inside your home. Your family could adorn a sunny spot with plants, pebbles, dried flowers, logs, verdigris figurines . . . perhaps even a battery-operated fountain.

Remembering loved ones

Prayers for people who died became important for Jews when they began to hope for life after death. This week, remember to pray for deceased relatives and friends.

Family time capsule

The Jewish people drew strength from recalling past experiences of God. Collect items that remind your family of happy times. Store the items in a decorated box. Set a date to open the box.

A Prayer for the Week

Lord, remind us that we do not have to face our struggles alone. We have you and our Christian brothers and sisters in heaven and on earth to help intercede for us. Amen.

Family Time

Something to Do . . .

On Sunday

Light a candle for someone in your family who is struggling, ill, or deceased. Ask God to give that person happiness and peace.

Through the Week

Take time to appreciate nature and the feelings of peace it inspires.

Visit Our Web Site

www.blestarewe.com

Something to Think About . . .

Believing in Life After Death

For if he were not expecting the fallen to rise again, it would have been useless and foolish to pray for them in death.

2 Maccabees 12:44

Believing in life after death is a basic tenet of our faith. This quote from the Old Testament refers to Judas Maccabeus, who prayed for the souls of fellow warriors who had died in the revolt against the Greeks. He showed his belief that our loving God does not stop loving people once their earthly lives end.

Understanding the belief in life after death is often difficult for children. But this belief can be a source of great comfort when children lose beloved older relatives. Explain that God is with us now and will only continue to be with us after death. Let children see you act in ways that show you have faith in this concept.

Something to Know About . . . Our Heritage in Ritual

Many Catholic churches feature rows of votive candles in front of statues or sacred images of Jesus and the saints. A churchgoer lights a candle and prays for a special intention. The burning candle suggests a continual rising of the intention toward Jesus or the saint who has been asked to pray.

Burning candles have a long history of religious symbolism. Candles or oil lamps burned outside saints' tombs in the third century. In the Middle Ages people sometimes lit candles as tall as themselves before they prayed to signify their coming into the light of faith. Lighting candles in a menorah is also an important part of the Jewish feast Hanukkah.

17 A New Life and a Coming Messiah

The King of the world will raise us up to live again forever.

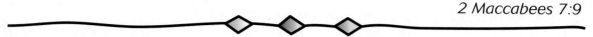

2 Maccabees 7:9

Share

Can you recall a time when you were very happy? What caused you to be happy? people you were with? a fun activity? a gift you received? No matter what makes us happy, if we had to choose between being happy and being sad, we all know what we would choose.

Now imagine what it would be like to enjoy happiness forever! Jesus promised us everlasting happiness and taught us how to achieve it.

Activity

Circle the things that make you happy, and draw a line through the things that are not important for your happiness.

_____	Winning a game
_____	Giving presents
_____	Having a lot of possessions
_____	Volunteering to help people
_____	Having name-brand clothes
_____	Making fun of people
_____	Being a good friend
_____	Getting away with breaking a rule
_____	Following Jesus
_____	Loving my family
_____	Respecting my parents
_____	Earning good grades in school
_____	People thinking I'm attractive

Now see how close you are to Jesus' idea of happiness. Write the letter *J* on the line next to the things that seem close to Jesus' way to happiness.

How many of your ideas of happiness seem to be the same as those of Jesus?

What would make the Jews of the Old Testament happy?

Scripture   The Struggles Under Greek Rule

The period before Christ's birth was difficult for the Jewish people. The Persian rule of Israel ended in 332 B.C., and the Jews came under the control of other foreign rulers, such as the Greeks. The Greeks did not worship the God of Israel. (People who worshiped other gods were called pagans or Gentiles.)

There sprang a sinful offshoot, Antiochus Epiphanes, son of King Antiochus, once a hostage at Rome. He became king in the year one hundred and thirty-seven of the kingdom of the Greeks.

In those days there appeared in Israel men who were breakers of the law, and they seduced many people, saying: "Let us go and make an alliance with the Gentiles all around us; since we separated from them, many evils have come upon us." The proposal was agreeable; some from among the people promptly went to the king, and he authorized them to introduce the way of living of the Gentiles. Thereupon they built a gymnasium in Jerusalem according to the Gentile custom. They abandoned the holy covenant; they allied themselves with the Gentiles and sold themselves to wrongdoing.

Then the king wrote to his whole kingdom that all should be one people, each abandoning his particular customs. All the Gentiles conformed to the command of the king, and many Israelites were in favor of his religion; they sacrificed to idols and profaned the sabbath.

In the year one hundred and forty-five, the king erected the horrible abomination upon the altar of holocausts, and in the surrounding cities of Judah they built pagan altars…Whoever was found with a scroll of the covenant, and whoever observed the law, was condemned to death by royal decree.

1 Maccabees 1:10–15, 41–43, 54, 57

Everlasting Joy

A group of devout Jews known as the Maccabees conquered the armies of the king. They took back the Temple, removed the pagan objects, and built a new altar. The Temple was rededicated, and according to tradition a one-day supply of lamp oil for the Temple lasted eight days. The eight-day Jewish feast of Hanukkah celebrates these events.

The belief in **resurrection** is gradually revealed in the Old Testament. The Maccabees believed that God's faithful people would have a rewarding life after death. The Maccabees prayed for the souls of fellow soldiers who were killed.

Catholics pray for the souls of the deceased. We believe we will be resurrected because of Christ's Resurrection. We believe that people who die in God's grace experience everlasting happiness, or **heaven**. Those who die in God's friendship but not without sin are purified in **purgatory**. A mortal sin is a serious act against God's law that is done purposely. It separates us from God's grace. It normally requires the sacrament of Reconciliation to be forgiven. People who do not repent of mortal sin before death are in danger of separation from God forever, or **hell**.

Praying for the forgiveness of souls in purgatory helps them enter heaven. The community of people in the Church, in purgatory, and in heaven is called the Communion of Saints.

GO TO page 360 to learn more about the Communion of Saints and everlasting life.

Faith Words

resurrection

Our bodies decay at our deaths, but our souls live forever. Resurrection is the new life given to us when our bodies reunite with our souls at the end of time.

heaven

Heaven is a life of everlasting happiness with God, and with all people who love God and others, after death.

purgatory

Purgatory is a final purification from sin after death.

hell

Hell is everlasting suffering and separation from God after death.

Activity

The Maccabees regained the Temple under the Lord's guidance, and the Jews dedicated the Temple to God again. They burned incense and lighted lamps. They bowed down and begged the Lord to spare them from such misfortune again. They asked God to protect them from sin. Then they celebrated joyfully for eight days, remembering all God had done for them. (See 2 Maccabees 10:1–6.)

Why should we too ask God to protect us from sin?

_____

_____

What help from God can we, too, celebrate in our lives?

_____

_____

How does the Holy Spirit lead us?

Hear & Believe

Praying for the Dead

Once, after a great battle, the Maccabees went off to bury their dead. To their surprise, some of the fallen soldiers were wearing pagan charms. These good soldiers had fought and died bravely for God's cause, but they had worshiped pagan idols.

The Maccabees prayed to God that the soldiers' sinful deeds might be erased. Then Judas Maccabeus, leader of the Maccabees, warned his men, "Keep free from sin. You have seen what has happened because of the sin of these fallen men."

Judas Maccabeus led the others in offering sacrifices for the dead soldiers' forgiveness. In this way, he showed that he believed in resurrection. He would not have prayed for the fallen soldiers if he did not hope that they would one day rise again. He prayed for the dead so that they might be freed from their sin and enjoy a heavenly reward.

Based on 2 Maccabees 12:38–46

The Maccabees trusted that God would listen to their prayers for the forgiveness of the otherwise good men. In the same way, we trust that God will hear our prayers for all the souls, both living and dead, in the Communion of Saints. We are especially hopeful because we know that God sent his Son, Jesus, to save all people.

Our Church Teaches

The Jews believed that God would send a messiah to bring peace, justice, mercy, and salvation to all. Jesus is the Messiah. God's promises to people in the Old Testament were completely fulfilled with Jesus Christ. Believing in Jesus Christ and in the Father who sent him is necessary for salvation from sin. Jesus Christ is both true God and true man, united in one divine person. Jesus said, "No one comes to the Father except through me" (John 14:6). God desires us to come to him through Christ so that we can be more Godlike. The Holy Spirit makes this possible. The grace of the Holy Spirit and our desire to be with God cause us to believe in Jesus and say, "You are the Christ, the Son of the living God."

The Holy Spirit inspired the Old Testament authors. The Holy Spirit is revealed in their writings. In the Old Testament, the Spirit is revealed in the Creation story, in promises of blessings from the Spirit, and in signs and revelations from God. The Spirit is revealed in the commandments, in the stories about the kingdom and the Exile, and in expectations of the Messiah. He is found in Isaiah's prophecies about Jesus Christ and in stories about the poor. If God had not revealed himself as Father, Son, and Holy Spirit, we never would have known about the Trinity, the central mystery of our faith.

GO TO page 358 to learn more about the Trinity.

> ## We Believe
> Jesus Christ makes everlasting happiness in heaven possible. Jesus is the Son of God and the Savior, as foretold in the Old Testament.

Activities

1. Why do Catholics pray for the dead?

_____

_____

"You are the Christ, the Son of the Living God." • "You are the Christ, the Son of the Living God." • "You are the Christ, the Son of the Living God." •

2. Explain why Jesus Christ is our Messiah.

"You are the Christ, the Son of the Living God." • "You are the Christ, the Son of the Living God." •

How can the saints help us in life and in death?

233

Saint Lucy

When you have a problem, it is good to talk to someone who understands how you feel. Praying is talking with God. We may ask saints to help us pray to God. We ask saints to pray for our special needs, too. But we do not pray *to* the saints the way we do to God.

Because saints overcame certain obstacles, many saints are patrons, or helpers, of people with certain needs or characteristics. Saint Joseph of Cupertino is the patron saint of students. The Church has assigned each saint a feast day. For example, we honor Saint Patrick, the patron saint of Ireland, on March 17. The feast day of Saint Lucy is December 13. Saint Lucy was a martyr. She lived in Italy in the third century after Christ's birth. Christians were being persecuted. Saint Lucy is the patron saint of people with blindness, eye disease, or throat infections. Here is the legend about why:

As a teenager, Lucy made a vow to live for Christ only. She did not want to marry the pagan nobleman her parents had chosen. Lucy prayed to Saint Agatha. Her mother was suddenly cured of a terrible illness. Then Lucy's mother respected Lucy's decision to devote her life to Jesus.

Lucy's fiancé was not happy that she rejected him. He reported Lucy to the authorities who persecuted Christians. Soldiers came to arrest Lucy, but she would not leave her house. They tried to pull her out by attaching a herd of oxen to her! But they could not move her. The soldiers decided to torture her. They poked out her eyes and tried to burn her, but by a miracle she would not burn. Then, one of the soldiers stabbed her in the throat. Her eyesight was restored before she died.

This girl is dressed as Saint Lucy for a Christmas tradition on Saint Lucy's feast day in Sweden. A parade takes place in the early, dark morning. The girl wears a wreath of candles because *Lucy* means "light." Other young people hold candles, sing, and pray.

Activities

1. On the line, write the name of the patron saint of your parish school, the saint you are named after, or your favorite saint. Then draw something you know about the saint.

Saint _____

2. Spiritual qualities that helped saints live the way Christ did are hidden in the mosaic below. To reveal them, shade in the spaces containing diamonds, stars, circles, and triangles, using a different color for each shape if you wish.

3. Name an everyday thing you can do to be a model of Christ.

_____

_____

How can the saints help us pray?

✝ Prayer Celebration

Praying with the Communion of Saints

Here are two litanies, one that requests help from the saints in heaven and one for the forgiveness of people who have died. After the leader speaks, pray the response while making the gestures shown.

Leader: Holy Mary,

Response: pray   for   us.

Leader:		**All:**	
Mother of God,		(response)	
Angels of God,		(response)	
Saint Peter and Saint Paul,		(response)	
All holy apostles,		(response)	
All holy martyrs of Christ,		(response)	
Saint Lucy,		(response)	
Saint (name a favorite saint),		(response)	
All holy men and women,		(response)	

Now we will pray to God for other people.
Lord, show us your kindness.

Response: Lord,   hear   our   prayer.

Leader: Save our friends and family.   **All:** (response)

For (name people you know)   (response)

Grant eternal rest to all who
have died, especially
(name people who have died).   (response)

Bring all people together
in trust and peace.   (response)

Lord Jesus, hear our prayer.   (response)

A **Write** sentences that explain the meaning of each word in the box.

1. _____

   _____

resurrection	heaven
purgatory	hell

2. _____

   _____

3. _____

   _____

4. _____

   _____

B **Complete** the litany below. It should ask the Communion of Saints to help you live a good life. Use your own words, and fill in the names of saints that you admire. Begin by writing a response that you will repeat throughout the prayer.

Response to repeat: _____.

Saint _____, help me _____.

Response: _____.

Saint _____, help me _____.

Response: _____.

All holy men and women, help me _____.

Response: _____.

Amen.

C **List** up to four things you did yesterday that made you happy. Then write the letter **J** next to the actions that were ways of following Jesus.

_____   _____

_____   _____

D **Complete** the sentences below, which relate Old Testament beliefs to Catholic beliefs today.

1. Some Jews came to believe in life after death. In the same way, we believe in _____.

2. The Maccabees prayed for their soldiers who had died in battle. In the same way, we pray for all souls, both living and dead, in the _____.

3. The Old Testament describes the Jews' hope that God would send a messiah. We believe that _____ is the Messiah.

4. The _____ inspired the Old Testament authors.

5. God revealed himself as Father, Son, and Holy Spirit in the Scriptures. This is how we know about the _____.

E **Respond** to the following.

1. How do saints help us?

_____

_____

2. Describe the problems that the Jews faced in the period before Christ's birth.

_____

_____

_____

Family Time

A choice of things to do at home

Baptism and Repentance

John the Baptizer prepared people for the Messiah, Jesus Christ. John preached repentance and the need to wash away one's sins in the waters of baptism. His story reminds us of the importance of sacraments and of our need to prepare spiritually for Christ. What helps your family live as people who are ready for God's kingdom?

The spirit of Advent

Preparation for Christ is appropiate any time of the year. Create an Advent wreath for next Christmas by inserting three purple taper candles, one pink taper candle, and some artificial greenery into a circular plastic foam base.

Feeling sorry

Using a marker and a small white poster board, together list feelings people might have after they do something wrong. What happens when people are forgiven? Have an adult dip the list into a shallow bowl of bleach, and see what happens.

Holy water in the home

Purchase bottles of holy water from a religious gift store. Invite family members to keep holy water in their rooms and bless themselves before praying.

A Prayer for the Week

God, thank you for the gift of Baptism and for all the sacraments, as they bring your life and love into our hearts.
Amen.

Family Time

Something to Do . . .

On Sunday

As you pray the Lamb of God, think of instances in which you need Christ's mercy.

Through the Week

When you know you are wrong or have hurt someone, quickly and graciously acknowledge it.

Visit Our Web Site

www.blestarewe.com

Something to Think About . . .

A Moral Guide to Humility

I am baptizing you with water, for repentance, but the one who is coming after me is mightier than I... He will baptize you with the holy Spirit and fire.
Matthew 3:11

 People would have readily accepted John the Baptizer as the Messiah, but he turned attention from himself and said that someone greater was coming. Later, Jesus came to John to be baptized. Jesus was sinless, but he turned attention from his holiness and was baptized.

Humility is a hard virtue to figure out. We know we should not be vain or boastful. We also know that a healthy self-esteem helps us accomplish things. So what does humility require? Jesus and John portray humility as the acknowledgment of one's purpose according to the plan of God, without dependence upon praises from people.

Something to Know About . . . Our Heritage in Scripture

During Christ's time, a Jewish sect believed to be the Essenes lived in Qumran near the Dead Sea in Israel. In 1947 shepherds stumbled upon jars filled with ancient scrolls in a cave near Qumran. A search of other caves turned up thousands of scroll fragments, which scholars have attempted to reconstruct. The scrolls date from the third century B.C. to A.D. 68. Written in Hebrew, Greek, and Aramaic, the scrolls include Old Testament books, books omitted from some versions of the Bible, and the religious writings of the commune believed to have been the Essenes. These Dead Sea Scrolls are the earliest known Bible manuscripts. They have inspired much interest and debate.

18 Baptism and Repentance

The Lord God says: I will give you a new heart
and place a new spirit within you.

Based on Ezekiel 36:26

Share

Think about your household when a holiday is coming. Your family will
make preparations so that everybody enjoys the holiday. Special meals
and activities are planned, especially if guests are visiting. Special
occasions are more special when we have time to get ready. God gives us
plenty of time to prepare ourselves for his kingdom—a lifetime!

Activity

This calendar shows events that require preparation. In each box
with an event, write something you would do to prepare for it.

Sunday	Monday	Tuesday	Wednesday	Thursday	Friday	Saturday
1 Mass	2	3 science test	4	5 piano lesson	6 sleepover party	7
8 cousin's baptism	9 Mom's birthday	10	11 gymnastic competition	12	13	14 receive sacrament of Reconciliation
15 Mass	16 book report due	17	18	19 doctor's appointment	20	21
22 friend's First Communion	23	24	25 vacation starts	26	27 sing carols at nursing home	28
29 Mass	30					

Who prepared
people for Jesus'
coming?

Worship   Advent Gospel Reading

About 2,000 years passed since Abraham first encountered the Lord. The Jews had survived the Exile and foreign rule. They still believed in Yahweh and the covenant. They tried very hard to obey God's laws. The **Pharisees** were Jews who were devoted to the commandments from the Old Testament. They also followed the spoken teachings of religious leaders. The **Sadducees** followed only the written laws from the Old Testament and valued the Temple rituals. The **Essenes** separated themselves from the rest of the Jewish community. They lived simply in the desert. They may have performed special washing rituals. They also believed in life after death. Some scholars think that John the Baptizer was one of them.

During Advent, we prepare to celebrate the birth of Jesus. The following passage is from a Gospel reading for the Second Sunday of Advent. It tells how John the Baptizer prepared people for the coming of Jesus.

A reading from the Gospel according to Matthew.

In those days John the Baptist appeared, preaching in the desert of Judea and saying, "Repent, for the kingdom of heaven is at hand!" It was of him that the prophet Isaiah had spoken when he said:

"A voice of one crying out in the desert,
'Prepare the way of the Lord,
    make straight his paths.'"

John wore clothing made of camel's hair and had a leather belt around his waist. His food was locusts and wild honey. At that time Jerusalem, all Judea, and the whole region around the Jordan were going out to him and were being baptized by him in the Jordan River as they acknowledged their sins.

When he saw many of the Pharisees and Sadducees coming to his baptism, he said to them, "Produce good fruit as evidence of your repentance…. Every tree that does not bear good fruit will be cut down and thrown into the fire. I am baptizing you with water, for repentance, but the one who is coming after me is mightier than I. I am not worthy to carry his sandals. He will baptize you with the holy Spirit and fire."

Matthew 3:1–8, 10–11

The Gospel of the Lord.
Praise to you, Lord Jesus Christ.

The Kingdom Is Coming

John the Baptizer prepared people to receive Jesus as the Messiah by telling them to repent, or be sorry for their sins and change their behavior. Some people believed that the coming of the Messiah was a sign of the final judgment of all humans and the resurrection of the dead. That was why John said, "The kingdom of heaven is at hand!" (Matthew 3:2)

We recognize Jesus as the Messiah. We are baptized in the Holy Spirit. At our baptisms, water and the words "I baptize you in the name of the Father, and of the Son, and of the Holy Spirit" give us the seal of eternal life and mark us as belonging to Christ. Confirmation deepens our baptismal commitment. It seals us with the gift of the Holy Spirit in oil and gives us grace to witness to our faith in word and deed. Baptism and Confirmation are called sacraments of initiation. They strengthen us to live as members of the Church and to spread Jesus' word.

Faith Words

Pharisees

Pharisees were Jewish people who accepted both the written law and spoken teachings and tradition.

Sadducees

Sadducees were Jewish people who accepted only the written law of the Old Testament and rejected spoken teachings and tradition.

Essenes

Essenes were devout Jewish people who lived simply in the desert.

Activity

John the Baptizer said, "Repent, for the kingdom of heaven is at hand!" He meant that there would be no room for sinful ways in the kingdom. Fill the box with words describing things that the kingdom *will* have room for, such as kindness and mercy. Add a design to the box that shows what you imagine the kingdom to be like.

What happened when John the Baptizer met Jesus at the Jordan River?

243

Hear & Believe

The Baptism of Jesus

John the Baptizer's preaching was so powerful that crowds flocked to the Jordan River to listen to him. Many people were in awe of John and thought *he* was the Messiah. But one day, a day for which John had long hoped, he stood in awe of another person, Jesus. As John was baptizing people, Jesus had stepped out of the crowd and asked John to baptize him. John did not feel worthy of baptizing him. He said to Jesus, "I need to be baptized by you, and yet you are coming to me?"

Jesus replied, "Allow it, please, so that God's plan of salvation can be fulfilled." And John did as Jesus asked. After Jesus emerged from the water, the heavens opened up, and the Holy Spirit descended like a dove upon Jesus. Then a voice was heard saying, "This is my beloved Son, with whom I am well pleased."

Based on Matthew 3:5–6, 13–17

Our Church Teaches

The sacraments of Baptism and Confirmation affect our souls permanently, so we never repeat them. On the other hand, we should celebrate the sacrament of Penance, or Reconciliation, frequently—at least once a year. This sacrament helps us spiritually in many ways. If we have committed a mortal sin, it reconciles us with God, giving us God's grace again. It also reconciles us with the Church. It excuses us from eternal punishment for mortal sins and from some of the punishment due for all sin after death. Finally, it brings us peace of mind, comfort, and the strength to avoid temptation. Through this sacrament, we prepare for the final judgment at the Second Coming of Christ.

Before confessing our sins to the priest, we carefully examine our consciences, reflecting upon how we have sinned. The Church teaches that we should confess all unconfessed serious sins to the priest. The Church does not require that venial, or less serious, faults be confessed, but it strongly recommends it. After we confess our sins and express our sorrow, the priest will absolve us, saying, "God, the Father of mercies, through the death and resurrection of his Son, has reconciled the world to himself and sent the Holy Spirit among us for the forgiveness of sins; through the ministry of the Church, may God give you pardon and peace, and I absolve you from your sins in the name of the Father, and of the Son, and of the Holy Spirit" (*Rite of Penance*).

Activities

1. Match the word to the sentence that describes it.

____ Sadducees   ____ Essenes

____ Pharisees   ____ Reconciliation

a) These Jews accepted both the written law and the spoken teachings and tradition.

b) These devout Jews lived simply in the desert.

c) This sacrament reconciles us with God.

d) These Jews accepted only the written law of the Old Testament.

2. Next to each event below, write how Christians prepare for it, based on what you have learned in this chapter.

Christmas _____

_____

the coming of the kingdom of heaven

_____

_____

the final judgment at the Second Coming of Christ _____

_____

the sacrament of Reconciliation

_____

_____

How do the sacraments lead us to holiness?

Respond

Activities

1. Fill in the missing information about the sacraments.

Type of sacrament	Sacrament	What is it?	Who may receive it?
Healing	Reconciliation		
	Anointing of the Sick	an anointing of Christians suffering from serious illness or old age, giving special graces, including forgiveness of sin	people who are sick or dying
Initiation	Baptism		babies or adults who have not been baptized
	Confirmation	the receiving of the gifts of the Holy Spirit	people who are ready to carry on the mission of the Church
	Eucharist		
Service of Communion	Matrimony	a lifelong commitment to love and serve a husband or wife and to raise and love children, teaching them to follow Christ	a man and a woman
	Holy Orders	a commitment to serve the Church as bishop, priest, or deacon	

 pages 361–363 if you need help with this activity.

2. Decode the prayer message using the code key.
   You will discover a prayer to help you prepare for the
   sacrament of Reconciliation.

Code Key

A:	1	H:	8	O:	15	V:	22
B:	2	I:	9	P:	16	W:	23
C:	3	J:	10	Q:	17	X:	24
D:	4	K:	11	R:	18	Y:	25
E:	5	L:	12	S:	19	Z:	26
F:	6	M:	13	T:	20		
G:	7	N:	14	U:	21		

Prayer Message:

_____   _____,
 8   15   12   25   19   16   9   18   9   20

_____
16   12   5   1   19   5

_____ _____ _____
 8   5   12   16   13   5   11   14   15   23

_____ _____. _____
13   25   19   9   14   19   8   5   12   16

____ ____ _____
13   5   2   5   19   15   18   18   25

_____ _____ _____
 6   15   18   20   8   5   13   23   9   20   8

_____ _____ _____.
 1   12   12   13   25   8   5   1   18   20

_____.
 1   13   5   14

How does prayer
renew us?

✝ Prayer Celebration

Lord, Send Your Spirit to Renew Us

What images from nature remind you of birth? The prophet Ezekiel told the Jewish people that God would make Israel "born again" after the Exile. At Baptism the following passage from the Book of Ezekiel may be read. The reading reminds us that Baptism gives us new life. Close your eyes and quietly listen to the passage. The leader will pause after each sentence and ask you to imagine a beautiful flower or plant growing step by step.

Leader: A reading from Ezekiel, chapter 36, verses 24 to 28. "For I will take you away from among the nations, gather you from all the foreign lands, and bring you back to your own land." *Imagine hands planting seeds in soil.*

"I will sprinkle clean water upon you to cleanse you from all your impurities, and from all your idols I will cleanse you." *Imagine a watering can over the soil and water sprinkling out.*

"I will give you a new heart and place a new spirit within you, taking from your bodies your stony hearts and giving you natural hearts." *Imagine tiny green sprouts shooting up from the soil.*

"I will put my spirit within you and make you live by my statutes, careful to observe my decrees." *Imagine a green stem beginning to grow, with buds and leaves slowly appearing.*

"You shall live in the land I gave your fathers; you shall be my people, and I will be your God." *Imagine the stem growing into a beautiful plant or a flower in full bloom, with sunlight shining on it. Imagine a meadow of flowers around it.*

All: Thank you, God, for the new life you gave us in Baptism. Help us grow in faith and love. Amen.

Chapter Review

A **Read** the Scripture verse below silently three times. Then, on the lines, explain how the verse relates to Baptism.

"I will give you a new heart and place a new spirit within you" (Ezekiel 36:26).

_____

_____

_____

B **Match** Column A with Column B by writing the correct number in the space provided.

A	B
1. Baptism	___ a commitment to serve the Church as bishop, priest, or deacon
2. Holy Orders	___ a celebration of God's forgiveness
3. Anointing of the Sick	___ a welcoming into the Church and receiving new life in Christ
4. Matrimony	___ receiving the gifts of the Holy Spirit
5. Reconciliation	___ the receiving of Christ's Real Presence in the form of bread and wine
6. Eucharist	___ an anointing that gives special graces to the sick and elderly
7. Confirmation	___ a commitment between a man and a woman to serve each other as husband and wife

C **Circle** the best answer.

John the Baptizer preached in the **(desert, community)** of Judea. He

(baptized, confirmed) many people in the **(Tigris, Jordan)** River. He

told people to **(repent, forgive)** and change their **(souls, behavior)**.

D **Complete** the sentences with words from the box.

| kingdom of heaven | Reconciliation | Confirmation | Baptism |

1. Baptism, Confirmation, and Reconciliation prepare us for the

   _____.

2. _____ excuses us from eternal punishment for mortal sin and brings us peace of mind.

3. Baptism and _____ affect our souls permanently.

4. Catholics receive _____ once in a lifetime.

E **Name** and describe the Jewish groups that existed after the Exile.

_____

_____

_____

_____

_____

_____

F **List** some things that you, your family, or your parish does to prepare for a special event, such as Confirmation, or a special holiday, such as Easter.

Name of event or holiday:

_____

Preparations:

_____

_____

_____

Family Time

A choice of things to do at home

Christians and the Reign of God

The New Testament story about the boy Jesus in wise conversation with Temple priests inspires us to reflect upon the great love of God, who let us share in his own divinity through a seemingly ordinary boy. When we value our dignity as Christians and God's children, we are able to understand that all people deserve our love and that *we* can become holy people and saints ourselves.

The star prayer

Have each family member draw an outline of a star and write *Holy Spirit* on the left and right of it, *Jesus Christ* in the center, and *God* above its top point. Inside the star, each person should jot down anything for which he or she would like to pray. With the help of the Holy Spirit, the "beams" of your prayers rise up to God through Jesus Christ.

You are special

The brightest star in the sky appeared at Jesus' birth. Although no special stars may have appeared, every person's birth has a special story behind it. Share stories about the times when family members were born, adopted, or became part of your family.

Temples of the Holy Spirit

How is each person in your family a temple of the Holy Spirit? At dinner, share examples of how each person has shown his or her goodness and holiness.

A Prayer for the Week

God, you became one of us and showed us how humans are to live. We will try to become the best family and best individuals we can be. Amen.

Family Time

Something to Do . . .

On Sunday

If your family normally just grasps one another's hands for the Sign of Peace, hug each other instead.

Through the Week

Look for the goodness inside people with whom you normally do not get along.

Visit Our Web Site

 www.blestarewe.com

Something to Think About . . .

A Moral Guide to Parental Worries

After three days they found him in the temple, sitting in the midst of the teachers, listening to them and asking them questions.
Luke 2:46

 Mary and Joseph lost track of Jesus on their journey from Jerusalem. But Jesus said, "Did you not know that I must be in my Father's house?" (Luke 2:49). Mary and Joseph learned a painful lesson about the supremacy of God's desires over our cares or worries. As their children grow older and more independent, parents may worry endlessly about whether the children will neglect every value they have learned in the home. But when parents have done their very best to teach, love, and protect, they can trust God to take care of the rest.

Something to Know About . . .

Our Heritage in Geography

A well-known path called Saints' Road winds through the Dingle Peninsula in County Kerry, Ireland. Beginning in the sixth century, monks traveled such paths to convert Christians to the monastic life. Christians lived, studied, and worshiped on the Dingle Peninsula between the sixth and tenth centuries. Ruins of early Christian settlements are abundant on the coast, from oratories to holy wells to Celtic crosses to small stone huts once belonging to the monks. Some sites remain remarkably intact from the time they

were abandoned in the twelfth century. Saints' Road connects the holy site of Mount Brandon to Gallarus Oratory, a stone church more than 1,100 years old (shown above).

19 Christians and the Reign of God

If we learn to love, we learn to be holy.

Mother Teresa

Share

Have you ever made something out of clay? From a lump of clay you can form something beautiful in any shape you want. If you do not like the way it comes out, you can reshape it until it seems perfect to you.

God lovingly shaped us in his own image, meaning that we are born with God's goodness and love within us. God gave each person beautiful gifts and talents. God sees beauty in all of us—inside and out. When we recognize the beauty of ourselves, we are better able to respect the inner beauty of others.

Activity

Each photograph shows a situation in which God's image was not respected. Choose one of the photographs, and draw an opposite situation in the box.

How do we show that we are all created in God's image?

Scripture   The Boy Jesus in the Temple

Each year, Jesus' parents went to Jerusalem for the feast of Passover, and when he was twelve years old, they went up according to festival custom. After they had completed the celebration, as they were returning, the boy Jesus remained behind in Jerusalem, but his parents did not know it. Thinking that he was in the caravan, they journeyed for a day and looked for him among their relatives and acquaintances, but not finding him, they returned to Jerusalem to look for him.

After three days they found Jesus in the Temple, sitting in the middle of the teachers, listening to them and asking them questions. All who heard him were astounded at his understanding and his answers.

When his parents saw him, they were astonished, and his mother said to him, "Son, why have you done this to us? Your father and I have been looking for you with great anxiety." Jesus said to them, "Why were you looking for me? Did you not know that I must be in my Father's house?" But they did not understand what he said to them. He went with them to Nazareth, and was obedient to them; and his mother kept all these things in her heart. And Jesus advanced in wisdom, age, and favor before God and man.

Based on Luke 2:41–52

Human and Divine

On the journey back to Nazareth, Mary would have traveled with the women, and Joseph with the men. Each parent probably thought Jesus was with the other one and did not realize he was missing right away. They were relieved to find Jesus but did not understand what he was doing in the Temple. The teachers in the Temple were amazed at Jesus' answers to their difficult questions.

Jesus was the Son of God, the Messiah. He was also a missing twelve-year-old Jewish boy with worried parents. He was both human and divine. We are created in God's image and share in God's divine nature through Jesus Christ. How special we are that God would make this possible! Our specialness is called **dignity**.

All people are equal because they have dignity as God's children. Human dignity gives people certain rights. People have a right to make moral choices, to have religious freedom, and to express belief in God. Like Jesus' family, all families have a special dignity. Families, formed by married men and women and their children, have the right to live peacefully, without being regulated by other groups.

Activity

Listed below are some ways of showing others that we respect their human dignity. As a follower of Jesus, how can you do each of the things listed? Give specific examples on the lines.

Helping others do what is right

_____

_____

Giving advice to those who are doubtful

_____

_____

Praying for others

_____

_____

Comforting the suffering

_____

_____

Forgiving people

_____

_____

Being patient with others

_____

_____

Why do we respect others' dignity?

Jonah, the Reluctant Prophet

Sometimes, respecting other people's dignity can be a struggle. Our own pride or prejudices can get in the way. In the Old Testament, the Book of Jonah tells the story of someone who struggled with God's call to help others do what was right.

Jonah was a prophet, but not a willing one. He tried to run away after the LORD told him, "Set out for the city of Nineveh, and preach against its people; their wickedness will be punished." God wanted Jonah to warn the citizens that if they did not repent, God would destroy them. But Jonah, like other Jewish people, did not like the wicked Assyrians who lived in Nineveh. He hoped that God *would* punish them. So Jonah refused to undertake his mission. He hopped aboard a ship headed in another direction.

But God had other plans. During Jonah's sea voyage, violent winds hurled the ship back and forth, until Jonah's passengers turned to him and said, "What is your business? Are you the source of God's wrath upon our ship?"

Jonah said, "Throw me into the sea so that it will quiet down for you. I know this violent storm is because of me."

After Jonah was thrown overboard, the LORD sent a large fish to swallow him. After three days, the fish heaved him upon the shore, and the LORD again told Jonah to go to Nineveh. Reluctantly, Jonah went and preached God's message. To his surprise, his hated enemies paid attention. They changed their wicked ways. Jonah's success really angered him. He asked God, "Why did I have to be the instrument of your mercy?"

The LORD answered, "Should I not care for the city of Nineveh, where more than a hundred thousand people dwell?"

Based on the Book of Jonah

From this story, we learn that God sends his mercy to everyone, including those whom we consider our enemies. We are called to respect the dignity of others, no matter what.

Our Church Teaches

We respect people's dignity by treating them with love and kindness. We can do this by practicing the **spiritual works of mercy**, loving deeds that fulfill the needs of other people. They are helping others do what is right, giving advice to those who are doubtful, praying for others, teaching the ignorant, comforting the suffering, forgiving people, and being patient with others.

 page 373 to learn about the corporal works of mercy.

Each Christian is a **temple of the Holy Spirit**. Saint Paul said, "Do you not know that you are the temple of God, and that the Spirit of God dwells in you?" (1 Corinthians 3:16). As temples of the Holy Spirit, we are called to respect our bodies. For example, God's gift of sex is noble and honorable and should be shared only by a husband and wife, for the creation of children and as an expression of love and commitment.

As temples of the Holy Spirit, we are also called to be saints, holy people who follow the example of Jesus. Holiness comes from living simply, as the saints did. The saints denied themselves possessions and avoided distractions from serving God. Holiness comes from the struggle of overcoming temptation and trying to imitate Christ. By pursuing holiness, we work toward experiencing the joy and peace of living the Beatitudes.

 page 370 to learn about the Beatitudes.

Activity

Complete the sentences.

1. Jonah refused his mission and was thrown into the _____.

2. Jonah preached a message of _____ to the Assyrians.

3. The people of Nineveh _____ after Jonah preached God's message.

4. We are called to show _____ to others.

We Believe

The spirit of Christ dwells in each one of us. We must respect our dignity as Christians and the dignity of all God's children.

Faith Words

spiritual works of mercy

The spiritual works of mercy are loving deeds to meet others' needs.

temple of the Holy Spirit

Each of us is a temple of the Holy Spirit because the Holy Spirit dwells within us. As temples of the Holy Spirit, we are called to respect our bodies and to become saints.

How can we use our gifts to help others?

257

What Is Wrong with Dad?

Ricky was shopping for a present for his dad's birthday. He went through the mall several times but could not find anything to buy. Ricky was getting frustrated. The fact that Ricky and his dad had been arguing a lot lately did not help. Nothing Ricky did seemed to please his father. "What is the matter with you?" his father would yell.

One day, Ricky asked his mother what he could do to make things better. "Well, Ricky," she said, "your dad is going through a tough time right now. Since he has been out of work, he does not feel very good about himself."

"But that is not my fault," said Ricky. "Does that give him the right to pick on me all the time?"

"No, it does not, and you should tell him that," she said. "But we all have to try to be patient with him. Can you understand how he feels?"

Ricky thought about this as he walked through the mall. Ricky realized that if his father felt better about himself, he would feel better about Ricky. His mother was right. Ricky's father needed his help.

In a store that sold coffee mugs, Ricky spotted a mug with a cartoon bull on it. The bull was alone in a meadow, with a strange expression on its face. The mug read, "Happy Birthday to someone 'out standing' in the field." The saying was funny. It reminded Ricky of his father's helpful advice: "The person who attracts the most attention is not the one who fits in, but the one who stands out." Ricky bought the mug and then some chocolate, his father's favorite candy.

In a birthday card, Ricky wrote, "Dad, I know things have been kind of rotten lately, but I still love you. I think you are 'outstanding.' Maybe we can talk sometime. I hope you have a happy birthday. Love, Ricky."

Ricky's small gesture did the trick.

Activities

1. Jesus said, "You are the light of the world... Your light must shine before others, that they may see your good deeds and glorify your heavenly Father" (Matthew 5:14, 16). Imagine that you are the lighthouse in the picture. Each boat is named with a difficulty it must overcome in order to see your light. On each light beam, write a gift you have that will guide each boat to shore unharmed.

   S.S. Ignorance

   S.S. Sorrow

   S.S. Poverty

   S.S. Hatred

2. You have learned many Old Testament stories about God, God's revelation to people, and God's covenant with the Jews. The New Testament tells us how God fulfilled his promises to the Jews by sending Jesus Christ. The Gospels in the New Testament are the books of Matthew, Mark, Luke, and John. The Gospels are the main source for our knowledge about the life and teachings of our Savior, Jesus. Why do you think we say Jesus fulfilled the Old Testament covenants?

   _____

   _____

   _____

What is a good prayer for holiness?

✝ Prayer Celebration

Let Your Light Shine!

Group 1: Lord, I pray that you may be a lamp for me in the darkness. Touch my soul and kindle a fire within it, that it may burn brightly and give light to my life.

Group 2: Thus my body may truly become your temple…. And may the light within me shine on my friends that it may drive away the darkness of ignorance and sin from them also.

All: Thus together let us be lights to the world, manifesting the bright beauty of your Gospel to all around us. Amen.

Based on a prayer by Saint Columbanus, A.D. 540–615

19 Chapter Review

A **Circle** the letter of the best answer.

1. Each year, Jesus' parents went to Jerusalem for the feast of
   _____.

   a. Christmas **b.** Passover **c.** Hanukkah **d.** Easter

2. After three days Jesus' parents found him in the _____,
   sitting in the middle of the teachers.

   a. Temple **b.** city **c.** church **d.** caravan

3. Jesus said to his parents, "Why were you looking for me? Did you
   not know that I must be in my Father's _____?"

   a. kingdom **b.** school **c.** shop **d.** house

4. Jesus returned with his parents to _____ and was obedient
   to them.

   a. Bethlehem **b.** Assyria **c.** Nazareth **d.** Nineveh

5. Jesus was both human and _____.

   a. old **b.** divine **c.** sinful **d.** selfish

B **Complete** the sentences.

1. We share in God's divine nature through _____.

2. _____ is the specialness of people because they are God's
   children.

3. All people have the right to make _____ choices.

4. All people have the right to have religious _____.

5. All people have the right to express _____ in God.

C **Complete** the list of qualities that show a person's
dignity as a child of God. Two answers are provided.

loving_____   _____   _____

forgiving_____   _____   _____

Write what it means to be a temple of the Holy Spirit.

_____

_____

_____

 Rewrite the prayer by Saint Columbanus from page 260 in your own words. Then silently pray what you have written.

_____

_____

_____

_____

_____

 Match each spiritual work of mercy shown in Column A with the example of how to accomplish it in Column B. Write the correct number in the space provided.

A

Spiritual Works of Mercy

1. helping others do what is right

2. teaching the ignorant

3. giving advice to the doubtful

4. comforting those who suffer

5. being patient with others

6. forgiving others

7. praying for others

B

Examples

____ telling a friend about the Good News

____ staying friends with someone who hurt you

____ willingly repeating an explanation

____ supporting a friend who tells the truth

____ asking for God's forgiveness of people who have died

____ sharing with a friend ways to grow in faith

____ showing concern for a sick person

Family Time

A choice of things to do at home

Hope for the Ages

Jesus, the hope of the ages, not only taught us how to pray in words but through his actions. Jesus ordinarily prayed alone in silence. He depended on prayer to help him through the most difficult moments in his life. Periods of silence and prayer may be rare in our lives, but Jesus' example shows us how to achieve a richer life of prayer.

Missionary family

The Catholic Church is a missionary church, long ago instructed by Jesus to spread his message of hope. Discuss together ways in which your family has been a family of Catholic missioners.

Our Father

Write each line of the Lord's Prayer (see page 383) on a separate slip of paper. Have each family member read a line out loud, and discuss its meaning together.

Quiet time

Designate a part of your family's usual "together time" as quiet time. This could be the first two minutes at the dinner table or the first two minutes of a car ride.

A Prayer for the Week

God, you were the hope of our ancestors and are our hope today. Help us show our faith in you by following Jesus' example.
Amen.

Family Time

Something to Do . . .

On Sunday

Listen to what the priest says just after the Lord's Prayer. What attitude should we adopt toward our worries and why?

Through the Week

View all your actions as examples of Christ's way of life, and see how your behavior changes.

Visit Our Web Site

www.blestarewe.com

Something to Think About . . .

Harboring the Strength of Christ

He went around all of Galilee, teaching in their synagogues, proclaiming the gospel of the kingdom, and curing every disease and illness among the people.
Matthew 4:23

We could say that Jesus led a very hectic life. He taught by example and by giving instruction. He healed by forgiving people's sins and by curing their physical ailments. After he ascended into heaven, his spirit came upon his disciples at Pentecost. This left Jesus' disciples with great strength to carry on his work. Our lives are not simple. We have to live out our mission in addition to many other things that are expected of us. But the strength of Jesus is always there for us.

Something to Know About . . . Our Heritage in Film

The films of late director Alfred Hitchcock often betray his Catholic roots. Educated at St. Ignatius College in London, Hitchcock often relied on Catholic imagery and plots about suffering for other people's crimes. In the 1953 film *I Confess*, his most overtly "Catholic" film, a parishioner confesses a murder to a priest. When the police learn that the murder victim had been trying to blackmail the priest, the priest becomes the main suspect. The sacred seal of confession, however, prevents the priest from revealing the truth. The priest is subjected to a trial and public humiliation. One scene depicts the priest walking past statues of Christ carrying the cross.

20 Hope for the Ages

May the God of Abraham, Sara, Isaac, and Esther,
May the God of Paul, Joseph, Mary, and John,
May the God of us all bless us
In the name of the Father, and of the Son, and of
the Holy Spirit.

Share

Parents or other adults who care for us love us and want us to be happy.
They do much more than meet our material needs. They are also there
to guide us when we need help making decisions. Just as Jesus, we have
two sets of guides: our earthly caregivers, and our heavenly one, God.
Mary and Joseph were Jesus' earthly parents, who guided him on earth.
God was Jesus' heavenly Father, who guided him spiritually. Jesus often
talked to God when he had a problem, and Jesus was obedient to God.

Activity

Fill out this certificate of achievement for an adult you love. List
three ways in which the person has done much more than meet
your material needs.

*This Certificate of Achievement
for an Outstanding Caregiver*
is Awarded to

_____

IN HONOR OF LOVING ACCOMPLISHMENTS,
ESPECIALLY...

1._____

2._____

3._____

This Award is Granted with Love on _____
DATE

Signed _____
YOUR NAME

How did
Jesus teach
us to pray?

✝ Scripture   Jesus' Ministry

Jesus came to Nazareth, where he had grown up, and went to the synagogue on the Sabbath day. He stood up to read a scroll of the prophet Isaiah. He read,

> "The Spirit of the Lord is upon me,
> because he has anointed me
>   to bring glad tidings to the poor.
> He has sent me to proclaim liberty to captives
>   and recovery of sight to the blind,
>   to let the oppressed go free,
> and to proclaim a year acceptable to the Lord."

The eyes of all in the synagogue stared at him. He said to them, "Today this Scripture passage is fulfilled in your hearing." And all spoke highly of him and were amazed at the gracious words that came from his mouth. But soon people in the synagogue became angry. They could not accept Jesus' claims that he fulfilled the prophecies from their Scriptures and that God's saving message was not just for themselves.

Jesus then went around all of Galilee, teaching in their synagogues, proclaiming the gospel of the kingdom, and curing every disease and illness among the people. Great crowds followed him. When he saw the crowds, he went up a mountain.

Jesus taught the crowds, saying, "When you pray, do not be like the hyprocrites, who love to stand and pray in the synagogues and on street corners so that others may see them. Amen, I say to you, they have received their reward. But when you pray, go to your inner room, close the door, and pray to your Father in secret. And your Father who sees in secret will repay you. This is how you are to pray:

> Our Father in heaven,
>   hallowed be your name,
>   your kingdom come,
> your will be done,
>   on earth as in heaven.
> Give us today our daily bread;
> and forgive us our debts,
>   as we forgive our debtors;
> and do not subject us to the final test,
>   but deliver us from the evil one."

Based on Luke 4:16–29 and Matthew 4:23, 25; 5:1–2; 6:5–6, 9–13

Jesus Taught Us How to Pray

The scroll of Isaiah referred to Jesus. Jesus was the one who had come to help the poor, heal people, teach people about God, and free people from sin. People flocked to hear Jesus preach. Jesus told them that just following the laws of their faith was not enough. He announced that God wanted *everyone* to know his love and forgiveness! Some people could not accept Jesus' messages.

In the Lord's Prayer, Jesus called the Lord "Father." Jesus actually used the word *Abba*, which means "Daddy" in Hebrew. Calling God "Daddy" would have seemed unusual to people. Jewish people would not even speak God's name. But Jesus taught people that God is a loving Father who looks after his children. Jesus said, "Your Father knows what you need before you ask him" (Matthew 6:8).

Praying in secret was an unfamiliar idea for people. Jesus said it was important to focus on God alone in silence. He said that people who wanted everyone to see how well they prayed and how much they gave to the poor were hypocrites, or people who are not sincere.

Activity

Jesus read a passage from the Old Testament prophet Isaiah. Isaiah's words described Jesus' ministry. In your book, especially in Unit 4, find the words of another Old Testament prophet. Then explain how the words describe Jesus.

_____

_____

_____

_____

What did Jesus teach about faith and prayer?

Hear & Believe

The Fruits of Prayer

Old Testament prophets sometimes performed miraculous acts to show people the lessons they were trying to teach. As you learned in Chapter 13, for example, the prophet Elijah called on God to send fire upon the people's sacrifice to teach them about their sinful ways.

Jesus also taught in this manner. In one Gospel story, a miracle of Jesus illustrates that if we pray to God with very strong faith, there is nothing that God cannot help us with. In this story, Jesus comes across a fig tree that is not producing any fruit, so he causes it to wither. When the disciples see this, they are puzzled and amazed, but Jesus tells them:

"Have faith in God. Indeed, if you say to a mountain, 'Be lifted up and thrown into the sea,' and do not doubt in your heart but believe that it will happen, it shall be done for you. Therefore, I tell you, with all that you ask for in prayer, believe that you will receive it, and it shall be yours. When you are about to pray, forgive anyone against whom you have a grudge so that your heavenly Father may in turn forgive your sins."

Based on Mark 11:20–26

Jesus used the fruitless tree to teach a lesson. He taught that our hearts should be in the right place when we pray to God. We need to have strong faith that will not be overcome by doubt, and we should be making a sincere effort in our daily lives to follow Jesus' example of goodness toward others.

Praying with sincere faith is like being a fig tree that produces lots of fruit. The fruit is all the good that can result.

Our Church Teaches

Prayers to God should be sincere. One way to pray quietly and sincerely is through **meditation**. This is a type of prayer in which we are silent and concentrate on our feelings, our imagination, and our thoughts of God.

Jesus did not teach the Lord's Prayer so that people would recite it without knowing what it means. He sent the Holy Spirit, who helps us desire to pray to God as "our Father." In the Lord's Prayer and every prayer, the Holy Spirit, through the Word of God, moves us to pray to God as our Father.

Activity

Write down five of Jesus' teachings about prayer that you have learned in this chapter.

_____

_____

_____

_____

_____

_____

We Believe

The Lord's Prayer, or the Our Father, comes from Jesus Christ. It is our model prayer.

Faith Words

meditation

Meditation is a type of prayer in which we are silent and concentrate on listening to God through our feelings, imagination, and thoughts. We can meditate by thinking about a Scripture story, art, or music.

The large photograph shows a fig tree. The small photograph shows some unripe figs on the tree.

How did Jesus pray for help?

Respond

Your Will Be Done, Father

As more people began to follow Jesus, his opponents became angry. Eventually this led to his suffering and death on the cross. (We do not blame Jewish people for Jesus' suffering or death.) Before Jesus died, he called on God in prayer. His final prayers are perfect examples of his obedience to and love for God.

Activity

Follow the trail of Jesus' prayers below. On the lines beneath each prayer, write what you think it means.

Jesus stopped to pray in a garden. Jesus knew he was about to be led to his death. He prayed, "Abba, Father, all things are possible to you. Take this cup away from me, but not what I will but what you will" (based on Mark 14:32–36).

_____

_____

_____

After the people voted to crucify Jesus, Jesus carried the cross up to the spot where he would be crucified. He prayed, "Forgive them, Father, for they know not what they do" (based on Luke 23:33–34).

_____

_____

_____

Even though it was daytime, darkness came over the land. Jesus was dying on the cross. He cried out, "My God, my God, why have you abandoned me?" (based on Mark 15:33–34)

_____

_____

_____

As Jesus breathed his last breath, he cried out in a loud voice, "Father, into your hands I entrust my spirit" (based on Luke 23:46).

_____

_____

_____

Women who followed Jesus came to his tomb after he died. But the tomb was empty. The stone in front of it had been rolled away. Jesus was risen! (based on Luke 24:1–7)

How does the Holy Spirit guide our prayers?

✝ Prayer Celebration

Come, Holy Spirit

After Jesus rose from the dead and ascended to heaven, the Holy Spirit gave Jesus' disciples the strength and wisdom to carry on Jesus' message. The Holy Spirit fills us with the desire to pray to our Father. We can ask the Holy Spirit to give us strength, wisdom, and the ability to pray.

Come, Holy Spirit, fill the hearts of your faithful
and kindle in them the fire of your love.
Send forth your Spirit, and they shall be created:
And you will renew the face of the earth.

Meditation:

Look at the painting on this page. It shows the Pentecost. On Pentecost, the Holy Spirit came to the disciples of Jesus to give them strength to carry out Jesus' mission. How do you think the disciples felt? What symbols for the Holy Spirit are in the painting? What do those symbols tell you about God's power?

A **Respond** to the following.

1. In what ways did Jesus fulfill the prophecy that he read from the scroll of the prophet Isaiah?

_____

_____

2. What did Jesus teach the people of Galilee about prayer?

_____

_____

3. How did Jesus use the example of a fig tree to teach us about prayer?

_____

_____

_____

4. What did Jesus say about people who wanted everyone to see how well they prayed and how much they gave to the poor?

_____

_____

B **Circle** the best answer.

1. Jesus had two sets of guides: God and (**Mary and Joseph, the temple leaders**).

2. Like Jesus, you have two sets of caregivers: parents and adults, who care for you, and (**God, teachers**).

3. These caregivers help you (**make decisions, comfort others**) and want you to be (**happy, proud**).

C **Match** Column A with Column B by writing the correct number in the space provided.

A

Jesus' prayers

1. Forgive them, Father, for they know not what they do (based on Luke 23:34).

2. Take this cup away from me, but not what I will but what you will (Mark 14:36).

3. My God, my God, why have you abandoned me? (Mark 15:34)

4. Father, into your hands I entrust my spirit (based on Luke 23:46).

B

Meaning

____ God, I give myself to you completely.

____ Oh, God, why have you allowed me to suffer like this?

____ Let me avoid this suffering, but only if it is your will.

____ Please forgive the people who are persecuting me. They are not aware of their sin.

D **Respond** to the following.

1. What is meditation? _____

_____

2. What is one way to meditate? _____

_____

3. Look at the painting on page 312 in your book. What does it show?

_____

4. Meditate by looking at and thinking about the painting. Write a prayer that asks the Holy Spirit to help you hear what God is saying to you as you pray.

_____

_____

_____

_____

WE CARE *About Ourselves*

A Person with a Bright Future

Javier lived in a poor, violent neighborhood. Most of the neighborhood kids joined a gang by the sixth grade.

Javier had been getting good grades in school all his life. He was also good at art projects. By the sixth grade, though, his friends were starting to drift away and join gangs, too. Javier was already worried about his future. Could he make it if he didn't join a gang like everyone else?

Javier's brother Jamie was in a gang. Jamie, who was only sixteen, had already been arrested for carrying weapons. He kept telling Javier that only a gang could protect someone in their kind of neighborhood. Jamie told Javier that gang members knew how to look out for each other. They knew how to get money for each other.

But then, late one night, Javier actually heard Jamie crying in his bed. Jamie said that his best friend was shot and killed that night.

That week, an organization called Jobs for a Future gave a presentation at Jamie's high school. Reverend Greg Boyle, S.J., started Jobs for a Future in 1988 for the youth in dangerous housing developments in Los Angeles, California. Its slogans were "Nothing Stops a Bullet Like a Job" and "Jobs, Not Jails." Jobs for a Future came to tell the high school students about Homeboy Industries. This was a collection of businesses that provided jobs for gang-involved youth.

Jamie decided to try making T-shirts for Homeboy Silkscreen. Jamie was proud of the designs he created. As he became busier with his job, he lost time for his gang. He started to encourage Javier to stay away from gangs. "You're creative," he told Javier. "Why don't you help out with the T-shirts, too?"

Javier watched his brother become happier and keep out of trouble. Javier decided he would stay away from the gangs.

Why was Javier's decision the right decision?

Think About It

Javier had a good mind and unique talents that would have been wasted if he had joined a gang. You, too, are an original, "handmade" by God. God gave special attention to your creation. God had a bright future in mind when he created you.

Describe something that could keep you from making a bright future for yourself.

_____

How can you prevent this from happening?

_____

_____

Learn About It

Jesus taught over and over that each of us is a special child of God. He backed up his teaching by treating everyone that way. It may be hard for you to recognize that you are special. You may seem to have average intelligence, looks, and abilities. But you are anything but average. No one is average.

What makes you special is your spiritual side, the part of you no one can really see, except God. You should feel pretty good about yourself. Everyone else is special too, so remember to treat them the same way Jesus would.

Do Something About It

Compose a T-shirt slogan that advertises <u>you</u> as a "handmade" creation of God. Be sure to include your talents and what is special about your personality.

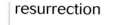

UNIT 5 Organizer

On the lines under each chapter title, write three words or phrases that you learned about in the chapter. Use all words and phrases from the box.

resurrection	Maccabees	spiritual works of mercy
Pharisees	temple of the Holy Spirit	John the Baptizer
Mary and Joseph	the Lord's Prayer	meditation
Essenes	Communion of Saints	Jesus' prayers

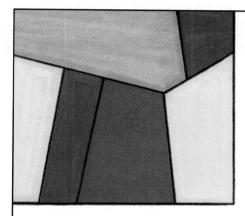

17
A New Life and a Coming Messiah

_____
_____
_____

18
Baptism and Repentance

_____
_____
_____

19
Christians and the Reign of God

_____
_____
_____

20

Hope for the Ages

_____
_____
_____

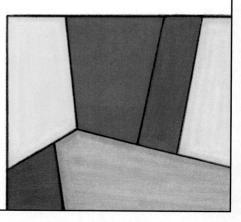

A **Complete** each sentence.

1. John the Baptizer said that to prepare for Jesus' coming
   people needed to _____.

2. The story of the Maccabees' praying for the souls of
   soldiers who were killed is an example of how belief in
   resurrection is revealed in the _____.

3. _____ sins must be confessed in the sacrament
   of Reconciliation.

4. God created us in his own _____.

5. Because the Spirit of Christ dwells in each one of us, we
   must respect the _____ of all God's children.

6. As _____ of the Holy Spirit, we are called to
   respect our bodies and to become saints.

7. The _____, the books of Mark, Matthew, Luke,
   and John, are the main source for our knowledge about
   the life and teachings of our Savior, Jesus.

8. We can ask the _____ to give us strength,
   wisdom, and the ability to pray.

9. After _____ baptized Jesus, the heavens opened
   up, and the Holy Spirit descended like a _____
   upon Jesus.

10. The Old Testament story of _____, who went
    reluctantly to preach God's message to the wicked
    people of Nineveh, teaches us that we are called to
    respect the dignity of others, no matter what.

Review

B **Match** Column A with Column B by writing the correct number in the space provided.

A	B
1. Advent	___ people who did not worship the God of Israel
2. patrons	___ the community of people in the Church, in purgatory, and in heaven
3. Reconciliation	___ helpers, such as the saints
4. Communion of Saints	___ the person who prepared people for the coming of Jesus by telling them to repent
5. Confirmation	___ the season in which we prepare to celebrate the birth of Jesus
6. pagans, or Gentiles	___ the sacrament in which we are sealed with the Holy Spirit in oil and given grace to witness to our faith
7. John the Baptizer	___ the sacrament that reconciles us with God and the Church and prepares us for the final judgment at the second coming of Christ

C **Write** the priest's words of absolution during the sacrament of Reconciliation.

_____

_____

D **Match** Column A with Column B by writing the correct number in the space provided.

A

1. dignity

2. Essenes

3. heaven

4. hell

5. meditation

6. Pharisees

7. purgatory

8. Sadducees

9. spiritual works of mercy

10. temple of the Holy Spirit

11. resurrection

B

___ everlasting happiness with God after death

___ prayer in which we are silent and concentrate on listening to God

___ devout Jewish people who lived simply in the desert

___ each of us, within whom the Holy Spirit dwells

___ everlasting suffering and separation from God after death

___ Jewish people who accepted both the written law and spoken teachings

___ Jewish people who accepted only the written law of the Old Testament

___ loving deeds to meet others' needs

___ a final purification from sin after death

___ the new life given to us when our bodies reunite with our souls at the end of time

___ the specialness of people because they are God's children

E **Write** the Come, Holy Spirit prayer on a separate sheet of paper.

FEASTS AND SEASONS

Advent

More than sentinels wait for the dawn,
let Israel wait for the Lord.

Psalm 130:6–7

The Second Coming of Christ

Jesus explained to his followers what would happen at the end of time. "No one except God knows the day or the hour," he told them, "but it will be similar to the way it was in the time of Noah. People were living their lives as they did every day, eating and drinking, marrying and being married. They did not know the end had come until the flood came and carried them all away. This is the way it will be when the Son of Man comes.

"Two men will be working in the field. One will be taken and one will be left. Two women will be grinding grain into flour. One will be taken and one will be left. So pay attention! You do not know when your Lord is coming!"

Finally, Jesus said to them, "If the owner of a house knew when a thief was coming, he would keep a careful watch on his house and not let it be broken into. You have to be the same way. The Son of Man will come when you least expect him."

Based on Matthew 24:36–44

During the season of Advent, the Church remembers that Jesus Christ will come again at the end of time. The four weeks of Advent also invite us to prepare our hearts for the celebration of the birth of our Lord at Christmas.

On the first Sunday of Advent, the Church proclaims the Gospel about Christ's Second Coming.

In the Gospel of Matthew we read that Christ's coming will be sudden and unexpected. The Gospel reminds us that no human being knows when Jesus Christ will come again. Jesus himself explained this to his apostles. To stress the idea that his return would happen when least expected, Jesus used the stories of the flood that completely changed the world, the workers in a field, and the women grinding grain. These stories also tell us that the Lord's return will change everything.

Again and again throughout the Gospels, we read that Jesus told his followers that his return would mean the end of everyday life as we know it. So, it is important that we live our faith, ready and waiting for the risen Christ's return.

While the Church always waits in hope and joy for Jesus Christ's return, it does so especially during Advent. We recall Jesus' birth at Christmas, and this reminds us that we will see him again at the Second Coming. The Church encourages us to take the time to think about our lives and our faith during Advent. By reflecting on what it means to be a Christian and a follower of Jesus, we will await his return with love and hope in our hearts.

Getting Ready

In the Gospels we read that Jesus wants his followers to be ready for his return. He wants us to draw close to him through the celebration of the sacraments and to live as part of his community. This Advent, will you reflect on what being a Christian means to you?

> Lord, we are waiting for your return. We know that you love us and care for us. May we be with you forever in your kingdom. Amen.

Activity

Color the stained-glass shapes marked with an asterisk to discover a hidden message. Then color the rest of the stained glass.

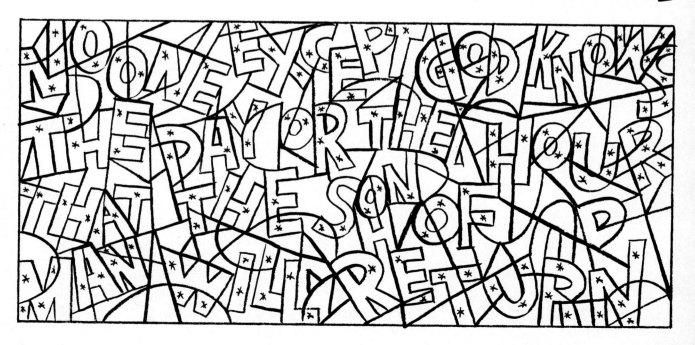

God Keeps His Promises

In the Bible we read about the many promises God made to his **chosen people**. He promised never to destroy the earth again by water, and then he set a rainbow in the sky as a sign of his promise. God promised Abraham and Sarah that he would make of them a mighty nation and that their descendants would be as many as the stars in the sky, and then Sarah, who was childless, became pregnant in her old age. God promised to deliver his people from slavery in Egypt, and then he led them into a land overflowing with milk and honey. These examples show God's generosity in keeping his promises.

Christians believe that Jesus is the **fulfillment** of God's promise to us. We believe that when the time was right, God sent his only Son to be our **Messiah** and to save all people from sin. Advent is the time in the liturgical year when we recall God's fulfilled promise and wait with joy for Jesus to return in glory at the end of time.

One way the Church recalls and awaits our Lord's Second Coming is by chanting the "O Antiphons" during Advent. During the liturgies of the last days of Advent, beginning on December 17, an antiphon, or short hymn verse, beginning with "O" is prayed and chanted. The O Antiphons come from Old Testament prophecies. Each antiphon calls for the coming of the Messiah. The popular hymn "O Come, O Come, Emmanuel" is based on the O Antiphons.

Here are the first two O Antiphons.

O Wisdom,
　　you came forth from the mouth of the Most High,
　　and reaching from beginning to end,
　　you ordered all things mightily and sweetly.
　　Come, and teach us the way of prudence.

O Lord of Israel,
　　you showed yourself to Moses in the burning bush,
　　and you gave him the holy law on Mount Sinai.
　　Come, stretch out your mighty hand
　　and set us free.

Based on Sunday Vespers at Advent, Liturgy of the Hours

284

Preparing for Christmas

The season of Advent consists of the four weeks before Christmas. During this time we prepare to celebrate Jesus' coming anew at Christmas. How do you prepare during the season of Advent?

Activity

Write your own "O antiphon" to praise God for his generosity. Remember to start your prayer with the word *O*.

_____

_____

_____

_____

_____

_____

_____

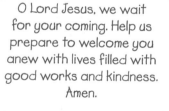

O Lord Jesus, we wait for your coming. Help us prepare to welcome you anew with lives filled with good works and kindness. Amen.

The Prince of Peace

Jesus is often called the Prince of Peace. Do you know why? In the Old Testament Book of Isaiah, there is a verse that describes the Savior. It says:

> For a child is born to us, a son is given us;
>   upon his shoulder dominion rests.
> They name him Wonder-Counselor,
>   God-Hero,
>   Father-Forever, Prince of Peace.
>
> *Isaiah 9:5*

The early Christians read the Jewish Scriptures, which are part of our Old Testament today. These Scriptures helped the first Christians understand their faith experience. The Book of Isaiah in particular helped the early Christians understand who Jesus was.

The Book of Isaiah was written several centuries before Jesus was born. Part of the book's message is that a good king for God's people would have special qualities. For example, a just ruler of God's people would bring peace to them. In fact, he would be known for ruling with peace. When the early Christians read passages from the Book of Isaiah that described this kind of leader, they immediately recognized Jesus. This is why we call Jesus the Prince of Peace.

When the risen Christ comes again in glory, the world will know peace. At the Second Coming of Christ, a new kingdom of peace and justice will begin. All the violence, confusion, misunderstanding, pain, and hurt that human beings experience will be wiped away. For now, Jesus Christ already touches our hearts with his peace whenever we celebrate the Eucharist together, and he guides us in making peace among people. We eagerly await the day when we will know his peace completely and for eternity. Until then, the Lord, our Prince of Peace, wants us to share the gift of peace with others. Whenever we help end an argument, solve a problem, or act generously toward others, we can feel peace within ourselves and bring peace to others. Every day, we have the chance to share the gift of peace with others. When we help bring peace to the world, we remind others that the Prince of Peace will come in glory, bringing his kingdom at last.

Sharing Peace

From the time of the early Church, Christians have called Jesus the Prince of Peace. They have shared in Jesus' gift of peace. When have you felt the gift of peace in your own life?

Activity

Suggest peaceful endings to the following situations.

1. Ryan and Ethan are having an argument in the cafeteria. At first, they are just saying mean things to each other. But then Ethan looks as if he is going to knock over Ryan's lunch tray. You

   _____

   _____

   _____ .

2. Ariel, Jennifer, and Danielle used to be good friends. Now they don't even want to speak to one another. You are assigned to work with them to complete a class assignment. You

   _____

   _____

   _____ .

3. Monica's younger brother Stuart goes into her bedroom and steals her CDs when she isn't home. Sometimes he even snaps them in half to make her angry. She tells you about this. You

   _____

   _____

   _____ .

O Lord, you bring peace to the world. May we know your peace in our hearts more each day. Help us know you as the Prince of Peace so that we may share your gift of peace with everyone we meet. Amen.

✞ Prayer Celebration for Advent

God's Promises

Leader: Each year during Advent we recall God's promises to his people, the people of Israel. We also recall that he sent his Son, Jesus, to live among us. Now we await Jesus' return in glory. Let us pray together.

Reader 1: Lord God, we await the coming of Jesus Christ. He fills our hearts with love and hope. He brings light to our lives and banishes darkness. When we light the candles of the Advent wreath, we look forward in hope to his return at the end of time. Lord, this Advent season, bring the light of hope to those who need it.

Reader 2: For all the people in the world who live in loneliness, we pray to the Lord.

All: Lord, hear our prayer.

Reader 2: For those who are ill and suffering, we pray to the Lord.

All: Lord, hear our prayer.

Reader 2: For people who have had arguments with one another, that they may be reconciled, we pray to the Lord.

All: Lord, hear our prayer.

Reader 2: For those who have many worries and troubles in their lives, we pray to the Lord.

All: Lord, hear our prayer.

Reader 2: For those who are fearful and need courage, we pray to the Lord.

All: Lord, hear our prayer.

Reader 2: For people throughout the world who need hope in their lives, we pray to the Lord.

All: Lord, hear our prayer.

Reader 3: You know the times in which we live. It is now time for us to wake from sleep, for our salvation is at hand. The night is nearly over; the day draws near. Let us live honorably and in peace, not in quarreling, violence, and jealousy *(based on Romans 13:11–14)*.

Leader:	Let us reconcile with one another with a sign of peace. *(Share a sign of peace.)*
Leader:	Let us pray together. Lord, thank you for your Son, Jesus. He is Emmanuel, the hope of all peoples. He is Wisdom, who teaches and guides us. He is our Savior. Bless us whenever we light the candles of our Advent wreath. May they be a sign of your promise to give your people salvation.
All:	Amen.

(You will now light candles on an Advent wreath.)

Leader:	May Jesus come quickly and not delay. We ask this through Christ, our Lord.
All:	Amen.

Based on the Blessing of the Advent Wreath, Book of Blessings

Christmas

The angel said to her, "You will bear a son, and you shall name him Jesus."

Based on Luke 1:31

The Birth of Jesus

This is how the birth of Jesus came about, according to the Gospel of Matthew. When Mary was engaged to Joseph, but before they were married, an angel appeared to Mary and told her that she was pregnant by the Holy Spirit. Joseph decided to break up with Mary quietly before anyone knew about it.

Then, in a dream, an angel appeared to Joseph and said, "Joseph, son of David, do not be afraid to make Mary your wife. It is through the Holy Spirit that she is going to have a child. She will have a son and you are to name him Jesus, because he will save people from sin."

All this happened because the Lord had told one of the prophets: "Behold, the Virgin shall bear a child, and they will name him Emmanuel." The name *Emmanuel* means "God is with us."

When Joseph woke up, he did as the angel had commanded. He and Mary were married. She bore a son, and they named him Jesus.

Based on Matthew 1:18–25

Did you know that only the Gospels of Matthew and Luke have stories about Jesus' birth? At the beginning of the Gospels of Mark and John, Jesus is already grown up.

The Gospels were written to help people believe in Jesus. Sometimes, the Gospel writers focused on different aspects of Jesus' story. According to the Gospel of Matthew, for example, the story of Jesus' birth was anything but ordinary. In this story, angels appeared and spoke in dreams to make sure that God's will was followed. Joseph married Mary even though he didn't completely understand what was happening.

The writer of the Gospel of Matthew reminds us that all these extraordinary events occurred because this birth was special. The writer even reminds us that a prophet had written about this special event long before it happened. The writer's message is that Jesus is no ordinary human being. From the beginning, even before he was born, there were signs that Jesus had a special role to play in the

world. In this way, the Gospel explains who Jesus really is: the Savior, the one whom God made promises about long ago. The writer of the Gospel of Matthew wanted to make it very clear from the beginning of the Gospel that Jesus is the Son of God, the chosen one, Emmanuel.

Angels and Dreams

The writer of the Gospel of Matthew tells us that God sometimes speaks in dreams. When Joseph dreamed that an angel was giving him a message, he discovered how to follow God's will. As described in Chapter 4 of your book, Joseph of the Old Testament also discovered God's will through dreams. Of course, there are many ways to find out God's will. What are some ways Christians can discover God's will for their lives?

Activities

1. Imagine that you have overheard Joseph talking about the angel he saw in his dream. What would you like to ask Joseph?

   _____

   _____

2. Do you think that the stories about Jesus' birth helped people believe that Jesus is the Savior? Why or why not?

   _____

   _____

   _____

> Lord, you always keep your promises to your people. From age to age, you have cared about us and loved us. Help us pay more attention to your will for us as we celebrate your Son's birth at Christmas. Amen.

Solemnity of Mary, Mother of God

Every year on January 1, the Church celebrates the Solemnity of Mary, Mother of God. This day is an important feast day honoring Mary. In the United States, it is a holy day of obligation. On this day U.S. Catholics are required to go to Mass.

Although the Solemnity of Mary, Mother of God, is one of many holy days that Catholics celebrate to honor Mary, a solemnity is an especially important holy day. This particular solemnity honors the special role Mary plays in the story of human **salvation**, because she is the mother of God. This holy day is celebrated one week after Christmas because it is only right that we celebrate Mary's motherhood as we honor the birth of Jesus.

On the Solemnity of Mary we remember who Mary is and what she has done for us. Of her own free will, Mary chose to accept the difficult challenge of being the mother of our Savior, Jesus. The angel Gabriel came to her and let her know God's will for her. Mary did not hesitate. Of course, at the time, she did not know everything that God would ask of her. But she loved and trusted God and was eager to do his will for her.

Mary said yes to God and, in this way, showed how much she loved us. By becoming the mother of God, Mary was giving us the chance to get to know her son. She was making it possible for salvation to enter the world. At a wedding in Cana, as described in John 2:1–12, Mary urged her son to make himself known through the miracle of turning water into wine. She helped encourage him to begin his public **ministry**.

Throughout her life, Mary continued to support her son. The Gospel of John tells us that she was at the foot of the cross when Jesus was crucified in Jerusalem. There, according to the Scriptures, Jesus entrusted Mary to the apostle John's care. In doing so, he was also giving Mary to us to be our mother.

Through the centuries, Christians have looked to Mary and thanked her for being the mother of God. They have prayed to her and devoted their lives to her. She is still with the Church today. She wants us to turn to her and ask her for help, strength, **guidance**, or anything else we need. As Jesus' mother, Mary continues to love us and take care of us.

This is why we celebrate a special holy day in her honor. On January 1, we recall that because Mary chose to say yes, we enjoy Jesus' love, peace, and joy in our lives. Mary, the Mother of God, brought hope into the world when she gave birth to Jesus.

Getting to Know Mary

Mary was probably about twelve years old when she told the angel Gabriel that she would do whatever God wanted. While none of us has such big challenges to face, there are many difficult situations that we face every day. For what kinds of problems can someone turn to Mary for help?

Activity

Write the name of the person, place, or thing described by each clue.

_____ the angel who appeared to Mary

_____ the name of Mary's son

_____ the name of Mary's husband

_____ the town where Mary and Jesus attended a wedding

_____ the apostle who took care of Mary after Jesus' death and Resurrection

_____ the month in which the Solemnity of Mary is celebrated

_____ an important title for Mary

_____ the city where Jesus was crucified

Mary, thank you for agreeing to bring God's Son into the world. May we find the strength and courage to say yes to God in our own lives. Remember us, O Mother of God, and take care of us, for we love you. Amen.

✝ Prayer Celebration for Christmas

Hark! The Herald Angels Sing

Leader: Some of the Christmas carols we love the most have interesting stories behind them. For example, "Hark! The Herald Angels Sing" came about almost by accident. Charles Wesley is famous for writing the words to more than 3,000 religious hymns, including the lyrics to the hymn we know as "Hark! The Herald Angels Sing." But Wesley didn't write the melody. Felix Mendelssohn was a famous composer who wrote a melody for a song about Johann Gutenberg, the inventor of the printing press. Mendelssohn wrote the song to celebrate that the first book ever printed was the Bible. Before the invention of the printing press, people had to copy books by hand.

In 1855, an English musician named William Cummings took the lyrics written by Charles Wesley and combined them with the melody written by Felix Mendelssohn. Both Wesley and Mendelssohn were dead by the time he did this, so they never knew that they had collaborated on one of the most famous Christmas carols of all time.

All: Hark! The herald angels sing,
"Glory to the newborn King!
Peace on earth, and mercy mild,
God and sinners reconciled."
Joyful all ye nations rise,
Join the triumph of the skies.
With the angelic host proclaim,
"Christ is born in Bethlehem."
Hark! The herald angels sing,
"Glory to the newborn King!"

Reader: Now there were shepherds in that area keeping watch over their flocks. The angel of the Lord appeared to them, and they were struck with fear. The angel said, "Do not be afraid. Behold, I bring you good news of great joy. For today in the city of David a Savior has been born unto you. You will find him wrapped in swaddling clothes and lying in a manger." Suddenly, there was a multitude of angels in the heavens, praising God.

Based on Luke 2:8–13

(Decorate the room with construction paper angels with prayers on them.)

Leader: Let us pray.
Group 1: Sing to the Lord a new song.
Group 2: Sing to the Lord all you peoples.
Group 1: Sing to the Lord; bless his name.
Group 2: Tell his glory among the nations.
Group 1: Tell of his wonderful deeds.
Group 2: Let the heavens be glad and the earth rejoice.
Group 1: Let the sea and the plains be joyful.
Group 2: Let all the animals rejoice.
Group 1: We rejoice in the Lord for he comes to rule the earth.
Group 2: He shall rule the world with justice.
Group 1: Everyone will know him and praise him.
Group 2: Sing to the Lord and bless his name.

Based on Psalm 96

All: Hark! The herald angels sing . . .
(Repeat lyrics of song.)

Lent

The Lord is the Spirit, and where the Spirit of the Lord is, there is freedom.

2 Corinthians 3:17

The Gift of forgiveness

Jesus knew that one of the gifts we would need most in our lives is the gift of forgiveness. Whenever we sin, either by doing something wrong or by failing to do the right thing, our relationship with God is weakened. Jesus knew that we would need a way to turn back to God and say that we are sorry. We would need a way to show this sorrow and ask for forgiveness.

The **sacrament** of Reconciliation is our celebration of God's forgiveness in our lives. This sacrament is called a sacrament of healing because when we celebrate it, we heal our relationship with God and one another. It also heals us of the pain and guilt caused by our sins. When we confess our sins and express our sorrow, we are *reconciled*, or brought back together, with God and the Church.

In order to experience God's gift of healing in the sacrament of Reconciliation, we need to do several things. We need to feel sorrow for our sins, to want to change the way we are living, and to confess our sins to a priest. In the sacrament, the priest will pray a prayer of absolution over us, which asks for God's mercy. The priest will also suggest a penance, an action or prayer to help us change our lives and avoid sin in the future.

The gift of forgiveness that we receive in the sacrament of Reconciliation is so powerful that Catholics have many different ways of describing this sacrament. It is described as a sacrament of *conversion*, a word that means "being changed." This name is fitting because this sacrament helps us change our lives and become united with God again. It is also called the sacrament of Penance, because in it we admit our wrongdoing and express our wish to make up for what we have done or failed to do. And it is called the sacrament of forgiveness, because we ask God to pardon us.

The forgiveness we experience in the sacrament of Reconciliation flows into the rest of our lives. Because we have been forgiven, we are better able to forgive others. We can forgive friends and family members when they hurt us. We can even learn to forgive our enemies—for if we can forgive them, we can learn to love them, as Jesus commanded us.

During the six weeks before Easter, a season we call Lent, the Church asks us to look at our lives and repent of our sins. Lent is an especially good time to celebrate the sacrament of Reconciliation.

Seeking God's Mercy

Lent is a time of penance and conversion. We are called to repent of our sins and turn back to God. The sacrament of Reconciliation is Jesus' special gift to the Church for doing just that. How can God's gift of forgiveness help you?

Activity

Complete the following sentences.

I think people are most likely to celebrate the sacrament of Reconciliation when _They are really sorry for their sins._

I think conversion means
is to turn back to God or if we have gone of his path to get back on God's path

One new thing I learned about the sacrament of Reconciliation is
that you should

To me, forgiveness means _To keep the forgiveness or not to just say that your sorry you really mean that your sorry_

> Jesus, thank you for your gifts of mercy and forgiveness. Help us forgive others as you have forgiven us. Guide us in making good decisions and avoiding sin. Amen.

Lent Is a Time of Preparation

In ancient times, people used numbers to symbolize, or stand for, important ideas. The Jewish people, for example, used the number forty to symbolize a long period of time. This is because centuries ago, most people only lived about forty years. So "forty" meant a long time. It also came to mean a period of testing, waiting, and change.

The number forty is important in both the Old Testament and the New Testament of the Bible. The Book of Exodus tells us that the Israelites, our ancestors in faith, wandered for forty years in the desert before they arrived in the **promised land**. Having been the slaves of the Egyptians, the Israelites trusted in God to lead them to freedom, so they endured many hardships to reach their goal. By the time they finally reached the promised land, their faith had become even stronger. They were changed people.

In the Gospels we read about Jesus and his stay in the desert. For forty days, Jesus prayed, fasted, and wrestled with temptation. And for forty days, God was with him, assuring him of his presence and faithfulness. When Jesus returned home from the desert, he was a changed person. He knew that he had been with God and that God had made clear to him who he was and what he was to do. Jesus left the desert prepared to help all people know what it means to live as the children of God.

The Church sets aside the forty days of Lent to remind us of our goals as Christians. During Lent, we prepare for Easter. We do this by considering how we can follow the Gospel message better and by reflecting on the challenges we experience in our lives. We try to become better Christians. We may try to follow the example of the "heroes" of our faith, such as saints or people of the Old Testament. They lived their faith in times of testing, waiting, challenge, and struggle.

Throughout Lent, we will hear Scripture readings at Mass that contain the number forty. These readings remind us that many people have gone through times of struggle and testing for their faith. The readings also inspire us to make good use of our own forty-day period of Lent so that we may grow closer to God and live our faith more completely. We try to become different people—people with new attitudes and a stronger willingness to live the Gospel.

Getting Ready

We have all experienced a time when something important is about to happen, such as moving to a new home, entering a new school, taking an exam, or playing in an important sports match. To prepare, we have to concentrate our efforts on our goal. Preparing for Easter during Lent also requires special effort. How do you prepare to celebrate Jesus' Resurrection?

Activity

Circle the ways you can use Lent as a time to deepen your faith.

Celebrate the Eucharist.

Forgive people who have hurt me.

Be more patient with others.

Give money to charity.

Pray the Rosary once a week.

Examine my conscience.

Spend several minutes in prayer and reflection every day.

Read about the life of a saint.

Celebrate the sacrament of Reconciliation.

Find ways to be generous to friends and family members.

Learn more about a charity or a group that helps those who are poor and homeless.

Jesus, be our strength. Help us spend the forty days of Lent preparing for the joy of Easter. We ask this in your name and Spirit. Amen.

Jesus Heals the Man Born Blind

One day while Jesus was walking with his apostles, he passed a man who had been born blind. In those days, people believed that such conditions could be punishments from God for sin, so the apostles asked Jesus, "Who sinned, this man or his parents, to cause him to be born blind?"

Jesus answered, "No one. He is blind so that God's works might be seen through him." Jesus smeared mud on the man's eyes and said to him, "Go and wash in the Pool of Siloam."

The man went and did as Jesus said. When the man came back, he could see. His neighbors were astonished. They asked him what happened and he told them, but he could not tell them who Jesus was.

Because Jesus had performed this healing miracle on a Sabbath day, the people were concerned. According to Jewish religious law, the Sabbath was supposed to be a day of rest. So the people took the man whom Jesus had cured to the **Pharisees**. The Pharisees were the religious authorities of the Jewish people in those days. The Pharisees were troubled and could not agree among themselves. One said, "The man who healed did not keep the Sabbath, so he can't be from God." Another said, "But he did good in helping his neighbor."

They asked the man who had been healed what he thought. He said, "The man who healed me is a prophet." They asked the man's parents, who could tell them nothing about what had happened to their son. Then they talked to the healed man again, but he got annoyed with them, saying, "Why do you want to hear my story again? I don't know where the man is from. If he wasn't from God, he wouldn't have been able to do this."

The Pharisees, annoyed with him for speaking to them this way, replied, "You were born in sin and now you are trying to tell us what to think?" They threw him out.

When Jesus heard what had happened, he went to the man he had healed and asked him to believe in the Son of Man. The man said, "I do believe, Lord," and worshiped him.

Some of the Pharisees overheard this conversation and spoke to Jesus about the healing. Jesus said to them, "If you were blind, you would have no sin. But since you have sight and are still not sure you believe in the Son of Man, your sin remains."

Based on John 9:1–41

This Gospel story, which is read at Mass during Lent, gives us the chance to think about our own attitudes about sin and belief. This Gospel reading reveals that the people of Jesus' time often thought that the troubles and challenges of life were the result of sin. They did not always recognize a sign from God when they saw it.

Through Jesus' conversations with the man he healed and with the Pharisees, we learn that it is important to have faith when we witness a sign of God's power in our lives.

Signs from God

God's generosity touches our lives. What signs from God could you pay more attention to?

Activity

Write a letter to the Pharisees about the man who was healed. Give your opinion about whether or not they should accept the healing as being from God. Give reasons for your opinion.

> Jesus, you are our Savior, Prophet, Priest, and King, we praise you. We believe you are the Son of Man sent by God to bring us into your kingdom. Help us recognize signs of your Father's love in our lives. Amen.

Dear Pharisees,

_____

_____

_____

_____

_____

_____

_____

_____

_____

Laetare Sunday

The Fourth Sunday in Lent is called Laetare Sunday. The word *Laetare* is a Latin word that means "rejoice." This Sunday in Lent got its name from part of a prayer said at the beginning of Mass: "Rejoice, Jerusalem!" (based on Isaiah 66:10). Why is this Sunday a day of joy if it is towards the end of Lent?

Lent can be a difficult time in our lives. If we are seriously reflecting on our actions and beliefs and if we are spending our time in prayer and acts of penance, towards the end of Lent we need a break. We need some time to remember that God acts in our lives with great love and generosity. As signs to us that the latter part of Lent is a time to enjoy ourselves a little, the priest may wear rose-colored vestments at Mass, the altar may have more flowers on it than usual, and hymns about rejoicing may be sung.

Laetare Sunday is also known as "Rose Sunday," partly because of the rose-colored vestments, but also because the pope traditionally blesses the "Golden Rose" on this day. The Golden Rose is an award made of solid gold in the shape of a rose. It is occasionally given to a notable Catholic person or group in thanks for special service or loyalty to the pope. This is an ancient custom. As far back as the eleventh century, the pope would carry a rose in his left hand when coming back from Mass on Laetare Sunday. By the fifteenth century, the pope's custom became to bless the rose and send it to someone in thanks for doing good.

On Laetare Sunday, priests wear rose-colored vestments such as the one shown in the center of the photograph.

In some countries, such as England, the Fourth Sunday in Lent is celebrated as "Mothering Sunday." Traditionally, on this day people would return to their native parishes and cathedrals as well as visit their mothers and spend some time with their family members.

Lent is almost finished when we celebrate Laetare Sunday. It is natural at this point during our season of reflection and penance to begin to feel a sense of joyful anticipation. We begin to grow more aware of the coming of Easter and spring. We look forward to the new life that awaits us during the Easter season.

Rejoicing a Little

On the Fourth Sunday of Lent we remember that God loves us. He blesses us with his mercy and generosity. What blessings do you enjoy in your life?

Activity

Create joyful words that relate to the season of Lent using the letters of the word *Laetare*.

L ent
a ct with ~~ein~~ kindness
e aster ~~on~~ sunday
t ime to reflect
a cept ~~to who~~ you are
r ejoice ~~ejocie ejoyce~~
e njoy times with family

> Lord, you bless us so much. You surprise us with your kindness and your love. May we share the joy you give us with others. We rejoice and we praise you for your goodness. Amen

✝ Prayer Celebration for Lent

For Repentance

(You will receive a colored piece of construction paper from your teacher before this prayer begins.)

Leader: As discussed in Chapter 12, there is a book in the Old Testament called the Book of **Psalms**. A psalm is a religious song from the Old Testament. Psalms were written centuries ago, some around the time of King David. Tradition says that King David actually wrote some of the Psalms. Today the Psalms are prayed and sung as a part of Christian worship. There are so many psalms that they are numbered. Some of the Psalms are so well known that they also have titles. Psalm 51, for example, is called "The Miserere." It is a psalm of repentance. Let us pray together verses from it now.

All: Have mercy on me, God, in your goodness.
In your great compassion, blot out my sins.
Wash away my guilt.
From my sin cleanse me,
for I know what I have done wrong.
My sin is always before me.
Against you alone have I sinned.
Create in me a clean heart,
and renew my spirit within me.
Drive me not from your presence.
Do not take your Holy Spirit away from me.
Give me back the joy of salvation,
and keep within me a willing spirit.

Based on Psalm 51:3–6, 12–14

Leader: Let us call to mind the things that we have done wrong and the right that we have failed to do. When you have spent several moments in reflection, come forward and place your slip of paper in one basket, and take a prayer card from the other basket. The construction paper slips are symbols of the emotions, struggles, and challenges that we live each day. We set them aside in the presence of the Lord and seek to put ourselves in a prayerful spirit.
(*Pause for reflection, then bring your construction paper slip foward when instructed*.)

Leader: We often read the Book of Isaiah when we want to remember the promises that God made to his people. Let us do so now.

Reader: Rejoice with Jerusalem and be glad because of her,
all you who love her;
Exult, exult with her,
all you who were mourning over her!
Lo, I will spread prosperity over her like a river
and the wealth of the nations like an overflowing torrent.
As a mother comforts her son,
so will I comfort you;
in Jerusalem you shall find your comfort.

Based on Isaiah 66:10, 12, 13

Leader: O Lord, thank you for taking care of us and being with us always. May we be mindful of your presence every day of our lives. May we always remember your great mercy and generosity. Thank you for your blessings, Lord. Continue to draw us near to you.

All: Amen.

Holy Week

It is in Christ and through his Blood that we have been redeemed and our sins forgiven.

Based on Ephesians 1:7

Celebrating Our Salvation

The events we recall during Holy Week are at the center of our lives as Christians. We believe that God loves us so much that he sent his only Son to suffer, die, and then rise to new life so that we might be free of sin and live with him forever. This belief is at the heart of Christianity.

Passion Sunday

Most Catholics call this day Palm Sunday. On Palm Sunday we recall Jesus' entry into Jerusalem by waving palm branches and singing "Hosanna." We proclaim the Gospel story of Jesus' Passion.

Holy Thursday

Holy Thursday evening is when we celebrate the Mass of the Lord's Supper. On the night before he died, Jesus gave us the gift of himself in the Eucharist.

Good Friday

The day on which we recall Jesus' suffering and death on the cross is called "good" not because Jesus suffered and died, but because his suffering and death brought about God's gift of **resurrection** and new life.

Holy Saturday

The morning and afternoon of this day in Holy Week are filled with silence and waiting. We recall Jesus' time spent in the tomb and God's promise of resurrection. The evening of the Easter Vigil is considered the holiest night of the year. At this first Mass of Easter, we praise and thank God for raising Jesus from death to new life. It is the time when we welcome new members into the Church.

Keeping Watch with the Lord

On every Good Friday we have the chance to deepen our faith by spending the hours between noon and three o'clock in prayer and reflection about Jesus. How do you spend the afternoon on Good Friday?

Activity

Answer the following questions about Jesus' last words.

1. Whom did Jesus promise to see in Paradise?

   _____

   _____

2. What might the writer of the Gospel of John have meant to show by having Jesus say, "It is finished"?

   _____

   _____

3. What two people is Jesus speaking to when he says, "Woman, behold, your son" and "Behold, your mother"?

   _____

4. What happened when Jesus said that he was thirsty?

   _____

5. What can we learn from Jesus' prayer "Father, forgive them, they know not what they do"?

   _____

   _____

   _____

> Lord, thank you for the writers of the four Gospels of the New Testament. Through them and the inspiration of the Holy Spirit, we deepen our understanding of your crucifixion. Thank you for your great sacrifice. Amen.

✝ Prayer Celebration for Holy Week

The Redeemer of the World

Leader: Jesus took all our sins upon himself and asked forgiveness for our offenses, placing his trust in God. According to the Scriptures, as Jesus died, he called out to God in the words of Psalm 22. We pray these words in the Good Friday liturgy.

Reader 1: My God, my God, why have you forsaken me,
 far from my prayer, from the words of my cry?
O my God, I cry out by day, and you answer not;
 by night, and there is no relief for me.
Yet you are enthroned in the holy place,
 O glory of Israel!

Reader 2: In you our fathers trusted;
 they trusted, and you delivered them.
To you they cried, and they escaped;
 in you they trusted, and they were not put to shame.
All the ends of the earth
 shall remember and turn to the LORD;
All the families of the nations
 shall bow down before him.

Reader 3: For dominion is the LORD's,
 and he rules the nations.
Let the coming generation be told of the LORD
 that they may proclaim to a people yet to be born
 the justice he has shown.

Psalm 22:2–6, 28–29, 31–32

Reader 1: Be compassionate and kind to one another, forgiving one another as God has forgiven you in Christ. Be imitators of God, beloved children. Follow the way of love, even as Jesus loved you. He gave himself for us as an offering to God, a pleasing gift.

Based on Ephesians 4:32—5:2

Group 1:	We worship you, O Christ, and we praise you.
Group 2:	We worship you, O Christ, and we praise you,
Group 1:	because by your cross you have redeemed the world.
Group 2:	We worship you, O Christ, and we praise you.
Group 1:	Glory be to the Father, and to the Son, and to the Holy Spirit.
Group 2:	We worship you, O Christ, and we praise you.

Based on prayers from the Good Friday liturgy, Roman Missal

Reader 2:	The Savior of mankind destroyed death by dying and restored life by rising. Let us pray.
All:	Make your people holy, Lord.
Reader 2:	Redeemer of the world, may we share in the glory of your Resurrection. Let us pray.
All:	Make your people holy, Lord.
Reader 2:	May we comfort others as you comfort us.
All:	Make your people holy, Lord.
Reader 3:	Reveal your saving power in the lives of your faithful people.
All:	Make your people holy, Lord.
Reader 3:	Give all who serve you the gifts of obedience and patience.
All:	Make your people holy, Lord.
Reader 3:	Bring us at last into the fellowship of the Communion of Saints.
All:	Make your people holy, Lord.

(*Share a sign of peace.*)

Leader:	Father, in your plan of salvation, your Son, Jesus Christ, trusted God, accepted the cross, and freed us from the power of evil. May we share in the glory of his Resurrection, for he lives and reigns with you and the Holy Spirit, one God, forever and ever.

Based on Evening Prayer for Wednesday of Holy Week, Liturgy of the Hours

All:	Amen.

Easter

Blessed are they who have not seen and have believed.

Based on John 20:29

God Raises Jesus to New Life

On Easter Sunday and throughout the Easter season, we rejoice in the Resurrection of Jesus. After Jesus died, God the Father glorified him, raising him to new life. Jesus did not return to his old life after the Resurrection. Instead, God saw fit to give him new life that would last forever.

Jesus shares that new life with us. No longer are we our old selves, returning to the same habits and sins of our old lives. We are now alive in Jesus, through his Passion, death, and Resurrection. We live in him, and he lives in us. Because we share this new life with Jesus, we have the chance to live better lives, open to the Spirit and growing closer to our heavenly Father every day.

Believing in Jesus' Resurrection requires faith. Jesus' first disciples struggled to understand Jesus' Resurrection and what it meant for them. They had locked themselves in a room out of fear, but Jesus came and stood before them. Wishing them the gift of peace, Jesus showed his friends the wounds in his hands and his side so that they would believe that he had risen from the dead. Today we do not have fear about what we believe because the Holy Spirit is with us. In the Spirit, we are free to live our faith and share it with others. Especially during Easter, we celebrate our belief in Jesus, and our hearts are filled with joy.

Easter is the time of the church year when we rejoice that God raised Jesus from death to new life. It is the most important celebration of the liturgical year. In fact, the Easter season lasts for fifty days. During that time we also celebrate Jesus' Ascension into heaven and the sending of the Holy Spirit on Pentecost. We praise and thank God for giving us his Son and for bringing us to new life in him. Easter is a new beginning for us because we are invited to change our lives. When we celebrate Jesus' gift of new life with the rest of the Church, we are invited to live every day as if it were Easter.

A Fresh Start

Our lives are full of new beginnings. Every birthday can seem like a new beginning, as can every new school year or every summer vacation. We see ourselves growing, changing, and becoming stronger, smarter, and more capable. Easter is a new beginning for us, too. It is a chance to live our new life in Christ.

Activity

Piece together the puzzle to discover the message from Saint Paul found in Romans 6:23.

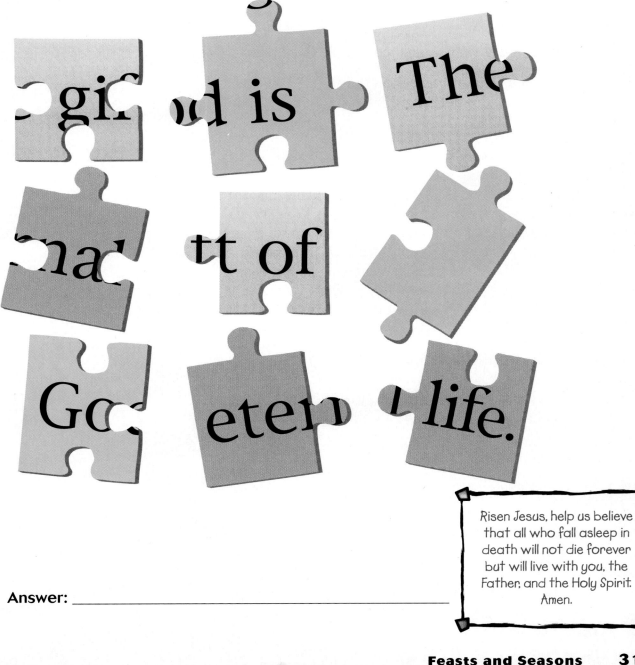

Risen Jesus, help us believe that all who fall asleep in death will not die forever but will live with you, the Father, and the Holy Spirit. Amen.

Answer: _____

Jesus Appears to His Apostles

Thomas was one of the Twelve Apostles, but he was not with them the first time Jesus appeared to them after his Resurrection. The other disciples told him that they had seen the Lord, but he did not believe them. Thomas said, "Until I see and feel the marks of the nails in his hands and touch the wound in his side, I will not believe."

A week later, the apostles were gathered, this time with Thomas among them. Even though the doors were locked, Jesus entered the room. He stood among them and said, "Peace be with you."

Then Jesus said to Thomas, "See my hands and touch them. Put your hand on the wound in my side. Do not be unbelieving. Believe."

Thomas touched Jesus' wounds and replied, "My Lord and my God!"

Jesus said, "Do you believe because you can see me? Blessed are those who have not seen and yet believe."

Based on John 20:24–29

The apostle Thomas thought that seeing was believing—a very human way of thinking. He heard the apostles say that Jesus had been raised from the dead, but he did not believe it. He wanted proof, and the proof he demanded was being able to touch Jesus and see Jesus' wounds for himself. We are sometimes a lot like Thomas. When we do not understand something, we doubt that it is real. We want proof and explanations for the things we do not understand. But belief is not always about getting the proof we want. This is why the story about Thomas ends with a blessing for all those who have not seen and yet believe.

The writer of the Gospel of John wanted to teach people about the importance of belief, especially people who had never met Jesus when he was on earth. This writer wanted everyone to understand that the apostles, who knew Jesus personally, and the later Christians who had never met Jesus shared the same faith. This is important because Christians in the early Church were worried about how faith in the Lord would continue after all those who knew Jesus personally had died. The writer of the Gospel of John is telling us that the Holy Spirit has made it possible for our faith to be the same as that of the apostles. The Holy Spirit is always with the Church, bringing us closer to God by strengthening our faith in his Son, Jesus.

Blessed Are Those Who Believe

The apostle Thomas is remembered for the story about his doubts. This is why we sometimes refer to a person who is suspicious about things until they are proven as a "Doubting Thomas." Just as Jesus helped Thomas overcome his doubts, he will help us overcome ours. When do you most need to have your faith strengthened?

Activity

Imagine you are a reporter interviewing the apostle Thomas about Jesus' Resurrection. Write the conversation you might have.

Reporter: _____

_____

_____

Thomas: _____

_____

_____

Reporter: _____

_____

_____

Thomas: _____

_____

_____

Reporter: _____

_____

_____

Saint Thomas, help us believe in Jesus, our Savior. When we are not sure what we believe, pray that we may overcome our doubts. Remind us of all that Jesus has done for us. Amen.

Living Our Faith

Easter is a time to strengthen our faith in God. How can we do this? We can receive the sacraments of Eucharist and Reconciliation regularly. We can also pray every day and read Scripture by ourselves and with our family. Another thing we can do is practice our faith through the choices we make every day. When we make choices that show our faith, we are making "acts of faith." We are living what we say we believe.

What is an act of faith? It is taking a chance and risking doing the right thing, even when there may be difficult consequences. Here are some examples of what Grade 6 students at Our Lady of Mercy School do to strengthen their faith.

Leighanne's teacher gave the class a geography test that was very difficult. As Leighanne and her classmates were taking the test, their teacher was called out of the room. Leighanne knew she could easily look up some of the answers in her textbook, but she decided not to cheat. Leighanne believes in honesty. This is part of her faith.

Ethan's parents told him to come home right after school, but he didn't. He stopped at his friend's house for a little while before going home. When Ethan's mother asked him where he was, Ethan told the truth even though he knew he would be grounded. He knew he had done wrong and decided not to do it again. Ethan believes in respecting his parents. This is part of his faith.

Jolinda had some money to buy a treat for herself at lunch in the cafeteria. All morning she looked forward to buying a package of chocolate chip cookies. Then, in the cafeteria line, Morgan did not have enough money to pay for her lunch. Jolinda heard herself saying, "Don't worry. Here's some money." Morgan thanked her gratefully. Jolinda was not able to get her cookies, but she believes in being generous. This is part of her faith.

Leslie's teacher arranged the class in groups to complete a literature assignment. Leslie didn't like one of the girls in her group. She wanted to tell this girl what she thought of her. But she decided not to. When the girl asked for help with one of the assignment questions, Leslie offered her help and even told the girl that she had good ideas. Leslie believes in speaking positively about others even when it's difficult. This is part of her faith.

It can be difficult to make acts of faith, but until you practice your faith every day, you don't show that you truly believe. When you put your beliefs into practice by being generous, patient, kind, and honest, you are living your faith. Then you begin to grow closer to God.

Making Good Choices

Although saints and other holy people are good models for living faithfully, we do not always know how to be faithful in ordinary, everyday situations. What are some examples of situations in which the right thing to do is not obvious?

Jesus, you trusted in your Father completely. Help us to trust our heavenly Father, too, especially when it is hard to be honest or to do the right thing. May we recall the events of Easter and turn to you as our model and our Savior. Amen.

Activity

Rate yourself on whether or not you have the qualities it takes to live your beliefs by placing a check mark below the appropriate heading.

	Never	Rarely	Sometimes	Frequently	Almost Always
Do you know the difference between right and wrong?	___	___	___	___	___
Are you a patient person?	___	___	___	___	___
Do you respect others?	___	___	___	___	___
Do you tell the truth?	___	___	___	___	___
Do you share what you have?	___	___	___	___	___
Do you enjoy making others happy?	___	___	___	___	___
Do you respect yourself?	___	___	___	___	___
Do you know what you believe in?	___	___	___	___	___
Do you want to make the world a better place?	___	___	___	___	___
Do you want people to get along?	___	___	___	___	___

What qualities would you like to see more of in yourself?

_____

✝ Prayer Celebration for Easter

Alleluia!

Leader:	Alleluia! Christ is risen!
All:	He has risen as he said. Alleluia!
Leader:	Rejoice and be glad for our Lord is raised to new life. Alleluia.
All:	The Lord has risen indeed. Alleluia.

Reader 1: The word *Alleluia* means "Praise God." From ancient times to the present, people have sung "Alleluia" to praise God with joy and thanksgiving. At Easter we celebrate the joy of new life in our lives. Alleluia, Alleluia.

All: Alleluia.

Reader 2: Give thanks to the Lord, for he is good.
His mercy endures forever.

All: Praise the Lord.

Reader 2: Let the house of Israel say,
"His mercy endures forever."

All: Praise the Lord.

Reader 2: The right hand of the Lord strikes with power.
The Lord's right hand is raised.

All: Praise the Lord.

Reader 2: I shall not die, but live,
and declare the works of the Lord.

All: Praise the Lord.

Reader 2: This is the day the Lord has made.
Let us rejoice in it and be glad.

All: Praise the Lord.

Based on Psalm 118:2, 16–17, 24–25

Reader 3: With joy in our hearts, let us call upon Christ, the Lord.
All: Christ is risen.

Reader 3: Lord, send your Spirit to us, for we proclaim your Resurrection.
All: Christ is risen.

Reader 3: May the whole earth be filled with the knowledge of your glory.
All: Christ is risen.

Reader 3: Jesus, you have triumphed over death. May we live only for you.
All: Christ is risen.

Reader 3: You were obedient to your Father, no matter what. Welcome us into your kingdom.
All: Christ is risen.

Reader 4: On the evening of the first day of the week, the disciples were gathered together behind locked doors. Suddenly, Jesus stood among them. He said, "Peace be with you."

Based on John 20:19

Leader: Alleluia.
All: Alleluia.

Leader: May the risen Lord touch our lives with his love and bring us joy and hope. May the risen Lord open our eyes so that we will follow him in his risen life. May the risen Lord heal our hearts so that we will share the joy of Easter every day.
All: Amen.
Leader: This is the day the Lord has made. Alleluia.
All: Let us rejoice and be glad. Alleluia.

Based on Morning and Evening prayer for Easter Sunday, Liturgy of the Hours

(*Create banners for the word* Alleluia.)

Holy Days

Praised be the God and Father of our Lord Jesus Christ, who has blessed us in Christ with every blessing.

Based on Ephesians 1:3

Archangels

Angels are God's messengers. They are spiritual beings who praise God continually. We read about these messengers of God in the Bible. They come to human beings in visions and in dreams, giving them warnings and telling them what God wants. In fact, so many angels are mentioned in the Bible that the tradition has been to group the angels into nine types, or orders: seraphim, cherubim, thrones, dominations, principalities, powers, virtues, archangels, and angels. Arranging the angels into nine orders is a way to describe these spiritual beings according to the roles and purposes they serve in Scripture. When we discuss angels, we most commonly talk about seraphim, cherubim, archangels, and a category of angels called guardian angels.

The word *archangel* means "chief angel." Tradition says that there are seven archangels: Michael, Gabriel, Raphael, Uriel, Raguel, Sariel, and the fallen archangel, Lucifer. Not all the names of the archangels are mentioned in the Bible. Some of the

stories about archangels have come down to us through writings that are not in the Bible.

The Church celebrates a feast day in honor of Michael, Gabriel, and Raphael on September 29. These three archangels are the most well-known angels in Christian writings.

Michael. Some stories about Michael say that he is the leader of all the angels. He is mentioned by name in the Book of Daniel, an Old Testament book. He is the protector of Israel. In art, he is often shown with a sword and with scales of justice because he is powerful. Over the centuries, some people have believed that Michael will take part in the judgment of souls on judgment day.

Gabriel. The archangel Gabriel is mentioned in the Book of Daniel. In the Gospel of Luke, he appears to Mary to tell her that she will become the mother of Jesus. He is also believed to be the angel of the Lord who came to Joseph in a dream. Over the centuries, some people have believed that on judgment day Gabriel will blow a trumpet to gather all the people of the world.

Raphael. This archangel is mentioned in the Book of Tobit, a book in the Old Testament. Over the centuries, some people have believed that Raphael is the chief of all guardian angels. Raphael is also known as the angel of healing. According to Tobit 3:17, he cured Tobit of blindness so that Tobit would once again see God's light.

Our belief in angels helps us recognize that God loves us and always takes care of us. We do not know very much for certain about the beings who surround God and praise him continually. Some of what is said about the angels may be legend, but all that has been said is meant to bring us closer to God. Some people think that believing in angels helps us put our faith in goodness and holiness.

Messengers of the Lord

In ancient times, angels were simply thought of as messengers of the Lord. In fact, the word *angel* means "messenger." The angels of ancient times did not have wings or carry swords or fit the imaginative descriptions that some people have of angels today. Can you recall anyone in Scripture who was visited by one of these messengers of the Lord?

Activity

In the space below, draw your image of a messenger of the Lord.

Heavenly Father, we praise you. We thank you for all the good things you give us. We thank you especially for your messengers, in whatever form and in whatever way they come to us. They guide us and help us do your will. Amen.

Christ the King

The Solemnity of Christ the King, an important holy day in the Church, was begun in 1925 by Pope Pius XI. The pope knew that people would never live in peace with one another if they did not look to Jesus as their Lord and Savior. He decided to help by starting a holy day that celebrated that Christ is our king, the head of the Church, and the Lord of all creation. Today we celebrate this feast at the end of the church year, on the last Sunday before Advent. (The first Sunday of Advent begins a new church year.)

Pope Pius XI also recognized something else. The year 1925 was the sixteen-hundredth anniversary of the important church Council of Nicaea. This council was a meeting of bishops that took place in the town of Nicaea (part of modern-day Turkey) in A.D. 325. At Nicaea, the bishops wrote the Nicene Creed, which states our belief in Christ, "of whose kingdom there shall be no end." This phrase about Christ tells us that Christ is our king.

In both the Old Testament and the New Testament, Jesus is described as a king. He is called the Son of David, Israel's great king. We read that Jesus Christ shall sit upon the throne of David. He will rule forever and be a just king. We are also told that our heavenly Father has given Jesus all power in heaven and on earth.

It is also important to remember that Jesus Christ is the head of the Church. The pope, the bishops, and priests are his representatives on earth. They help us recognize Jesus' rule in our hearts and in our lives.

On the Solemnity of Christ the King, we celebrate the reign of Jesus Christ in our world. We recall that we are members of the Church and that we must spread the good news of Jesus. We are encouraged to help everyone in the world know that Jesus Christ is our Savior and our Lord. We are called to proclaim Christ's kingly power and turn to him with love. We should give him honor, serve him, and be faithful to him because he is our king.

Jesus Christ will reign over all human beings in a new, perfect society at the end of time. Until he returns to us in glory, he will reign in our minds when we believe in his teachings. He will reign in our hearts when we love God and put him first in our lives. And he will reign in our wills when we obey his laws and live a life of love.

The Coming of the King

Christians believe that at the end of time, Jesus Christ will come again in glory to establish his kingdom. Until then, the Church is his kingdom on earth. What does it mean to you to say that Jesus Christ is King?

Activity

Write a prayer to express your faith in Jesus Christ as King.

_____

_____

_____

_____

_____

_____

_____

_____

_____

Jesus Christ, Lord, Savior, and King, we honor you and thank you for your love and care. Help us live according to your law of love. Amen.

The Feast of the Presentation of the Lord

Jesus was born into a family that cherished its Jewish traditions and practices. In the time and culture of Jesus, male babies were especially welcomed. It was the firstborn son's responsibility to care for his aging parents. Jewish people believed that the firstborn son belonged to God.

Jewish families were required by religious law to offer a sacrifice in thanksgiving for the birth of a son. In the Gospel of Luke, we read that when Jesus was forty days old, Mary and Joseph took him to the **Temple** in Jerusalem to present him to God, according to Jewish custom. There they made an offering of a pair of turtledoves, or pigeons. Today we remember Mary and Joseph's act of thanksgiving for Jesus' birth on the Feast of the Presentation of the Lord. The Church celebrates the Presentation of the Lord on February 2.

The writer of the Gospel of Luke included the story of the Presentation because he wanted to show that Jesus, like other Jews, was at the Temple early in his life. For the writer of the Gospel of Luke, the city of Jerusalem and the Temple are symbols of God's promises and the relationship God has with his people. Jesus is the link between the Jewish people and the future God wants for all people.

According to Luke's Gospel, while Mary, Joseph, and Jesus were at the Temple, they met an old prophet named Simeon. Simeon held the baby Jesus in his arms. He had waited all his life to see the Messiah. He knew that God had finally fulfilled his promise. Mary, Joseph, and Jesus also met a prophetess named Anna. She too had been promised by God that she would see the Messiah before she died. When she saw Mary and the baby Jesus, she cried out in praise to God. She gave thanks to God and spoke about how Jesus would be the one to save the Jewish people.

The Feast of the Presentation of the Lord is a chance for us to celebrate how God keeps his promises to his people. He promised to send a Messiah, then sent his Son, Jesus. We praise and thank God for the gift of his Son. We remember the Jewish people and their long wait for the Messiah, and we look forward to Jesus' return in glory.

Welcoming the Messiah

Simeon and Anna had been promised that they would see the Messiah before they died. When they saw the baby Jesus, they both praised God for keeping his promise to them and to the rest of his people. If you had been with Simeon and Anna, what would you have prayed?

Activity

Complete the following sentences.

1. When Jesus was about forty days old, his parents took him to the _____.

2. At the Temple, they offered a _____ of turtledoves, or pigeons.

3. They did this to give _____ to God.

4. While they were at the Temple, they met a prophet named _____.

5. They also met a prophetess named _____.

6. God promised to send his people a _____.

7. _____ is the Messiah God sent.

8. Today we celebrate the Feast of the _____ _____ _____ _____ in the Temple.

Loving God, from age to age you remember your people. You promised to send them a Messiah, and you gave the world your Son, Jesus. Help us make our lives an offering to you. Amen.

Feast of the Immaculate Heart of Mary

Christians have a special place in their hearts for Mary, the mother of Jesus. One way we give glory to God is by showing respect for Mary, the mother of his Son. The Feast of the Immaculate Heart of Mary is one of the holy days the Church celebrates in Mary's honor. In 1942, in the middle of World War II, Pope Pius XII dedicated the world to the Immaculate Heart of Mary. In this way, he entrusted the world to Mary's care. In 1944, the pope started the Feast of the Immaculate Heart of Mary and encouraged Catholics to pray to Mary for peace on earth.

The Feast of the Immaculate Heart of Mary takes place each year on the Saturday following the second Sunday after Pentecost. It celebrates that Mary is without sin and that she stands before God in heaven to protect and help us. Mary brings us closer to God. On this day, we pray for the conversion of sinners and freedom for Catholics around the globe.

Another way of honoring Mary is to practice the "first Saturday devotion," which means going to Mass and receiving the Eucharist on the first Saturday of the month for five months in a row. United with her son through the Eucharist in this way, we show Mary that we love her.

Mary inspires us and guides us. She is our spiritual mother. Our devotion to Mary also helps us commit ourselves to living our faith and growing closer to God. Respecting and honoring Mary helps us put God first in our lives. In doing so, we will be able to make good decisions for ourselves. We will be kind and generous to others.

Mary, the Mother of God

Mary is called the mother of God because she gave birth to Jesus, the Son of God. Over the centuries, Christians have honored Mary by praying for her help, doing good works in her name, and practicing other religious devotions, such as saying the Rosary and going to Mass on the first Saturday of the month. How do you show respect and honor to Mary?

Activity

Complete the following prayer to Mary.

O _____ Virgin, you said yes when Gabriel

asked you _____. We thank you for being

_____. You are our spiritual _____

who never stops caring about us. Just as you followed

Jesus to the cross, be with us when we _____.

We know that you will always help us _____.

Mary, _____, protect and guide us whenever

_____. Never forget us. We thank you for your

_____. Amen.

> O Mary, you are our spiritual mother who loves us and cares for us. Remember us, and help us be faithful to your son, Jesus. Guide us when we face difficult decisions. May your son give us the courage to live our faith. Amen.

Mary

My soul proclaims the greatness of the Lord. My spirit finds joy in God my Savior.

Based on Luke 1:46–47

Letter from Miriam of Nazareth

Miriam is my Jewish name. You know me by my Greek name, Mary.

I was only about twelve years old when God asked of me something extraordinary. In my time we were considered adults by age twelve, so God knew what he was doing! Anyway, I was not yet married, and I hadn't even thought about having a baby. But God spoke to me through his messenger, the angel Gabriel. Gabriel told me not to be scared. God had a great plan for me, if only I would trust him and say yes.

Can you even imagine all the things that were going through my head? I didn't know what to think. And what would Joseph, my husband-to-be, think? We were only engaged at the time. How could I explain this to him when I didn't understand it myself? But with God, all things are possible, if we only believe.

You know how it all turned out. Jesus, my son, is also the Son of God. As Jesus was growing up, I thought about how special he was and how privileged I was to have been called by God to be his mother. Of all the women in the world, God chose me, an ordinary Hebrew girl, to do something so extraordinary for him.

I'll let you in on a secret: God calls everyone to be extraordinary. By being the person God intends you to be, you too will do extraordinary things for God. Just trust him to know what he's doing, and say yes to his plans for you.

With a mother's love,

Miriam

Vocations

As Christians, we believe that we are called to a "vocation" by God. This means that God calls us to a particular type of service to one another and in the Church. Some Catholics serve the Church as priests, deacons, or religious sisters or brothers. Many other Catholics serve the Church community as "lay ministers" or "**laity**." They may help at the liturgy, teach religion to children, care for people who are sick or poor, or assist people in other ways. What might God be calling you to do in the Church?

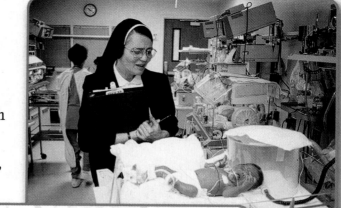

Activity

Write about what you think your vocation might be.

_____

_____

_____

_____

_____

_____

_____

_____

_____

_____

Mary, mother of Jesus, pray for us, your children. Help us see God's hand in our lives as you did. May we trust in him so that we may do extraordinary things for him. Amen.

Mary, Our Intercessor

There was a wedding in Cana in Galilee. Jesus, his mother, and his disciples were all there. During the feast, there was not enough wine. Jesus' mother said to him, "They have no wine."

Jesus replied, "What has this got to do with me?"

Jesus' mother told the servers, "Do whatever he tells you."

Jesus told the servers to fill six large stone jars with water. When the headwaiter tasted the water, he found that it had become very good wine.

This was one of the first signs Jesus performed, and his disciples began to believe in him.

Based on John 2:1–11

The story of the wedding in Cana, found in the Gospel of John, is one of the Gospel stories that show Jesus taking care of people by providing them with food or drink. These stories are meant to show us how generous God is. They are also meant to show us that when the Lord is with us we should celebrate.

In the early Church, Christians began to honor Mary as the mother of God. They recognized that because she was the mother of God, Mary had a unique role to play in God's plan for us. She is an intercessor for us. An intercessor is someone who acts on behalf of another.

At the wedding in Cana, Mary saw that there was going to be a problem: The wine was going to run out. So she asked Jesus to help the couple who were being married. In the same way, Mary asks Jesus to help us. Because she is Jesus' mother, Mary is in a special position to help us. She is closer to her son than we are. We can turn to her and she will intercede with her son for us, or act on our behalf. Whenever we are in need, we can depend on Mary to be there for us.

Catholics understand that there is even more to Mary's role at the wedding in Cana. Mary was Jesus' mother and his closest and best disciple. She believed in her son and knew that he was sent by God to bring salvation to his people. The story of the wedding in Cana is important for another reason, as well. This story is one of the few stories in which Mary, Jesus' mother, is mentioned in the Gospels.

As our intercessor, Mary acts on our behalf to bring us closer to her son. She helps us understand that we should celebrate and be joyful, because God has done many good things for us. Our heavenly Father loves us and takes care of us. We should praise him and give thanks with full hearts.

A Sign of the Kingdom

Jesus came to bring the kingdom of God to us. Mary, his mother, has a special role to play in drawing us closer to her son. Have you tried to grow closer to Jesus through Mary?

Activity

Draw a line from the first half of the statement to its correct second half.

Column 1	Column 2
Jesus went to a wedding	in Cana.
Mary, the Mother of God,	the Gospel of John.
Mary encouraged Jesus to	were with Jesus at the wedding.
The story of the wedding at Cana is found in	is our intercessor.
Mary and the disciples	was turned into wine.
The water in the stone jars	do something about the lack of wine.
Mary has	a unique role to play in God's plan.

Mary, at the wedding in Cana you asked your son to show us a sign of God's glory and love for us. Help us recognize the signs of God's love in our lives. May we always depend on you as a child relies on a parent. Amen.

Our Lady of Lourdes

In 1858, Bernadette Soubirous was fourteen years old and lived in Lourdes, France. Her family was very poor. Bernadette was not a good student, and she was often ill. But she worked very hard to help her family. She collected firewood and searched for food, such as plants and berries. One day in February, when Bernadette was out collecting supplies for her family, she saw a lovely lady near a grotto, or cave-like mound of rock.

Later, Bernadette described what she saw: "She was wearing a white dress, which reached down to her feet, but I could see her toes. On each foot was a yellow rose. She also wore a white veil that came down over her shoulders and arms, almost to the bottom of her dress. The sash of the dress was blue."

Bernadette also said that the lady carried a Rosary. The chain was yellow, but the beads were big and white. Bernadette began saying the Rosary with the lady.

Over the next several months, Bernadette saw the lady eighteen times. People began going to the grotto with Bernadette, but only Bernadette could see Mary. She told Bernadette, "Pray to God for sinners!" She also told Bernadette to kiss the ground as a penance for sinners. On one occasion, people who had gone with Bernadette suddenly saw her scratch at the ground and then try to drink and wash. Mary had told Bernadette to uncover a stream. The stream appeared and, much later, became the site of many miraculous cures.

More and more people were showing up at Lourdes. The authorities wanted to put a stop to the commotion that Bernadette and her visions were causing. But Bernadette continued to see Mary. Bernadette's parish priest told her to ask the lady who she was. On March 25, the Feast of the Annunciation, Mary told Bernadette, "I am the Immaculate Conception." Only several years before, the pope had declared that Mary had been conceived without original sin. By calling herself the Immaculate Conception, the lady in Bernadette's vision had declared the same thing. This made many people believe that the lady appearing to Bernadette was truly Mary.

In July 1858, Mary's visits to the grotto stopped. Then church leaders investigated the matter thoroughly, questioning Bernadette very carefully and closely. They concluded that everything that had been said was true. Mary had indeed appeared to Bernadette at Lourdes. In 1866, Bernadette entered a convent. She died in 1879 at the age of thirty-five after being ill for a number of years. She was canonized in 1933, and her feast day is April 16. Lourdes became an important shrine to Mary. Thousands of pilgrims visit the French shrine each year, many of them seeking a miraculous cure at the waters of Lourdes.

The Power of Mary

Mary's appearances at Lourdes brought many people back to their faith. People began to take their faith more seriously. In this way, Mary led people back to her son, Jesus. Has your faith been strengthened by learning about Bernadette and Mary at Lourdes?

Activity

Design a banner to celebrate the appearance of Mary at Lourdes in 1858.

Saint Bernadette, Mary appeared to you and spoke to you. Many people have become stronger in their faith because of you. Thank you for bringing Mary into our lives. Help us grow closer to her son, Jesus, too. Amen.

The Assumption

On August 15, Catholics celebrate the Feast of the Assumption. This is an important holy day that honors Mary. On this day we celebrate the church teaching that at the end of her life, Mary was taken up, body and soul, into heaven. Although the Bible does not tell us what happened to Mary, Christians have believed throughout the centuries that the end of Mary's earthly life was special because she was without sin.

The Feast of the Assumption of Mary was celebrated in Syria as early as the fifth century. By the twelfth century, Christians throughout the Mediterranean world, including Spain, Italy, and France, were celebrating it. In 1950, Pope Pius XII declared the doctrine of the Assumption in a formal ceremony in St. Peter's Square before 500,000 people. Our belief in the Assumption recognizes that since Mary was Jesus' mother, she shared, body and soul, in his Resurrection and his glorification at the right hand of his Father.

Saint John Damascene, who lived centuries ago, wrote an interesting story about the Assumption. According to his story, the Eastern Roman Emperor Marcian asked Saint Juvenal, the bishop of Jerusalem, for Mary's body. He wanted to create a magnificent tomb for her. But Saint Juvenal wrote to the emperor explaining that there were no remains of Mary. From the time of the apostles, it had been known that Mary had been taken up into heaven.

The Immaculate Conception by El Greco (1613)

Our belief in the Assumption of Mary is very important. The Church teaches that human beings die because they sin and are not perfect. But Mary was not born into original sin and never sinned in her life. She was full of grace and is the mother of God, so she shared in Jesus' Resurrection in a special way.

334

The Assumption of Mary into heaven gives us hope in our own resurrection at the end of time. Catholics believe that when Jesus comes again, all of us who serve our heavenly Father will be raised to eternal life with him. When we celebrate our belief in Mary's Assumption every year on August 15, we are also celebrating our belief in the resurrection of the dead. Mary went before us to show us how it will be for us when we follow the Lord as completely as she did.

Honoring Mary

Throughout the liturgical year, there are many holy days that honor Mary. We celebrate the Assumption, the Annunciation, the Immaculate Conception, and the Solemnity of Mary Mother of God, just to name a few. What is your favorite holy day in Mary's honor?

French sculpture, 1500s, titled "La Vierge à l'Enfant"

Activity

How much do you know about Mary?
Write **True** or **False** beside each statement.
Correct the statements that are false.

1. _____ Mary was born without original sin.

2. _____ Mary is never called the mother of God.

3. _____ Catholics believe that Mary was taken body and soul into heaven.

4. _____ Mary is not the best model of faith and holiness.

5. _____ Mary never committed a mortal sin but she may have committed venial sins.

6. _____ Mary was full of grace throughout her life.

7. _____ Mary is called the Immaculate Conception because she was conceived without sin.

8. _____ Mary was the mother of John.

O holy Mother, you gave the world the Savior, Jesus Christ. In your life and Assumption we see that all of God's promises will be fulfilled. Thank you, Mary, for all that you do for us. Amen.

Saints

O God, you are my God whom I seek;
For your kindness is a greater good than life.

Psalm 63:2, 4

Saint Rafka

Some saints are known for solving problems that the Church faced. Others are known for being great preachers or teachers. Still others are known for their heroic example of suffering. These holy people accepted suffering in their lives to bring others to God.

Saint Rafka of Lebanon is one of these special people. She was born around 1832 in Lebanon, a country in the Middle East. She was named Pierina. Her mother died when she was seven, and her father remarried. When Pierina grew up, her stepmother and her aunt wanted her to get married. But Pierina knew she was called to another life.

Pierina went to a convent. She felt peaceful there and heard a voice telling her that she would be a nun. When Pierina's parents came to get her, she refused to leave. Pierina took the name Agnes and became a teacher in a nearby village. She made her final vows as a nun in 1856.

Most of the people in the Middle East follow the religion of Islam, but there are some Christians. During Agnes's lifetime, Christians faced persecution by Muslims. There were many changes in Lebanon after the persecution. For one thing, the religious order that Agnes belonged to was merged with another order. Agnes left to join the Lebanese Maronite Order of Saint Anthony instead. She took the name Rafka, or Rebecca, which had been her mother's name.

When Rafka was in her fifties, an eye infection caused her to go blind. Next, she became mostly paralyzed and had terrible headaches. Rafka never complained. Instead, she offered up all her pain to God and prayed constantly. Her hands were not paralyzed, so she could still knit stockings and do some work. Everyone could see how holy Rafka was.

One day, Rafka prayed that God would let her see for just one hour. God granted her prayer. For an hour, Rafka was able to see her room and all those around her. She died in 1914 when she was eighty-two, and she was canonized on June 10, 2001.

The Challenge of Suffering

From Saint Rafka we learn to accept everything, including suffering, with faith. We are called to accept the difficulties of life with patience and joy. Do you patiently trust God when you experience sufferings or difficulties?

Activity

Check the statements that are true for you.

_____ Having to wait in line bothers me.

_____ When someone doesn't help me right away, I treat him or her badly.

_____ When my parents tell me to do something I don't want to do, I talk back.

_____ I hate it when I don't get what I want for my birthday.

_____ I won't eat things I don't like.

_____ When I'm mad, I let people know it.

_____ I feel that I should do what I want when I want.

_____ I understand when someone else is having a bad day.

_____ I try to be polite to everyone I meet.

_____ I don't mind making little sacrifices so that others are happy.

_____ When people are rude to me, I try to say something nice to turn the situation around.

_____ I try to make the best of what I have.

_____ I can wait to get something I really like.

_____ I treat my teachers and parents with respect most of the time.

If you chose most of the responses in the top of the list, perhaps you might think about practicing more patience in your life.

Saint Rafka, you accepted suffering willingly. Help us get through the tough times in our lives patiently. From your example, may we learn that God never abandons us. Amen.

Saint Andrew Kim Taegon and the Korean Martyrs

In most countries, the story of how the Catholic Church grew usually goes like this: Catholic missionaries arrived to spread the good news of Christ, and people decided to join the Catholic Church. The story of the Catholic Church in Korea, however, is different. In Korea, the Church was established by Korean laypeople who had been anxious to learn as much about the rest of the world as possible. It was years before any Catholic priest even arrived in Korea.

The first Korean Catholics spread the faith to others in their country. When Father James Tsiou, a Chinese Catholic priest, finally arrived in Korea in 1794, he found that there were nearly 4,000 Catholics already there. The Catholics of Korea faced many challenges and dangers. The Korean rulers were deeply suspicious of foreigners, and they certainly did not like the spread of this foreign religion. By the time Father Tsiou came to Korea, there had already been several martyrs for the faith.

Nevertheless, the Catholic Church in Korea grew. When young men wanted to become priests, they were sent to Macao, then a Portuguese colony that had been seized from the Chinese. Andrew Kim Taegon was a young man from a noble Korean family. Andrew's father was martyred for the faith, and when Andrew was fifteen, he traveled 1,300 miles to study at the seminary in Macao. There he was ordained. In 1845, he set out for Korea to begin his work among Korean Catholics. Andrew Kim Taegon was the first Korean priest and pastor.

Father Andrew was arrested almost immediately by the Korean authorities, who had begun persecuting members of the Church about six years earlier. In prison, Andrew continued his work. He met and prayed with missionaries from Europe and other Korean Catholics who had been arrested. He was martyred in 1846 for his faith.

Between 1839 and 1867, thousands of Catholics were persecuted for their faith in Korea. The Church has recognized 103 of these people as saints. We remember and honor Saint Andrew Kim Taegon and all the martyrs of the Korean Church on September 20.

Courage and Faith

The martyrs of the Catholic Church show us what it means to be courageous. Throughout the world, even in faraway places such as Korea, Catholics are living their faith. What does the example of Saint Andrew Kim Taegon mean to you?

Activity

Complete the sentences in the paragraph by using the words in the box.

father	4,000
Catholic Church	pastor
Korea	Macao
priest	Saint Andrew Kim Taegon
persecution	September

The story of the _____ _____ in Korea is not the same as in in other countries. The Church in _____ was started by laypeople. The first priest to visit Korea found that _____ Catholics were already there. Catholics in Korea faced _____ by their rulers. Saint Andrew's _____ was martyred for his faith. Saint Andrew decided to become a _____. He traveled to the seminary in _____ when he was only fifteen. When he returned to Korea, he was the first Korean priest and _____. In 1846, _____ _____ _____ _____ was martyred for his faith. Today all the Korean martyrs are honored on the twentieth of _____.

Saint Andrew, although your life was brief, your faith was strong. When we are not sure whether or not to depend on our beliefs, help us. May your courage inspire us to do what is right even when we are faced with challenges. Amen.

Saint Edith Stein

Born in 1891 in eastern Germany, Edith Stein was one of eleven children. Edith's family was Jewish and owned a lumber business. She and her brothers and sisters were raised in a faith-filled and loving home. Edith went to college, eventually receiving her doctorate in 1916.

At this time, discrimination against Jews was spreading rapidly in Edith's part of the world. It was almost impossible for a Jewish woman to obtain a teaching position at a college or university. Edith was very discouraged. She longed to share her knowledge with young students.

For a while Edith struggled with questions about the meaning of life. At one point, she even questioned the idea of God. Then, while staying with some friends, Edith came across a copy of the autobiography of Saint Teresa of Ávila. Edith's search for meaning in her life had ended. She met Jesus in Teresa's writings and wanted to become a Christian. Edith was baptized in 1922 and soon began teaching in a Dominican convent school.

In 1934, Edith joined the Carmelite Order and took the religious name of Sister Teresa Benedicta of the Cross. In 1938, Sister Teresa moved to Holland to avoid the persecution of Jewish people. Eventually, she was joined there by her sister Rosa, who had also become a Catholic.

Holland was occupied by the Nazis, who persecuted the Jewish people. When the Dutch bishops condemned the Nazis for this, the Nazis were angry. They rounded up all the Jews who had become Christians, including Edith and Rosa.

Edith and Rosa were taken to Westerbork concentration camp. While there, Edith spent her time helping and comforting the other women. Later, Edith and Rosa were taken to Auschwitz, another concentration camp, where in 1942 both sisters died in the gas chambers.

On October 11, 1998 Pope John Paul II canonized Sister Teresa Benedicta of the Cross.

Discovering Faith

Some people of faith learn about Jesus at a very early age. Others, like Saint Edith Stein, discover Jesus later in life. What has your experience been?

Activity

Complete the survey below.

Faith Survey

1. How old were you when you first learned about God? _____

2. Who first introduced you to God? _____

3. How would you have described God when you were a young child? _____

   _____

4. How would you describe God now? _____

   _____

5. How does Jesus fit into your life? _____

   _____

6. If you didn't believe in Jesus, how might your life be different?

   _____

   _____

7. How would you describe who Jesus is to someone who has never been introduced to him? _____

   _____

   _____

   _____

Saint Edith Stein, pray that we may remain faithful to the God who calls each of us to follow him. Amen.

Saint Ignatius of Antioch

In the time of the early Church, the authorities of the Roman Empire were very suspicious of Christians. They thought Christians were troublemakers because they did not worship gods, as most people did in those days. Christians were persecuted for their faith. From time to time they were arrested and put to death for their belief in Jesus Christ. Martyrs are those Christians who gave up their lives for their faith. Ordinary Christians were martyrs, but so were church leaders.

In the city of Antioch, across the Mediterranean Sea from Rome, there was a good bishop named Ignatius. His exact date of birth is uncertain, but he died around A.D. 107. Ignatius called himself Theophorus, which means "God-bearer." Ignatius was arrested for being the leader of the Christian community in Antioch and was sent to Rome to be executed. Execution was not always the punishment for Christians, but because Ignatius was a leader in the early Church, the Roman authorities felt that he should become an example of what could happen to Christians. Ignatius was chained and put on board a ship to Rome.

Guarded by Roman soldiers, Ignatius began writing letters to the Christian communities at the cities where the ship stopped on its way to Rome. He wrote letters to Christians in Ephesus, to the churches of Magnesia and Tralles, and to the Christians in Rome. From these letters we know what Ignatius was thinking and experiencing. For example, Ignatius told the Ephesians how to live. He said, "Let others learn from your lives. In the face of people's hatred, be patient. Faced with their boasts, be humble. Answer their insults with prayers." Ignatius is also the first person known to have used the term *Catholic Church* in Christian writings.

Ignatius was allowed to receive visits from his friends, such as Bishop Polycarp of Smyrna, who was later martyred and became a saint. At the cities where Ignatius's ship stopped, Christians, who did not want to see Ignatius killed, greeted him. They begged the captors to release him. But Ignatius believed in suffering for his faith. He told them, "Let me follow the example of the suffering of my God."

Ignatius arrived in Rome on the last day of the public games. The Romans hurried him to the amphitheater, where he was attacked by lions as the crowd cheered. Many Christians mourned his loss. His feast day is October 17.

Living Our Faith

Saint Ignatius of Antioch not only remained true to his faith until the end, but he showed great courage and strength. Even though he knew he was going to his death, he kept encouraging others to be faithful Christians and live good lives. What do you think of his example?

Activity

Write a letter to Saint Ignatius about your faith and how you live as a Christian.

_____
_____
_____
_____
_____
_____
_____
_____
_____
_____

Saint Ignatius, teach us about being faithful to our belief in Jesus Christ. When we waiver in our beliefs, help us be strong the way you were strong. May we learn from your example what it means to encourage faith in others. Amen.

Saint Charles Borromeo

Some people are born into wealth and power. A few of them use these gifts to make the world a better place. Saint Charles Borromeo was such a man. He was not brilliant or even handsome. He also had a speech impediment. Yet he was born into a noble family, and his uncle was elected Pope Pius IV. Because of his family's influence, Charles was named Archbishop of Milan when he was just twenty-three. In those days, the archdiocese was huge. It extended as far Geneva, Switzerland, and had nearly a million people in it.

At first, Charles did not spend much time in Milan. He was in Rome, helping his uncle run the Church. Charles lived during a very important time in the history of the Church. We call this time the Catholic Reformation, a time of great change and improvement. During the first part of the sixteenth century, some Christians objected to many of the corrupt practices that had become part of the Church. Instead of working within the Church to change it, however, they created their own religious beliefs and left the Catholic Church. We call these people Protestant Christians. There were Christians who stayed in the Church and tried to improve it. Charles was one of the most important of these Christians.

One of the first things that Charles did was help his uncle, the pope, bring a successful end to the Council of Trent, one of the most important church councils in the history of the Church. Charles wrote the Roman Catechism, an important document that set forth the teachings of the Church in a clear form. He also worked in Switzerland to help bring Protestant Christians back to the Church.

As archbishop of Milan, Charles sold off much of the Church's property to help the poor people of Milan. Next, he improved seminary education for priests so that they could help people better. He was also very concerned about the education of children. He began the Confraternity of Christian Doctrine, an association that would be important in religious education for generations.

Some Catholics did not like all the changes Charles made. Several of these people, one of whom was a priest named Jerome Donati Farina, tried to assassinate Charles. Farina shot at Charles with a pistol while he was praying. The bullet went through his clothes but only bruised him. When Farina was captured, Charles asked that he be treated fairly and mercifully.

One of the bravest things that Charles did took place during an epidemic that swept through the city of Milan in 1576. Since medical care was poor in the sixteenth century, once an epidemic started in a city, many people died. Sometimes as much as 50 percent of the population would be wiped out. Wealthy and important people fled whenever there was a threat of an epidemic. But Charles stayed in Milan and helped those who were ill. He and those who were with him fed and cared for the people who were sick. Charles went into debt to help these people. He even had fabrics from his own home made into clothing for those who needed it.

Saint Charles Borromeo died in 1584 when he was forty-six after a lengthy illness. His feast day is November 4.

For the Good of Others

The story of Saint Charles Borromeo reminds us of the great good that people can do when they are in a position to help others. Power and wealth need not always lead to corruption. What good do you do for others?

Activity

Answer the following questions.

1. What are two of the accomplishments of Saint Charles Borromeo?

   _____

   _____

2. If there was one thing you could ask Saint Charles, what would it be?

   _____

3. How might he respond? _____

   _____

4. In your opinion, why did the Church make Charles Borromeo a saint?

   _____

   _____

> Saint Charles, thank you for all you did to help the Church and to make the world a better place. Help us use our talents and influence to make a difference today. May we be willing to be responsible and take the role of leaders in the Church. Amen.

Holy People

Rejoice in hope, be patient under trial, persevere in prayer. Be generous in offering hospitality.

Based on Romans 12:12–13

Pope Pius XII

The pope is the leader of the Catholic Church throughout the world. He must explain church teachings, stand up for what is right, and help bring peace to the world. Being pope is difficult at any time in history, but it was especially difficult for Pope Pius XII because he was pope during and after World War II.

The man who would become Pope Pius XII was born Eugenio Maria Giuseppe Giovanni Pacelli in Rome, Italy, in 1876. His father was an important canon lawyer for the Church. Canon law is the law of the Church. Eugenio Pacelli also studied canon law, but he decided that he wanted to become a priest. He was ordained in 1899. But instead of becoming a parish priest, Pacelli spent most of his career working as a church diplomat, traveling throughout Europe and the rest of the world to help governments understand Catholics and the Church. He traveled often at a time when few people had the chance to do so, and the American press called him the "Flying Cardinal."

In 1939, when Pacelli was sixty-three, he was elected pope. Out of respect for the previous pope, Pope Pius XI, with whom he had worked closely, Pacelli took the name Pius XII. As pope, he faced many challenges. The greatest of these was Nazi Germany. During World War II, the Nazis in Germany killed about 16 million people, 6 million of whom were Jewish. This is known as the Holocaust. It is one of the greatest tragedies in history. Under the evil chancellor of Germany, Adolf Hitler, the world was torn apart by war. Americans fought alongside the British and French to defeat Hitler's Nazis.

In Vatican City in Italy, Pope Pius XII worked for peace. He had no armies to command, but he did everything he could to resist and defeat Hitler. When the Germans conquered Italy, they tried to make Pope Pius XII obey them. But he wouldn't. This made Adolf Hitler angry. He once said, "Pius XII? That is the only human being who has always contradicted me and who has never obeyed me."

Even more important, Pope Pius XII worked to save the Jewish people. He told bishops, priests, and nuns to help the Jewish people whenever they could. He gave Jewish people Vatican citizenship and helped them escape Europe. He may have saved several hundred thousand Jews from being killed in the Holocaust.

After the war, Pope Pius XII worked against the spread of Communism, a political system whose dictators were dominating Russia and Eastern Europe. He was the first pope to use radio and television to speak to the peoples of the world. He also declared the doctrine of the Assumption. Pope Pius XII died in 1958. Some people believe that he should be made a saint for his courage and sense of justice.

Respecting Our Church Leaders

Every pope faces the great challenge of teaching people throughout the world to stand up for what is right. What challenges does the pope face today?

Activity

Write a brief explanation of each term.

pope _____

_____

_____

canon law _____

_____

_____

Holocaust _____

_____

Communism _____

_____

_____

GO TO page 386 to pray a prayer by Pope Pius XII.

O Heavenly Father, bless the leaders of your Church, especially the pope. Give him wisdom to understand the world, courage to speak the truth, and patience to never give up doing what is right. Amen.

Ita Ford and Companions

Ita Ford was born in Brooklyn, New York, in 1940. When she grew up, she became a religious sister who belonged to the Maryknoll order. But she had many health problems and had to leave the order after three years. Ford then worked for seven years as an editor of children's textbooks. In 1971, when her health improved, she became a Maryknoll sister again. In 1973, the Maryknoll order sent Ford to Chile to work among the poor in the city of Santiago, the capital of the country, and she and another Maryknoll sister settled in the ghetto.

Ford lived in Chile during a time of great violence and civil unrest. She once wrote, "Am I willing to suffer with the people here . . . ? Can I say to my neighbors, 'I have no solutions . . . I don't know the answers . . . '? . . . Can I look at and accept my own poorness as I learn it from the poor ones?" She did not give up. She stayed with the people she was trying to help.

In 1980, Ford was sent to El Salvador to help Archbishop Oscar Romero. But by the time she and others arrived, Romero had been killed by people who opposed his political views and his activism for the poor. In spite of this, Ford stayed in El Salvador.

Ita Ford (left) and Maura Clarke (right)

Soon, Ford began working with Sister Maura Clarke in El Salvador. They tried to help people who had become refugees because of the civil violence and bad government policies. During the war in El Salvador, which lasted for more than a decade, 75,000 people were killed. Sadly, the violence touched Ita Ford and Maura Clarke personally. On December 2, 1980, Ita Ford, Maura Clarke, and two other women, Dorothy Kazel and Jean Donovan, were kidnapped, raped, and shot to death at night. Their bodies were discovered alongside a road. They were killed because they were helping to fight for justice in El Salvador.

Today Ita Ford has not been forgotten. The Maura Clarke-Ita Ford Center, founded in 1993 in Brooklyn, New York, honors the memory of the two women killed in El Salvador. It does so by serving poor women who need to learn English and receive job training.

Faith in Practice

From the example of Ita Ford and her companions, we learn about the price of doing what is right. Some people say that politics and religion do not go together. But Ita Ford knew that if there was to be justice, politics and religion had to go together. She believed in this principle so strongly that she gave her life for it. What price would you pay for what you believe?

Activity

Write words or phrases that describe examples of justice on the lines of the sunburst below.

JUSTICE

Lord, you called Ita Ford and her friends to heaven. They worked for you and for the sake of justice in the world. From their example, help us learn to always seek justice and help others. Amen.

Blessed Francis Seelos

Bavaria is a province in Germany. In 1819, Francis Xavier Seelos was born there. He was one of twelve children. He was often ill as a child, so his mother would tell him stories and encourage him to pray. Francis was always a generous person and had a good sense of humor. Even at a young age, he was noticeably holy. Later, while he was in college in Munich, he told his brother he was receiving visions of Mary.

Francis decided to become a priest and joined the Redemptorists, a religious order that was serving German-speaking immigrants in America. In 1843 he arrived in America and was soon ordained. He worked in Pittsburgh for nine years. There, for three years, he was the assistant pastor to another holy priest, John Neumann, who later became a saint.

Francis was kind, understanding, and very prayerful. While some priests preached that God would punish people for their sins, Francis Seelos spoke about God's mercy and forgiveness. Francis recognized how important a priest's role in leading people to God was. He wrote: "A long experience has taught me the great lesson that God leads men in a human manner by other men whom he appointed to be in His place." Francis himself was a good example of what a priest should be. He was patient with people and gave them good advice. He was also able to reach beyond language barriers to help many immigrants. His homilies were powerful but easy to understand. Soon, people were standing in line for two hours to confess their sins to him.

Word soon got around that when Francis prayed for something, it happened. In fact, from his earliest days as a priest, he seemed to be able to bring people God's gift of healing. It became known that, often, when Francis prayed for someone who was ill, the person was cured. He cured those suffering from cancer and epileptic seizures, as well as people with pneumonia and those who thought they would have to spend the rest of their lives walking with crutches. In 1865, a man who had fallen from a scaffold was brought home to die. He had internal injuries and a broken hip and ribs. The doctors could not save him. Francis knelt with the man's children and prayed with them. Then he announced that the man would not die but would recover. And sure enough, he did.

350

In 1866, Francis was sent to serve the people of New Orleans. When he was there only a year, he fell ill with yellow fever, a disease that can cause liver and kidney failure. Although he was dying, he still kept his sense of humor. When asked if he had been in touch with his brothers and sisters about his family inheritance, he explained that everything had been arranged before he came to America, saying, "I get nothing and they get nothing."

Francis Seelos died at the age of forty-eight in 1867. Hundreds attended his funeral. Sick people who touched his body were reportedly cured. And ever since his death, there have been reports of people who were cured when they prayed to him. He was beatified on April 9, 2000.

The Blessing of Healing

Most saints and holy people, though they possess many gifts, are known for one particular gift. Francis Seelos was a good and holy priest whom we honor especially for the gift of healing. For what type of healing would you pray to Blessed Francis Seelos?

Activity

Write a prayer to Blessed Francis Seelos.

_____

_____

_____

_____

_____

_____

_____

Lord, you share your gifts with those of us whom you have chosen to do your will in a special way. Thank you for Blessed Francis Seelos. Through him your gift of healing is shared with the world. Amen.

Benedictines

What does it mean to lead a holy, prayerful life? How would a good person go about trying to lead such a life? What would he or she do every day?

Saint Benedict of Nursia had answers to these questions. Saint Benedict was born around the year A.D. 480. He tried to lead a holy, simple life. Soon men began coming to him for advice and modeling their own search for holiness on the way he was living. To help these men, known as "monks," Saint Benedict wrote a description of what people needed to do to find God in their lives. We call his description the Rule of Saint Benedict. This rule was a list of the ways that people could combine work and prayer, get along with one another, and seek God in simple, everyday situations. It outlined how to respect and forgive one another and how to take care of the material things that God blesses us with. For example, Saint Benedict said that we should treat the kitchen dishes with the same respect and care that we treat the vessels used on the altar.

While he was alive, Saint Benedict helped his monks live the life he described in his Rule. By 529, enough monks had gathered together to live a common life that the religious order of Saint Benedict, the Benedictines, was founded. Benedict's sister, Saint Scholastica, founded a monastery for nuns around the same time so that women could also follow the Rule of Saint Benedict. For most of the Middle Ages, anyone who was a monk or a nun in Europe was probably a Benedictine. The Benedictines were great teachers. They kept knowledge alive in the worst times because they copied books and had great libraries.

Today, almost 1,500 years later, the Rule of Saint Benedict is still being followed. The Benedictines are one of the greatest religious orders in the Church. There are about 10,000 Benedictines throughout the world. Monks and nuns of this order lead simple lives of work and prayer. While some Benedictines teach, many lead lives of prayer in their monasteries.

Benedict did not mean to found a religious order; he just wanted to create a way of life that would lead to holiness. He taught that a person does not have to do unusual things to become holy. He believed that holiness is found in the way simple, everyday things are done. Saint Benedict's feast day is July 11.

A Simple Kind of Spirituality

Benedictines are known for leading simple, spiritual lives. Saint Benedict created a rule that was easy to understand and very practical. He wanted people to find holiness every day. Can you find holiness in your life or in the lives of others around you?

> Saint Benedict and Saint Scholastica, help us find God in ordinary, everyday situations. May we learn to do the little things well and leave the big things up to God. Amen.

Activity

To reveal the great motto of the Benedictines, color spaces with the number 1 in red and spaces with the number 2 in yellow.

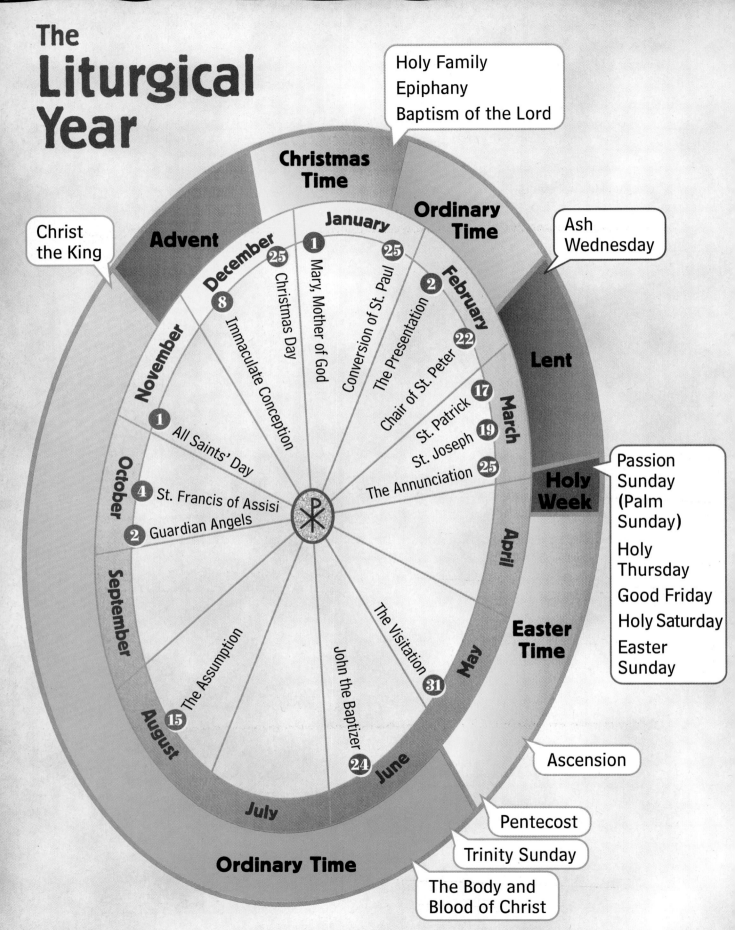

The Liturgical Year

OUR CATHOLIC HERITAGE

WHAT CATHOLICS BELIEVE

We share a common faith based on Sacred Scripture as found in the Bible and on the tradition of the Church founded on the teachings of the Twelve Apostles.

ABOUT THE BIBLE

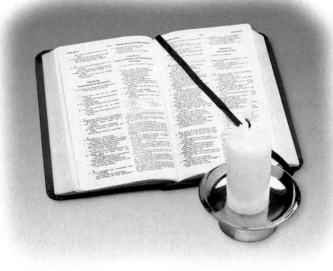

Catholics believe that the Bible is the word of God. The Bible contains the story of God and his people.

We believe that God is truly the author of the Bible because the Holy Spirit inspired the people who wrote it.

Although we usually see the Bible as one volume, it is actually a collection, or a library, of 73 books. The Bible is divided into two parts. The first is called the Old Testament. There are 46 books in the Old Testament, which includes stories, laws, history, poetry, and prayers. The Old Testament tells the story of our salvation before the birth of Christ. In the Old Testament we can read the words of the prophets that foretold the birth of Jesus.

The Old Testament books are usually listed in four sections. When we see them referenced, their titles are often abbreviated.

The second part of the Bible is called the New Testament. There are 27 books in the New Testament, which includes the four Gospels, the letters of Saint Paul, and other writings of the apostles and early Christians. After Jesus ascended into heaven, the apostles and the early Christians naturally talked about him. In order to instruct new converts, many of the important sayings and events of Jesus' life were written down.

These writings are called the Gospels. Many of Jesus' teachings were also related in letters to the early Christians. Jesus' teaching spread throughout the world.

Finding a Bible Text

When we hear a part of the Bible, it is usually introduced or followed by a Scripture reference, such as, "The Gospel of John, chapter 6, verse 3." This Scripture reference tells what book the passage comes from and which chapter and verse, or verses, of the book are being quoted. The following examples of Scripture references and their meanings will help you learn how to look up passages from the Bible.

Gn 2:5–11—the second chapter of the Book of Genesis, verses five to eleven

Lk 15:1–17—the fifteenth chapter of the Gospel of Luke, verses one to seventeen

Catholics are encouraged to read the Bible daily. Every chapter in your religion book contains information from the Bible. Catholics believe that one way that Jesus is present is in God's word, the Bible.

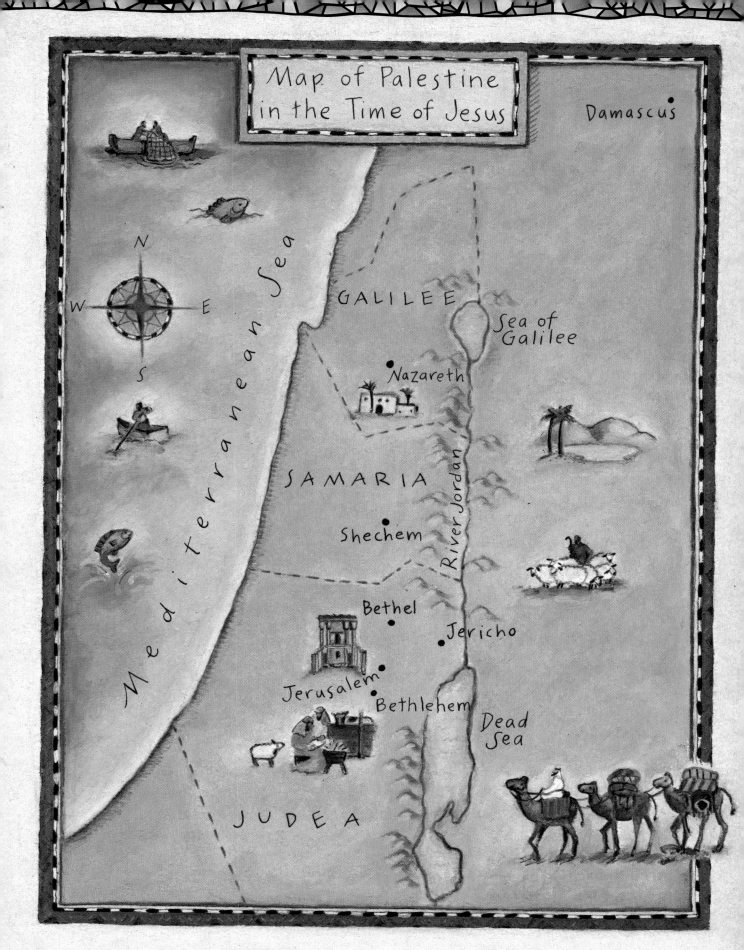

Map of Palestine
in the Time of Jesus

Damascus

N
W E
S

Mediterranean Sea

GALILEE

Sea of
Galilee

Nazareth

SAMARIA

River Jordan

Shechem

Bethel

Jericho

Jerusalem

Bethlehem

Dead
Sea

JUDEA

THE TRINITY

We believe there is only one God, who is revealed to us as three divine Persons. The three Persons are the Father, the Son, and the Holy Spirit. We call the three divine Persons the Blessed Trinity.

God, the Father

God is the Supreme Being, who always was and always will be. We believe human beings are made in the image and likeness of God. We share the gift of God's life in us. We believe that all men and women desire God because they are created by God and for God. Only in God will we find real truth and happiness.

We believe that God is the Creator of all things. God is all-good, all-holy, and all-knowing. God is always just and merciful. We believe that God speaks to us in many ways, especially through Jesus Christ, the Scriptures, and the teachings and life of the Catholic Church.

Jesus taught us to call God "Father," because of the loving care that his Father has for everyone and everything. Jesus told us to tell our Father our needs in prayer, and he said that God would always be listening.

Jesus Christ, the Son

Jesus Christ is the Father's greatest gift to us. Jesus Christ is God's Son. By the power of the Holy Spirit, Jesus was born of the Virgin Mary. Jesus has a divine nature and a human nature. We believe that Jesus is God who became human like us in all things but sin and lived among us. This belief is called the **Incarnation**.

We believe that Jesus' mission was to announce the Good News. Jesus carried out his mission by teaching, healing, forgiving, and working miracles as signs of God's love. He gathered his followers into a group of disciples who became the Church. Jesus is our Savior. Jesus loved us so much that he died on the cross for all our sins. Jesus was buried, and on the third day he rose from the dead. Catholics believe the truth of the Resurrection is that death is not an ending but leads to everlasting life. We receive grace when we share in the divine life of the risen Jesus. We believe that Jesus Christ ascended into heaven, where he lives and reigns with the Father and the Holy Spirit. One day, Jesus will return to judge the living and the dead.

God, the Holy Spirit

The Holy Spirit is the love that is shared by the Father and the Son. The Holy Spirit has been at work in the world since creation. Jesus Christ sent the Holy Spirit to guide his Church and the consciences of his people until the end of time. The Holy Spirit comes to us in Baptism and the other sacraments to help fill us with God's life and lead us to be true followers of Jesus.

ABOUT
THE CATHOLIC CHURCH

We believe in** one, holy, catholic, **and** apostolic **Church.

We call these the four marks, or qualities, of the Church. They distinguish the Catholic Church and show its truth and origin in God.

The Church is one. We believe in one God, Father, Son, and Holy Spirit, one faith, and one Baptism. We believe that the Catholic Church is one because we are united in Jesus Christ. We are also one in our celebration of the same sacramental life. We pray to the Holy Spirit to strengthen our unity as one Body of Christ.

The Catholic Church is holy because Jesus Christ, together with the Father and the Holy Spirit, is holy, and because of God's grace we too are holy. We believe that our holiness will increase through our participation in the sacramental life of the Church.

The Church is catholic, or universal, because Christ is present in the Church and because we welcome all people as Jesus does. Membership in the Catholic Church is open to all, regardless of race, nationality, or culture. We especially welcome those who are poor and disadvantaged into our community of hope.

The Church is apostolic because it is founded on the teachings of Jesus Christ and the apostles. We believe the chief teacher of the Church is the pope. The pope is the successor of Peter, the apostle Christ chose to lead the Church. Peter was the first bishop of Rome. The pope is the Vicar of Christ. As Jesus' representative in the world, he leads and serves God's people on earth. The pope, with the bishops, priests, and deacons, helps us understand God's word, celebrate the sacraments, and serve others.

Catholics believe that when the pope speaks officially for the Church to define a matter of faith or morals, he speaks without error. We call this the doctrine of papal infallibility. This doctrine assures us that the pope teaches with the guidance of the Holy Spirit.

ABOUT
MARY AND THE SAINTS

Mary, the mother of Jesus, is our greatest saint. Mary was filled with grace from the first moment of her life. She was conceived without original sin. This mystery is called the Immaculate Conception. Mary lived a sinless life on earth. Catholics honor her as the mother of Jesus and the Mother of the Church.

Because she always followed God's plan, supported Jesus in his ministry, and offered her strength and holiness to the early Church, Mary is our most important model of faith.

Catholics believe that Mary was taken body and soul into heaven. This belief is called the Assumption.

Catholics also believe in the virginity of Mary, in giving birth to Jesus, throughout her life, and for all time.

Saints are holy people whose example shows us how to live as Jesus taught us. As

Catholics, we honor the saints and ask them to pray to God for us. We believe that one day we will live with all the saints forever with God.

ABOUT
LIFE EVERLASTING

We believe that the kingdom of God will be completed at the end of time. The Catholic Church teaches that at the end of time, Jesus Christ will come again to restore all things in peace, love, and justice.

Jesus teaches us that if we live as he taught us, we will have life everlasting. This means that we will live forever with God in heaven. Jesus told us that heaven is unending happiness with God and all who love God.

All who die in God's grace and friendship but still have faults and imperfect love will be united with God forever in heaven, but first they must undergo a purification. The Church has given the name *purgatory* to this purification.

We believe that we are united with all those who believe in Jesus Christ in this world and the next. All those who have gone before us into everlasting life and who share in God's wonderful grace and all those who are being purified in purgatory are joined with us in the Communion of Saints. Together we make up the membership of the Church.

We have always included those who are in purgatory as part of the Communion of Saints. We pray regularly for those who are in purgatory that they will soon enjoy the happiness of heaven. Our prayers and good works can gain for us and for the souls in purgatory indulgences, which remove some of the punishments we must suffer in purgatory for the effects of sins.

Those who deliberately refuse to love God and their neighbor freely choose to separate themselves from God for all eternity. We call this separation hell.

HOW CATHOLICS WORSHIP

We celebrate our faith in worship when we give honor and praise to God. Worship is so important for us that the Church calls it the first "work" of God's people. The official public worship of the Church is called "liturgy."

ABOUT
THE SACRAMENTS

We place the sacraments into three groups to better understand their purpose. The first group is called the *sacraments of initiation.*

ABOUT
THE SACRAMENTS OF INITIATION

We become full members of the Catholic Church through the *sacraments of initiation:* Baptism, Confirmation, and Eucharist. These three sacraments are most often received at different times, as a person grows from infancy to maturity. Before being received into the Catholic community, older children and adults go through a period of formation called the catechumenate to prepare for Baptism, Confirmation, and Eucharist.

Baptism

In the sacrament of Baptism, we receive the Holy Spirit and are anointed with the Sign of the Cross. Through the waters of Baptism, which represent life and death, all sin is washed away and we rise with Christ to new life.

The grace of Baptism makes us conscious of our faith and ready to accept God's call.

Confirmation

In the sacrament of Confirmation we stand with a sponsor before the church community and proclaim our faith and our readiness to respond to God's call to discipleship. We should be in a state of grace and old enough to understand the commitment we are making.

When we are confirmed the bishop or priest says, "Be sealed with the gift of the Holy Spirit" (*Rite of Confirmation*). The bishop or priest places his hand on our head and anoints our forehead with the oil of chrism. Our baptismal faith is strengthened through the coming of the Holy Spirit.

The grace of Confirmation gives us the courage to live our faith and to be committed to the work of the Catholic community.

Eucharist

The Eucharist is the sacrament of the Real Presence of Jesus Christ with us under the appearances of bread and wine. The changing of bread and wine into the Body and Blood of Jesus Christ is called **transubstantiation**. When we worship together at Mass, we celebrate the Eucharist. The word *Eucharist* means "thanksgiving." During the Mass we praise and thank God for all our gifts, especially the gift of God's Son, Jesus Christ.

At Mass, Jesus is present in the bread and wine, in his word, in the people gathered, and in the priest who celebrates.

THE SACRAMENTS OF HEALING

The second group of sacraments is the *sacraments of healing*.

Reconciliation and Anointing of the Sick are sacraments of healing because they celebrate God's healing and forgiveness.

Reconciliation

Reconciliation is the sacrament that celebrates God's loving forgiveness. God always loves us and is ready to forgive our sins. When we sin, we freely choose to turn away from God and one another. The sacrament of Reconciliation reunites us with God and the church community. We may celebrate Reconciliation whenever we need God's mercy and peace and are sorry for our sins. We may celebrate the sacrament individually or with others.

We prepare for the celebration of Reconciliation by examining our consciences.

When we meet the priest, he welcomes us in the name of Jesus and the Church. He may read a story or lesson from the Bible. Then we confess, or tell the priest our sins. The priest may suggest ways we can improve and grow closer to God. He then asks us to do some act of service or to pray a particular prayer or prayers. This is called an act of penance. The priest then asks us to tell God we are sorry for our sins by praying an act of contrition.

Then, on behalf of the Church, the priest extends his hands over us and prays, "I absolve you from your sins in the name of the Father, and of the Son, and of the Holy Spirit" (*Rite of Penance*). This action is called "absolution." Then, with the priest, we praise God for his mercy. The priest tells us to go in peace and that our sins are forgiven. We respond, "Amen."

Anointing of the Sick

In the sacrament of Anointing of the Sick, we follow the custom of the early Church described in the Letter of James. The Church prays for the healing and forgiveness of the person who is ill, and the priest anoints him or her with holy oil as a sign of the healing power of the Holy Spirit.

The grace of Anointing of the Sick is the comfort brought about by the prayer of the Church, which can ease the suffering of mind and body.

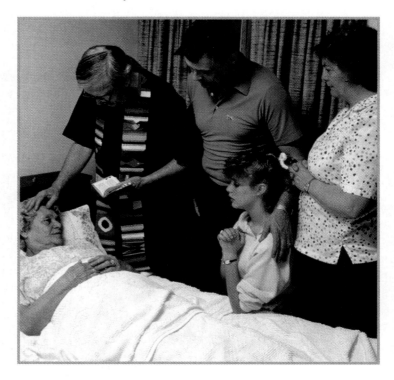

THE SACRAMENTS AT THE SERVICE OF COMMUNION

The third group of sacraments is the *sacraments at the service of communion.* These sacraments are Holy Orders and Matrimony.

Holy Orders

Holy Orders is the sacrament that celebrates the ordination of deacons, priests, and bishops to serve the Church in a special way. The word *ordain* means "to set aside or to empower a person to carry on the work of the apostles." Bishops carry on the work of the apostles and serve the Church by leading a diocese. Priests are ordained by the bishop to assist him in ministering to the people of the community by celebrating the sacraments, proclaiming God's word, and guiding the parish community. Deacons are also ordained by the bishop. Deacons assist with the work of the parish. They may read the Gospel and give the homily at Mass, baptize, witness marriages, and preside at funerals. Transitional deacons are men who have been ordained deacons as the final step before becoming priests. Permanent deacons have the same ministries as those of transitional deacons but can be married.

At the celebration of Holy Orders the bishop prays a special prayer asking God to bless the man being ordained. The bishop asks God to help this person preach the Gospel, celebrate the sacraments, and serve others. At the celebration of Holy Orders the bishop lays his hands on the head of the person being ordained.

Matrimony

The sacrament of Matrimony celebrates the commitment of a man and a woman to each

other for as long as they live. In the sacrament of Matrimony, the man and woman's love for each other is a sign of Christ's love for the Church. In the sacrament, God gives them special grace to sustain them and to help them grow in their love for each other. Through their physical love, which is the complete giving of themselves to each other and a sharing in God's creative power, they become one. This is why Catholics believe that sexual love is reserved for married couples only.

Catholic parents accept the responsibility of sharing their faith with their children. The love and care that parents give to their children are a reflection of God's love.

In the celebration of the sacrament of Matrimony, the man says to the woman, "I take you to be my wife." The woman says to the man, "I take you to be my husband." The couple confer the sacrament on each other in the presence of a priest or deacon and the Christian community.

ABOUT
THE MASS

Our Greatest Prayer

The greatest and most important prayer of the Catholic Church is the Mass. At Mass, we gather to celebrate the saving actions of Jesus. Jesus is present with us at Mass in the priest who leads our worship, in the word of God that is read, in the bread and wine that have become the Body and Blood of Jesus Christ, and in the community that gathers in his name.

The Introductory Rites

The Entrance Procession

The priest and other ministers enter the church. As the procession begins, we sing a gathering song.

The Greeting

The procession pauses before the altar to show reverence, and the priest, deacon, and servers move to their places. The priest and deacon kiss the altar to show reverence for the table on which the bread and wine will be offered.

We begin our worship. The priest welcomes us by saying, "The Lord be with you." We answer, "And also with you."

The Penitential Rite

As a community, we confess that we have sinned, and we thank God for the gift of forgiveness. Then we say or sing, "Lord, have mercy."

The Gloria

We say or sing this hymn of praise.

The Opening Prayer

The priest prays a prayer that helps us focus on the theme of the Mass for that day.

The Liturgy of the Word

The First Reading

The lector reads a story about God's love for us. The first reading is usually from the Old Testament. We sit quietly and listen to God's word.

The Responsorial Psalm

The cantor sings a psalm, and we sing the response.

The Second Reading

The lector reads a reading from the New Testament. The second reading is usually from one of Saint Paul's letters. We sit quietly and listen to God's word.

The Gospel Acclamation

Before the Gospel is proclaimed, we sing the "Alleluia" or another acclamation.

The Gospel

The priest or deacon reads the Gospel. In honor of Jesus, who speaks to us in the Gospel reading, we stand as it is read.

The Homily

The priest or deacon explains the meaning of the readings and the Gospel to the community. We sit quietly and pay attention as the homily is given.

The Profession of Faith

We stand and profess our faith in our Catholic beliefs. We pray the Nicene Creed together as a community of faith.

The General Intercessions

We pray for the Church, our country, and the needs of God's people. We also pray for those who are sick and for those who have died.

The Liturgy of the Eucharist

The Preparation of the Altar and the Gifts

As the altar is prepared, members of the community bring the gifts of bread and wine in procession to the priest. At this time we also give our prayers and offerings to God.

The Eucharistic Prayer

In this prayer of praise and thanksgiving, the priest praises God our Father and invites us to lift up our hearts to the Lord in prayer. We join with the angels and say or sing the "Holy, Holy, Holy."

The priest prays to the Holy Spirit, asking that the bread and wine become the Body and Blood of Jesus. Then in the words of Jesus himself at the Last Supper, the priest says the prayers of consecration, and Jesus Christ becomes truly present in the bread and wine.

The Memorial Acclamation

After the consecration, we proclaim the mystery of our faith by singing or saying these or similar words of joy and promise: "Christ has died, Chist is risen, Christ will come again."

The Great Amen

At the conclusion of the Eucharistic Prayer, the people respond, "Amen."

The Communion Rite

The Lord's Prayer

We pray the prayer that Jesus taught us.

The Sign of Peace

We offer each other a sign of peace to show that we wish goodness for our brothers and sisters in Jesus.

The Breaking of the Bread

As the priest at the altar breaks the bread, we say or sing, "Lamb of God, you take away the sins of the world: have mercy on us."

Communion

We reverently go up to the priest, deacon, or Eucharistic minister to receive the Body and Blood of Jesus in the Eucharist. When we receive the eucharistic bread, the priest, deacon, or eucharistic minister says, "The Body of Christ." We respond, "Amen." When we receive the cup, the priest, deacon, or Eucharistic minister says, "The Blood of Christ." We respond, "Amen." We return to our places, sing the communion song, and spend time in quiet prayer and thanksgiving.

Concluding Rite

Blessing

The priest blesses us in the name of the Father, and of the Son, and of the Holy Spirit. We answer, "Amen." Our celebration ends when the priest or deacon tells us to go in peace to love and serve God and one another. We respond, "Thanks be to God."

Dismissal

The servers, lector, deacon, and priest leave the altar in procession as we sing a song of praise and thanksgiving.

ABOUT
RECONCILIATION

In the sacrament of Reconciliation, we celebrate God's forgiveness. We ask the Holy Spirit to help us better live as Jesus taught us.

Preparation ▶

I examine my conscience by thinking of things I might have done or said on purpose that were harmful to myself or others. I remember that I may have sinned by not doing something good when I should have.

Rite of Reconciliation of Individuals

Priest's Welcome

The priest welcomes me in the name of Jesus and the Church.

Reading from Scripture

The priest may read a part of the Bible or tell me a story from the Gospels. He talks to me about the importance of living as Jesus taught and caring for others as God wants.

Confession

I tell the priest my sins. The priest asks me to do a kind act or to say a prayer, to show that I am sorry for my sins and to remind me to be more loving.

Prayer of Sorrow

I tell the priest that I am sorry for all my sins. The priest asks me to say an act of contrition. I say aloud a prayer of sorrow for sin.

Absolution ▶

On behalf of the Church, the priest extends his hands over me and asks God to forgive me. The priest gives me absolution in the name of the Father, Son, and Holy Spirit.

Prayer of Praise and Dismissal

With the priest, I say a prayer of praise. The priest tells me to go in peace. I answer, "Amen."

ABOUT
THE LITURGICAL YEAR

The prayer life of the Church revolves around the events of the life, death, and Resurrection of Jesus. Catholics celebrate these events in the life of Christ in the seasons of the liturgical year. During each season, the ministers, the altar, and the interior of the church are often clothed in a particular color that symbolizes the meaning of the season.

Advent

The liturgical year begins with the First Sunday of Advent. Advent is a time of waiting in which we celebrate the coming of Christ at Christmas and at the end of time. During the four weeks of Advent, we recall the prophets' words that foretold the birth of Christ. The liturgical color for Advent is violet, as a sign of joyful waiting.

Christmas

During the Christmas season we celebrate the birth of Jesus Christ; the Feast of Mary, Mother of God; the Epiphany; and the Baptism of Jesus. The liturgical color for the Christmas season is white, which is a sign of joy.

Lent

The season of Lent is a forty-day period of prayer and sacrifice. This season prepares us to celebrate the great feast of Easter. Lent begins with Ash Wednesday. The sixth Sunday of Lent is Palm Sunday, which is the beginning of Holy Week. The liturgical color for Lent is violet, as a sign of penance.

The Triduum

The **Easter Triduum** begins with the celebration of the Lord's Supper on Holy Thursday. Next we celebrate Good Friday, the day on which Christ died. The high point of

the Triduum is the Easter Vigil, which takes place on Holy Saturday night. The liturgical color for Good Friday is red, and the other days of the Triduum are celebrated in white.

Easter

The Triduum ends with the evening prayer on Easter Sunday. After Easter Sunday, we continue to celebrate the Resurrection of Jesus and we also celebrate his Ascension into heaven. During this time we prepare for the great Feast of Pentecost. The liturgical color for the Easter season is white, and the color for Pentecost is red.

Ordinary Time

The liturgical year has two periods of Ordinary Time. The first begins after the Baptism of Jesus and lasts until the day before Ash Wednesday. The second begins with the Monday after Pentecost and lasts until the Saturday before Advent. During Ordinary Time, we celebrate all that Jesus taught us during his public ministry. The liturgical color is green.

HOW CATHOLICS LIVE

Living as Jesus taught us is not easy, but God gives us lots of help. Our conscience and other special gifts help us. When we turn away from sin and make good choices, we live as children of God.

ABOUT
CONSCIENCE

Our conscience is a gift from God. Our conscience helps us know what is right and what is wrong. We must learn ways to form a good conscience. As Catholics, we believe the Beatitudes, the Ten Commandments, the teachings of Jesus, and the guidance of the Church help us develop a good conscience.

One of our greatest blessings is free will. Free will is our freedom to choose to do what is right or what is wrong. We can pray to the Holy Spirit to guide our choices, but we must always take responsibility for our actions.

ABOUT
THE THEOLOGICAL AND MORAL VIRTUES

The Holy Spirit gives us gifts that are so wonderful they help us become more like God. These gifts include the theological and moral virtues.

Virtues are often called habits. The more we practice virtues, the more natural they seem to us and the easier they are to live out.

The theological virtues are faith, hope, and charity. Faith helps us believe in God. Hope allows us to trust in God's promises. Charity prompts us to show our love for God and others.

The moral virtues are prudence, justice, fortitude, and temperance. Prudence is the habit of making good judgments and decisions. Justice is the practice of treating others fairly. Fortitude is the courage to do what is right. Temperance is the habit of living in moderation and controlling desires.

ABOUT

SIN AND MERCY

The Bible tells us that Jesus came to show mercy to sinners. Before Jesus was born, an angel told Joseph, Mary's husband, "You are to name him Jesus, because he will save his people from their sins" (Matthew 1:21).

Sin

Sin is a free choice to turn away from God's love. We sin by doing what we know is wrong. Sin keeps us from living as Jesus taught us. Sin turns our hearts away from God.

Mortal sin is a very serious refusal to love God. There are three ways to know when a sin is mortal.

1. The action must be seriously wrong.

2. We must know that the action is seriously wrong.

3. We must make a free choice to commit the sin.

Less serious sins are called venial sins. Venial sins weaken but do not completely destroy our relationship with God and the church community.

Mortal and venial sins committed by individuals are called personal sins. Our personal sins are always our choices. But some of our personal sins may tempt others to sin. We have a responsibility for the sins committed by others when we cooperate in them.

Social sins are those that reflect the unjust and oppressive wrongs in our society. Some examples of social sins are racism, failure to

pay just wages, abortion, unjust wars, sexism, ignoring the poor, and prejudice in any form. As Catholics, we must work to put an end to these sins wherever they exist.

Mercy

Even when we sin seriously, we can remember that God's mercy never leaves us. Mortal sins must be confessed in the sacrament of Reconciliation. Through Christ we receive God's forgiveness, and we are reunited with the church community.

God loves us so much and wants to forgive us even more than we want to be forgiven. When we share in God's life of love, we receive the grace to live good and holy lives. The Holy Spirit helps us turn away from sin. The Holy Spirit helps us form our conscience so that we know when something is right or wrong.

ABOUT
THE BEATITUDES

Jesus gave us the Beatitudes to teach us how to love God and others. The Beatitudes are Jesus' way of telling us what life will be like in the kingdom of heaven. When we live the Beatitudes, we can be truly happy.

The Beatitudes	Living the Beatitudes
Blessed are the poor in spirit, for theirs is the kingdom of heaven.	We know that we need God more than anything else. We obey God and trust in God's goodness.
Blessed are they who mourn, for they will be comforted.	We try to help those who are in sorrow or those who are hurting. We know the Holy Spirit is with them and will comfort them.
Blessed are the meek, for they will inherit the land.	We try to be gentle and patient with others. We try to please God more than anyone else. We believe we will share in God's promises.
Blessed are they who hunger and thirst for righteousness, for they will be satisfied.	We try to be fair and just toward all people everywhere. We share what we have with those in need.
Blessed are the merciful, for they will be shown mercy.	We forgive those who are unkind to us. We accept the forgiveness of others.
Blessed are the clean of heart, for they will see God.	We try to keep God first in our lives. We show our love for God by loving our neighbor. We believe we will live forever with God.
Blessed are the peacemakers, for they will be called children of God.	We try to bring God's peace to the world. When we live peacefully, we are known as God's children.
Blessed are they who are persecuted for the sake of righteousness, for theirs is the kingdom of heaven.	We try to do what is right even when we are made fun of or insulted. We believe we will be with God forever.

Matthew 5:3–10

370

ABOUT
THE COMMANDMENTS

The Ten Commandments are God's law of love. God gave the Ten Commandments as a gift to help people live in peace with one another. The Ten Commandments are a guide to help us live as children of God. Jesus told us that it is important to obey the commandments.

The Ten Commandments	Living the Ten Commandments
1. I am the Lord your God. You shall not have other gods besides me.	We believe in God. We only worship God. We love him more than everyone and everything else. We offer God prayers of adoration and of thanksgiving.
2. You shall not take the name of the Lord, your God, in vain.	We never use the name of God or Jesus in an angry way. We use the names of God, Jesus, Mary, and the saints with respect at all times.
3. Remember to keep holy the Sabbath day.	On Sunday we honor God in special ways. We worship him by celebrating the Eucharist with our family and friends.
4. Honor your father and mother.	We love, honor, respect, and obey our parents and all adults who care for us.
5. You shall not kill.	We believe that God gives us the gift of life. We must protect the lives of children not yet born, the sick, and the elderly. We respect the life and health of others. We must live peacefully and prevent harm from coming to ourselves and others.
6. You shall not commit adultery.	God created man and woman in his image. God calls each to accept his or her identity. The Church teaches that chastity is important for us to be healthy and happy. We must respect our bodies and the bodies of others. We honor the lifelong marriage covenant.
7. You shall not steal.	We take good care of the gifts that God has given us and share them with others. We want others who come after us to have them, too. We do not cheat.
8. You shall not bear false witness against your neighbor.	We must not tell lies, or mislead others on purpose. We must not hurt others by what we say. If we have misled somebody, then we must correct what we have said.
9. You shall not covet your neighbor's wife.	We respect the promises married people have made to each other. We must always dress and act in a decent way.
10. You shall not covet anything that belongs to your neighbor.	We are satisfied with what we have. We are not jealous, envious, or greedy. The Gospel teaches us to place God first in our lives.

Based on Exodus 20:2–17

The Great Commandment

Jesus told us that all of God's laws can really be summed up in the Great Commandment: "Love God with all your heart, with all your soul, with all your mind, and with all your strength, and love your neighbor as yourself" (based on Mark 12:30–31). The Great Commandment teaches us that God's laws are based on love of God and love of neighbor.

The New Commandment

Jesus told us that besides wanting us to keep the Great Commandment, he also wanted us to keep a New Commandment. The New Commandment Jesus gave us is, "Love one another as I have loved you" (based on John 13:34). We are called to live as followers of Jesus. When we love others and treat them as Jesus taught us, we live in happiness and freedom.

ABOUT THE GIFTS OF THE HOLY SPIRIT

The seven gifts of the Holy Spirit help and guide us. Below is a list of the gifts of the Holy Spirit and what they do for us.

1. Wisdom helps us know how God wants us to live.

2. Understanding helps us know what God teaches through Jesus, the Bible, and the Church.

3. Knowledge helps us know and appreciate that God is more important than anything else in life.

4. Right judgment helps us make good decisions in our everyday lives.

5. Courage helps us be strong when we face problems.

6. Reverence helps us love God more than anything else.

7. Wonder and awe help us to be thankful for all that God creates.

ABOUT
THE WORKS OF MERCY

Jesus expects us to care for the poor and those who are in need. Jesus wants us to live in peace and to be just. Jesus even wants us to love our enemies. Catholics call these ways to show love for others the spiritual works of mercy and the corporal works of mercy. These acts are described in Matthew 25:31–46 and in 1 Corinthians 12:4–11.

The Spiritual Works of Mercy
Help others do what is right.
Teach the ignorant.
Give advice to the doubtful.
Comfort those who suffer.
Be patient with others.
Forgive injuries.
Pray for the living and the dead.

The Corporal Works of Mercy
Feed the hungry.
Give drink to the thirsty.
Clothe the naked.
Visit those in prison.
Shelter the homeless.
Visit the sick.
Bury the dead.

ABOUT
THE PRECEPTS OF THE CHURCH

The Catholic Church also gives us some very specific duties and responsibilities. These are called the precepts of the Church. They are:

- Celebrate Mass on all Sundays and Holy Days of Obligation.
- Confess your sins at least once a year.
- Receive the Eucharist at least during the Easter season.
- Fast and abstain on the days appointed by the Church.
- Contribute to the Church to provide for its material needs.

ABOUT
VOCATIONS

Many of us were baptized when we were infants. Our parents and godparents wanted to give us the opportunity to grow in faith, hope, and love within a Catholic Christian community. They knew that we would need strong values and guidelines in order to live a full and happy life.

As we get older, we begin to think about what choices we will make in the future. Because of our life in the Church, we know that those choices will include devoting time to service in the Catholic Christian community. We call the choices we make about our place in the Church our vocation—what we feel we are called to do by the Gospel message of Jesus.

All Christians have a vocation. Although people live different lifestyles—single, married, living in community—all of us are called to hear and respond to the same Gospel message.

Many Ways of Serving

Many people devote some of their time to service within the Christian community. They choose a particular ministry in their parish or diocese, such as caring for the poor, teaching, planning and leading the liturgy, helping with parish management, or inviting others to join the Church.

Some women and men choose to devote their lives completely to the ministry of the Catholic Christian community. Many decide to join religious communities of sisters or brothers who take vows, which are promises of poverty, chastity, and obedience. The vows help them be completely devoted to their ministries. Each religious community chooses to concentrate its efforts on a particular ministry, such as teaching, working with the sick and the poor, preaching, prayer and contemplation, or parish work.

In the Catholic Church there are also ordained ministers—bishops, priests, and deacons. Men who feel that they are called to the priesthood have the special vocation of leading the community in worship as well as serving in other ways. There are diocesan priests who serve as pastors of parishes, as educators, and as counselors or in other capacities. There are priests who, like sisters and brothers, belong to religious communities. They may also be assigned as pastors or as teachers or to lead a particular ministry of their community.

There are also men who are ordained as permanent deacons. They can assist the pastor by leading the celebrations of Baptism and Matrimony, giving the homily at Sunday Mass, and helping with parish management. They are called to serve the poor. Deacons can be married and live with their families.

Discernment

In what ways are we being called to serve? Answering this question is called **discernment**, which means determining, with God's help, God's will for our lives. We should pray that God will help us understand what the Gospel is calling us to do. We should also try to know more about the possibilities for us in the Christian community. Talk to a priest, teacher, parish minister, or religious brother or sister to find out more about how God's invitation can be answered.

ABOUT
PRIESTS

Priests are men who have been ordained, or set apart. They have received the sacrament of Holy Orders. Priests preside at eucharistic celebrations and administer the sacrament of Reconciliation, as well as the other sacraments. They also proclaim the Gospel and give homilies. Priests may or may not be members of religious orders. Priests do not marry. Rather, they devote their lives to serving the People of God, the Catholic community.

Diocesan Priests and Religious Order Priests

Father Pat is a priest of Our Lady of Mercy parish. He was ordained a priest five years ago and was assigned to Our Lady of Mercy parish right after his ordination. He has been there ever since. Father Pat is a diocesan priest.

Father Tom is a religious order priest. He is a priest at St. Peter's parish, but he is also a member of the Fathers of the Holy Name, a religious order of priests founded in the 1700s.

Both Father Pat and Father Tom are parish priests, but one belongs to a religious order, and one does not. They told us why they chose their particular styles of priesthood.

Father Tom: As I was growing up in a small town in the Midwest, I was an altar boy at my parish church. The priests at my parish were very prayerful in the way they presided at Mass. And they always greeted people outside the church before and after each Mass. There were many activities in my parish as I was

growing up, and the parish priests were always involved. Very often there was a group of parishioners talking with them, joking around, or sharing a concern.

These priests were well liked and very good at what they did. But there was another side to their lives that interested me. They lived in a rectory they called a friary. I soon realized that these men had a special group identity and communal relationship with God.

As I continued to learn more about these priests, I discovered that they were part of a religious order that had many parishes all over the country as well as in other parts of the world. As a matter of fact, when I was in the eighth grade, some members of the order who had just come back from their missions in Africa told my class about their work there. I was fascinated by their sincerity and joy. That experience taught me that these priests were part of a large family that went beyond their little friary.

I liked the fact that there were many Fathers of the Holy Name all over the world and each friary was their home. I also learned that they took the same three vows of poverty, chastity, and obedience that religious sisters and brothers took. Those shared vows put an even greater emphasis on the community, and I found that very appealing. Those experiences left lasting impressions on me, and I maintained contact with my parish priests and eventually joined their order.

Father Pat: I cannot believe how similar our stories are. We both chose to become priests because we were impressed with what priests did and how they lived. When I was in high school, I worked in the front office of the parish rectory. What I remember most is the number of phone calls that came in for the priests. So many people wanted to talk to them. It seemed the priests were always checking in for their messages and then going out to see how they could respond. I thought it was great that their lives were so busy and they received so much energy from their work.

Because I grew up in a large parish in a big city, there were many families, and every night something was happening in or around the parish. One of the priests was going to a parish meeting, and another was going to a wake service at a nearby funeral home. There were always groups meeting in the parish hall with one of the priests. The mornings and weekends were just as busy. Between the many Masses, funerals, and meetings—not to mention the weekend weddings and marriage preparations—those priests were constantly on the go. They really knew the local area and knew people all over the diocese. Many of the priests from

the neighboring parishes even knew one another and helped one another out whenever they could.

That's what appealed to me—staying in one area or diocese and getting to know it well by working within it.

Father Pat and Father Tom are involved in the same ministry, yet their lives are not identical. Father Tom gets support from his fellow priests in the friary and is able to minister in different parts of the world. Father Pat finds strength and support from the priests and people of the diocese in which he lives and works. It is wonderful that the Church offers these two possibilities of priesthood for young men to consider.

HOW CATHOLICS PRAY

When we pray, we are expressing our faith in God. We can pray privately. We can also pray with others in the church community when we gather to worship.

ABOUT
PRAYER

Prayer is talking and listening to God. We pray to praise the goodness and love of God. We pray to thank God for the many gifts we have received. We pray to ask God for special blessings for ourselves and others. Sometimes we ask Mary or one of the saints to pray to God for us.

We believe God always hears our prayers. We believe God always answers our prayers in the way that is best for us.

Sometimes we may find it difficult to pray. We may be distracted by all the things we do in our daily lives. We may even forget to pray. It is important to set aside a special time or place to pray each day. Then, as we mature in our Christian life, we will have already formed a habit of daily prayer.

ABOUT
KINDS OF PRAYER

Just as we have different ways of talking and listening to our friends, we have different ways of praying. Praying is not always asking God for something. Our prayers should include praise and thanksgiving, too.

Quiet Prayer

It is always possible to pray. We can pray without saying words. When we are quiet and think about God, we are praying. This is a very good way to pray because the Holy Spirit speaks to our hearts.

We can pray quietly and think about a Bible story. We might imagine ourselves being in the crowd when Jesus preached.

Beautiful sights in nature remind us of God's wonderful gifts. When we see a sunrise or sunset, smell the ocean or a flower, see the colored leaves in autumn, or even play with our pets, we can pray a quiet prayer of thanks to God.

Prayers with Words

Sometimes we pray by using our own words. We talk to God just as we would speak to our friends or parents. Sometimes when we pray with others at home or in religion class, we might be invited to lead the prayer.

We also learn and pray the prayers that are part of our Catholic heritage. Some of these prayers are the Lord's Prayer, the Hail Mary, the Glory Be to the Father, the Act of Contrition, the Prayer to Our Guardian Angel, and the Prayer to the Holy Spirit.

As Catholics, we begin our prayers with the Sign of the Cross. The Sign of the Cross reminds us that we offer our prayers in the name of the Father, the Son, and the Holy Spirit. We end our prayers with "Amen," which means "I believe."

ABOUT THE ROSARY

The Rosary is a prayer that honors Mary, the mother of Jesus, and helps us meditate on the life of Christ. We pray the Rosary using a set of beads. A group of ten beads is called a decade. Before each decade, recall one of the mysteries, or important times in the lives of Mary and Jesus. There are twenty mysteries, shown at right. The prayers for the beads are shown below.

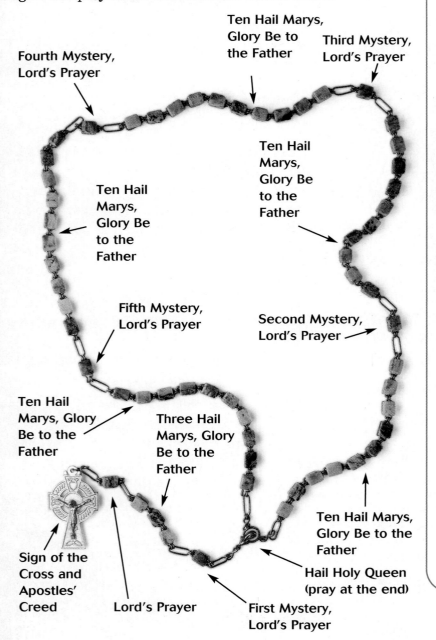

Fourth Mystery, Lord's Prayer

Ten Hail Marys, Glory Be to the Father

Third Mystery, Lord's Prayer

Ten Hail Marys, Glory Be to the Father

Ten Hail Marys, Glory Be to the Father

Fifth Mystery, Lord's Prayer

Second Mystery, Lord's Prayer

Ten Hail Marys, Glory Be to the Father

Three Hail Marys, Glory Be to the Father

Ten Hail Marys, Glory Be to the Father

Sign of the Cross and Apostles' Creed

Lord's Prayer

First Mystery, Lord's Prayer

Hail Holy Queen (pray at the end)

The Mysteries of the Rosary

The Joyful Mysteries

1. The Annunciation
2. The Visitation
3. The Birth of Jesus
4. The Presentation of Jesus in the Temple
5. The Finding of Jesus in the Temple

The Luminous Mysteries

1. The Baptism of Jesus
2. The Wedding at Cana
3. The Proclamation of the Kingdom of God
4. The Transfiguration
5. The Institution of the Eucharist at the Last Supper

The Sorrowful Mysteries

1. The Agony in the Garden
2. The Scourging at the Pillar
3. The Crowning with Thorns
4. The Carrying of the Cross
5. The Crucifixion

The Glorious Mysteries

1. The Resurrection
2. The Ascension
3. The Coming of the Holy Spirit at Pentecost
4. The Assumption of Mary
5. The Crowning of Mary as the Queen of Heaven

ABOUT
THE STATIONS OF THE CROSS

1. Jesus is condemned to death.

2. Jesus accepts the cross.

3. Jesus falls the first time.

4. Jesus meets his mother.

5. Simon helps Jesus carry the cross.

6. Veronica wipes the face of Jesus.

7. Jesus falls the second time.

8. Jesus meets the women of Jerusalem.

9. Jesus falls the third time.

10. Jesus is stripped of his garments.

11. Jesus is nailed to the cross.

12. Jesus dies on the cross.

13. Jesus is taken down from the cross.

14. Jesus is buried in the tomb.

15. Jesus Christ is risen.

ABOUT
MEDITATIVE PRAYER

Meditation is praying without words. In meditative prayer we pay close attention to our thoughts and our feelings. We pray silently so that God can speak to us in our minds and hearts.

Meditative prayer begins with thinking about a single subject. We may begin by reading a Bible story or by thinking about a holy person whom we respect. We may also pay very close attention to something beautiful in the world, such as a sunset or the ocean waves. All the while we concentrate on God's relationship to this single subject. This is how to pray in a meditative way. Another way to meditate is to call upon the Holy Spirit to help us think about how we are living. Are we truly living as followers of Jesus? Are there some things we think we need to correct? We can think about how we can better our relationship with God. We can think about how we can show our love for God in our everyday lives.

Then, we sort out our thoughts and feelings. We think about what God wants us to do. We use our imaginations to think about different ways we can serve God. Our prayer ends with a better understanding of what God wants us to do as followers of Jesus.

THE LORD'S PRAYER

Jesus taught his followers to pray. He gave us the Lord's Prayer so that we can honor God and remember his love for us. This prayer teaches us many important lessons about how God wants us to live.

Jesus said, "This is how
you are to pray . . ."

Matthew 6:9

The Lord's Prayer

Our Father, who art in heaven, hallowed be thy name;

God is our Father. We praise and thank God for all the wonderful gifts he has given us. We pray that God's name will be spoken with respect and reverence at all times.

thy kingdom come;

Jesus told us about God's kingdom in heaven. We pray that everyone will live as Jesus teaches us to live. We look forward to the day when God's kingdom will finally come about.

thy will be done on earth as it is in heaven.

We pray that everyone will obey God's laws. We know that Jesus has taught us how to live as his followers. We wish to show others how to live as Christians.

Give us this day our daily bread;

God cares for us. We know that we can pray for our needs. We know that we must pray for the needs of the poor. We ask God for the good things we can share with others.

*and forgive us our trespasses
as we forgive those who trespass against us;*

We ask God for forgiveness when we have done something wrong. We forgive those who have hurt us.

and lead us not into temptation,

We pray that God will help us make good choices and do what is right. When we have difficult choices to make, we can pray to the Holy Spirit for guidance.

but deliver us from evil.

We pray that God will protect us from what is harmful. We know that we should care for our own health and the well-being of others.

Amen.

When we say, "Amen," it means "I believe."

CATHOLIC PRAYERS

The Lord's Prayer

Our Father, who art in heaven,
 hallowed be thy name;
thy kingdom come;
thy will be done on earth
 as it is in heaven.
Give us this day our daily bread;
and forgive us our trespasses
 as we forgive those
  who trespass against us;
and lead us not into temptation,
 but deliver us from evil.
Amen.

Act of Contrition

My God,
I am sorry for my sins with all my heart.
In choosing to do wrong
and failing to do good,
I have sinned against you
whom I should love above all things.
I firmly intend, with your help,
to do penance,
to sin no more,
and to avoid whatever leads me to sin.
Our Savior Jesus Christ
suffered and died for us.
In his name, my God, have mercy.
Amen.
Rite of Penance

Hail Mary

Hail Mary, full of grace,
 the Lord is with you.
Blessed are you among women,
 and blessed is the fruit
 of your womb, Jesus.
Holy Mary, Mother of God,
 pray for us sinners, now,
 and at the hour of our death.
Amen.

Glory Be to the Father

Glory be to the Father,
 and to the Son,
 and to the Holy Spirit.
As it was in the beginning,
 is now, and will be forever.
Amen.

Nicene Creed

We believe in one God,
 the Father, the Almighty,
 maker of heaven and earth,
 of all that is seen and unseen.

We believe in one Lord, Jesus Christ,
 the only Son of God,
 eternally begotten of the Father,
 God from God, Light from Light,
 true God from true God,
 begotten, not made, one in Being with the Father.
 Through him all things were made.
 For us men and for our salvation
  he came down from heaven:

By the power of the Holy Spirit
 he was born of the Virgin Mary, and became man.

For our sake he was crucified under Pontius Pilate;
 he suffered, died, and was buried.
 On the third day he rose again
  in fulfillment of the Scriptures;
 he ascended into heaven
  and is seated at the right hand of the Father.

He will come again in glory to judge the living and the dead,
 and his kingdom will have no end.

We believe in the Holy Spirit, the Lord, the giver of life,
 who proceeds from the Father and the Son.
 With the Father and the Son he is worshiped and glorified.
 He has spoken through the Prophets.
 We believe in one holy catholic and apostolic Church.
 We acknowledge one baptism for the forgiveness of sins.
 We look for the resurrection of the dead,
  and the life of the world to come.

              Amen.

Act of Faith

O my God,
I firmly believe that you are one God in
Three Divine Persons,
Father, Son, and Holy Spirit.
I believe that your divine Son became man
and died for our sins,
and that he will come to judge the
living and the dead.
I believe these and all the truths which the
Holy Catholic Church teaches,
because you have revealed them,
who can neither deceive
nor be deceived.

Amen.

Hail Holy Queen

Hail Holy Queen,
Mother of Mercy;
our life, our sweetness, and our hope!
To you do we cry,
poor banished children of Eve;
to you do we send up our sighs,
mourning and weeping
in this vale of tears.
Turn, then, most gracious advocate,
your eyes of mercy toward us;
and after this exile,
show to us
the blessed fruit of your womb, Jesus.
O clement, O loving, O sweet Virgin Mary!

Amen.

Act of Love

O my God,
I love you above all things,
with my whole heart and soul,
because you are all good and worthy
of all love.
I love my neighbor as myself
for the love of you.
I forgive all who have injured me,
and I ask the forgiveness of
all whom I have injured.

Amen.

Vocation Prayer

Lord, show me how to be of service,
in your Church and in the world.
Help me see what you want me to do.
Give me vision, courage, and friends
who encourage me to do your work.

Amen.

Grace Before Meals

Bless us, O Lord, and these your gifts,
which we are about to receive
from your goodness,
through Christ our Lord.

Amen.

Prayers for Peace

The Prayer of Saint Francis of Assisi

Lord, make me an instrument of your peace.
   Where there is hatred, let me sow love;
   where there is injury, pardon;
   where there is doubt, faith;
   where there is despair, hope;
   where there is darkness, light;
   and where there is sadness, joy.
Grant that I may not so much seek
      to be consoled as to console;
      to be understood as to understand;
      to be loved as to love.
For it is in giving that we receive;
   it is in pardoning that we are pardoned;
   and it is in dying that we are born to
      eternal life.

                              Amen.

For Justice and Peace

Almighty and eternal God,
may your grace enkindle in all of us
a love for the many unfortunate people
      whom poverty and misery reduce to
      a condition of life
      unworthy of human beings.
Arouse in the hearts of those who call
      you Father
      a hunger and thirst for justice
      and peace,
      and for fraternal charity in deeds
      and in truth.
Grant, O Lord, peace in our days,
peace to our souls, peace to families,
      peace to our country,
and peace among nations.

                              Amen.

Pope Pius XII

Prayer for Peace

O Lord Jesus Christ,
who said to your apostles:
"Peace I leave with you,
      my peace I give to you,"
regard not my sins
      but the faith of your Church,
and deign to give her peace and unity
according to your will:
      who live and reign, God,
      world without end.

                  Amen.

Glossary

altar An altar is a raised place where sacrifices are offered. The altar used for the center of worship during the Mass is also a table. *(page 18)*

amen *Amen* is a word we usually say at the end of our prayers. It means "I believe" or "So it is." *(page 157)*

ark of the covenant The ark of the covenant was a special box that held the stone tablets of the Ten Commandments. *(page 87)*

catholic The word *catholic* means "universal." With a capital *C*, it describes the Church founded by Christ's apostles. *(page 121)*

chosen people In the Old Testament, the chosen people were Abraham and his descendants, whom God had selected to receive his word. People who choose to follow God's will today are also chosen people. *(page 99)*

commitment A commitment is a pledge to completely accomplish a promise. *(page 33)*

conscience A conscience is an ability to know what is right and what is wrong. *(page 145)*

covenant A covenant is an agreement or relationship sealed by a ritual or ceremony. In the Old Testament, the covenant was a loving, sacred agreement between God and his people to be faithful to each other. *(page 30)*

dignity Dignity is the specialness of people because they are God's children. *(page 254)*

discernment Discernment is discovering, with God's help, God's will for our lives. *(page 101)*

Easter Triduum The Easter Triduum is the holiest celebration of the liturgical year. It begins on Holy Thursday evening and concludes with the evening prayer on Easter Sunday. The Triduum includes the Mass of the Lord's Supper on Holy Thursday, the remembrance of Jesus' crucifixion on Good Friday, and the celebration of Jesus' Resurrection at the Easter Vigil. *(page 367)*

Essenes Essenes were devout Jewish people who lived simply in the desert. They believed in special washing rituals and life after death. *(page 242)*

exile Exile is the forced removal of people from their homeland to another land, or a person who has experienced such removal. *(page 186)*

Exodus The Exodus is the Old Testament story of how God freed the Hebrews in Egypt. *(page 63)*

faith Faith is the assurance of things hoped for, the conviction of things not seen. It means believing and trusting in God. *(page 6)*

fidelity Fidelity is faithfulness and loyalty to something or someone. *(page 43)*

fulfillment Fulfillment is the accomplishment of a promise. Jesus was the fulfillment of God's promises in the Old Testament. *(page 31)*

guidance Guidance is help in making the right choices. *(page 145)*

heaven Heaven is a life of everlasting happiness with God, and with all people who love God and others, after death. *(page 231)*

hell Hell is everlasting suffering and separation from God after death. *(page 231)*

Incarnation The Incarnation is God's Son becoming man, one like us, Jesus Christ, who is both human and divine. *(page 358)*

laity Laity are people who serve in the church community and are not clergy or religious brothers or sisters. *(page 119)*

liturgical year The liturgical year is the Church's yearly calendar of celebrations and seasons that honor the Paschal mystery. *(page 74)*

manna Manna is the breadlike food that God gave the Israelites in the desert. *(page 86)*

meditation Meditation is a type of prayer in which we are silent and concentrate on listening to God through our feelings, imagination, and thoughts. We can meditate by thinking about a Scripture story, art, and music. *(page 269)*

messiah A messiah is a person chosen to save people from a particular fate. The word means "savior." Jesus Christ is our Messiah, chosen by God to free us from sin and death. *(page 186)*

ministry A ministry is a way of serving and caring for others in Christ's name. *(page 119)*

moral virtues The moral virtues are four spiritual qualities—temperance, prudence, justice, and fortitude—that we receive through the Holy Spirit. They help us avoid sin. *(page 201)*

original sin Original sin is the sin of the first man and woman, passed on to all human beings. Because of it, we are weakened in our ability to resist sin and do good. *(page 177)*

Paschal mystery The Paschal mystery is the way that Jesus' Passion, death, Resurrection, and Ascension saved us from sin and gave us life after death. *(page 75)*

Passover Passover is the Jewish celebration of the Exodus from Egypt. *(page 75)*

patriarch A patriarch, a term meaning "father," is a great leader of the Hebrews from early Scripture times. A patriarch is also the male leader of a family or tribe. *(page 7)*

persistence Persistence is the act of continually pursuing something in spite of obstacles. *(page 211)*

Pharaoh Pharaoh is the title for a ruler of ancient Egypt. *(page 42)*

Pharisees Pharisees were Jewish people who accepted both the written law of the Old Testament and spoken teachings and tradition. *(page 242)*

piety Piety is putting God above everything else. *(page 43)*

precepts Precepts are teachings about our obligations. Two precepts of the Church are that we attend Mass on Sunday and Holy Days and that we receive the Eucharist at least once a year. *(page 201)*

promise A promise is a pledge to do something. *(page 19)*

promised land The promised land is Canaan, the sacred place God promised to Abraham, Isaac, Jacob, and the Israelites in Egypt. God led his people out of Egypt to this holy land, and God's people formed a Hebrew nation there. The term can also refer to heaven. *(page 63)*

prophet A prophet is a person sent by God to speak out against accepted behavior that does not follow God's will. *(page 174)*

psalms Psalms are religious songs and prayers from the Old Testament. Many psalms express praise for God and are believed to have been written by David. *(page 155)*

purgatory Purgatory is a final purification from sin after death. *(page 231)*

resurrection Our bodies decay at our deaths, but our souls live forever. Resurrection is the new life given to us when our bodies reunite with our souls at the end of time. *(page 231)*

revelation Revelation is God's act of revealing who he is and inviting us to respond with faith. *(page 9)*

reverence Reverence is honor and respect. *(page 157)*

sacrament A sacrament is a sacred sign and cause of grace instituted by Christ in the Church to continue the saving action of Christ through the Holy Spirit. *(page 130)*

sacramental A sacramental is a symbolic prayer, blessing, object, or action instituted by the Church that can lead us to a fuller participation in the grace of the sacraments. Examples include holy water, blessed candles, and the Sign of the Cross. *(page 133)*

sacramental grace Sacramental grace is the unique gift of God's love that we receive in each sacrament. Sacramental grace helps us respond to the challenge of the sacraments. *(page 145)*

sacrifice A sacrifice is an act of unselfish giving. It is also the act of making an offering at an altar. *(page 18)*

Sadducees Sadducees were Jewish people who accepted only the written law of the Old Testament and rejected spoken teachings and tradition. *(page 242)*

salvation Salvation is freedom from the pain of sin. *(page 175)*

spiritual works of mercy The spiritual works of mercy are loving deeds to meet the needs of other people. *(page 257)*

supplication Supplication is humbly and earnestly asking for help. As a form of prayer, supplication is praying to God in a time of need. *(page 211)*

Temple The Temple was the Jewish place of worship that Solomon built in Jerusalem. It contained the ark of the covenant and became an important center of worship for the Israelites. *(page 131)*

temple of the Holy Spirit Each of us is a temple of the Holy Spirit because the Holy Spirit dwells within us. As temples of the Holy Spirit, we are called to respect our bodies and to become saints. *(page 257)*

theological virtues The theological virtues are three spiritual qualities—faith, hope, and charity—that come from God and help us become more holy. They connect us with the Trinity. *(page 201)*

transubstantiation Transubstantiation is the sacred mystery in which bread and wine are changed into the real presence of Jesus Christ. *(page 361)*

Yahweh Yahweh is the most sacred name of God, spoken to Moses. It means "I am who I am." *(page 62)*

Index

as Son of God, 7, 65, 68, 77, 233, 254, 265, 267, 270, 358

teachings of, 266, 267, 356, 358, 359, 360

Jews, 7, 243, 248. *See also* Chosen People, Hebrews, Israelites.

beliefs of, 230, 231, 242

and covenant with God, 230, 259

customs and rituals of, 36, 73, 132–133, 148, 210, 215, 242, 324

feasts of, 73, 148, 215, 230, 254

prayers of, 79, 80, 103, 148, 192, 210, 211, 215

revolt by, 230

and the Sabbath, 24, 36, 199

Job, 212

Jobs for the Future, 275

Jochebed, 62

John the Baptizer, 104, 130, 242, 243–244

Jonah, 244

Jordan River, 98, 102, 130, 242

Joseph, Saint, 254, 265

Joseph (son of Jacob), x, xi, 42–43, 46, 62, 63

Joseph of Cupertino, Saint, 234

Joshua, x, 98–99, 118

Juan Diego, Saint, 100

Judah, 43, 174, 187, 198, 202, 230

Judges, of Israel, x

Judgment, final, 243

Justice, 201, 368

K

Kaddish, 192

Kiddush, 36

Kielburger, Craig, 78

Kingdom of God, 119, 131, 242–243

Korean Martyrs, 338–339

L

Laetare Sunday, 302–303

Laity, 119, 329

Last Supper, 19, 74, 75, 80

Laws, 230, 242

Lay ministers, 329, 365

Laying on of hands, 29

Lent, 75, 296–303, 367

prayer celebration for, 304–305

Life after death, 63, 65, 68, 231, 242

Litanies, 134, 180, 236

Liturgical colors, 367

Liturgical year, 74, 75, 354, 367

Liturgy, 7, 18, 75, 186

of the Eucharist, 365

of the Word, 157, 364

Lord's Prayer, 266, 267, 381–382, 386

Lord's Supper, Mass of the, 74, 367

Lourdes, 332–333

Lucy, Saint, 234

M

Maccabees, 231–232

Magnificat, 48

Manna, 86, 215

Maps

Babylonian empire, 198

Exodus, 57

Journey of Abraham and Sarah, 1

Palestine in the time of Jesus, 357

Route of exiles to Assyria and Babylon, 169

Twelve Tribes of Israel, x

Marks, of the Church, 121, 359

Marriage, 33. *See also* Matrimony.

Martyrs, 34, 234

Mary, 7, 8, 48, 254, 328, 330, 331, 332–335, 358

feasts of, 292, 326, 327, 332, 334, 335, 367

honoring, 292, 330, 331, 332, 333, 334, 335, 360, 378

and Jesus, 254, 265, 290

Mass, 18, 19, 33, 75, 134, 148, 157, 224, 306, 361, 364–365

of the Lord's Supper, 74

Matrimony, 246, 363. *See also* Marriage.

Meditation, 269, 380

Mercy, works of, 164, 255, 369, 373

Messiah, 186, 187, 233, 243, 254, 284, 324–325

Micah (prophet), xi, 174, 175, 187

Ministry, 119

Miriam, 63, 67

Moral decisions, 201

Moral virtues, 201, 368. *See also* Fortitude, Justice, Prudence, Temperance.

Mordecai, 210

Mortal sin, 231, 245, 369

Moses, 62–63, 74, 86–87, 92, 98

Mount Sinai, 215

Mount Zion, 131

N

Naomi, 202, 203

Nativity, 290

Nazareth, 254, 266, 328

New Commandment, 372

New Testament, viii, 65, 259, 356, 357, 364

Nicene Creed, 364, 384

Noah, 32–33

O

"O Antiphons," 284

Oil lamps, 230

Old Testament, viii , 12, 65, 66, 99, 130, 131, 135, 155, 202, 233, 242, 243, 259, 284, 356, 364

Ordinary time, 134, 363, 367

Ordination, 134, 363. *See also* Holy Orders.

Original sin, 130, 142, 175, 360

Orpah, 202

Our Father. *See* Lord's Prayer.

P

Pagans, 230

Parable, xiv, 214

of the Persistent Widow, 214

Paschal mystery, 75

Passion Sunday, 306–307

Passover, 73, 74, 75, 254

Patriarch, x, 7, 30, 31, 63

Patrick, Saint, 234

Patron saints, 234

Paul, Saint, 7, 34, 35, 257, 356, 364

Penance, 145, 147, 245, 362, 367. *See also* Reconciliation.

Penitential Rite, 148

Pentecost, 272, 367

Persecution, of early Christians, 34

Persians, 199

Persistence, 211, 212, 214

Personal sin, 369

Peter, Saint (apostle), 120, 359

Petition, 211

Pharaoh, 42, 62, 63

Pharisees, 242, 243

Piety, 43

Plague, 62

of death, 62, 73, 74, 75

Pope, 117, 134, 346, 358

Potiphar, 42

Prayer, 101, 236, 266–272, 383–386. *See also* names of individual prayers.

CELEBRATING CATHOLIC SCHOOLS

CATHOLIC SCHOOLS IN AMERICA
Mother Frances Cabrini

Teacher of Immigrants

Maria Francesca Cabrini was born on July 15, 1850 in northern Italy. As a child, Maria knew she was destined to help people.

Maria's parents helped her receive an education. She received her teaching certificate as an adult and began her career as a teacher in a neighboring town. Maria wanted to teach people in faraway lands about Jesus. She also wanted to become a Franciscan nun. Her bishop encouraged her to become a religious sister. He also told her to start her own religious order because he was unaware of any nearby Franciscan orders. With seven other women, Maria founded the Missionaries of the Sacred Heart of Jesus. She became known as Mother Frances Xavier Cabrini when she became a nun.

Mother Frances Xavier Cabrini wanted to go to China. However, the pope told her to aid the Italian people arriving in America. On March 31, 1889, Mother Cabrini and six sisters arrived in New York City. Many people, especially poor people, were sick. Many children's parents had died. Mother Cabrini opened a home to take care of these children. Because there was so much sickness, Mother Cabrini also opened a hospital for the poor.

Mother Cabrini believed that the children and their parents needed to learn English. She started schools to teach the children both English and Italian. The sisters in her order held classes to teach the adults English. The sisters also taught the adults how to sew, cook, clean, and perform other tasks that would help them get jobs. All of Mother Cabrini's schools taught people about the love of Jesus.

Mother Cabrini traveled across the United States. In 1909 she became a U.S. citizen. By the time of her death in 1917, she had opened sixty-seven Catholic institutions, including schools, orphanages, and hospitals. She was the first American citizen to become a saint. Her feast day is November 13.

✝ Prayer Celebration for Catholic Schools Week

The Gift of Education

Mother Cabrini helped people in many ways, but she made an especially important contribution to society as an educator. Catholic education helps people become productive citizens while growing in their Catholic faith.

All: In the name of the Father, and of the Son, and of the Holy Spirit.

Reader: Different people have different roles in helping others. Some people become missioners, others become parents, and still others become health-care and public safety workers. Some become teachers who instruct youths in the truths of God. And finally, some people are students who seek to learn about God and his created world. All people work together to make the world a better place and to give glory to God.

Leader: Let us pause briefly to examine our lives as students.

Group 1: Now there are a variety of gifts, but the same Spirit, and there are a variety of services, but the same God.

Group 2: There are a variety of good works, but it is the same God who inspires them in everyone.

Group 1: To one is given through the Spirit the gift of wisdom, and to another the gift of knowledge.

Group 2: All these are inspired by one and the same Spirit, who gives to each one individually according to God's will.

Based on 1 Corinthians 12:4–11

All: God, you gave us the example of Mother Cabrini, who brought the word of God and truth to many people. We acknowledge that you have called us to be students. We pledge to follow this vocation faithfully by following the directions of our parents and teachers. We ask that you send your Spirit to guide us in our work. We ask all this through Jesus, our Brother and Teacher. Amen.

GRADE 6 FAVORITES

The school year is just about over. You have learned a lot in your religion classes. Think about the things you have studied and celebrated this year, and answer the following questions.

Which Bible story in this book did you enjoy the most?

_____

_____

_____

_____

What did you learn from this story?

_____

_____

_____

_____

Which person from the Bible stories in this book is your favorite? Why?

_____

_____

_____

_____

_____

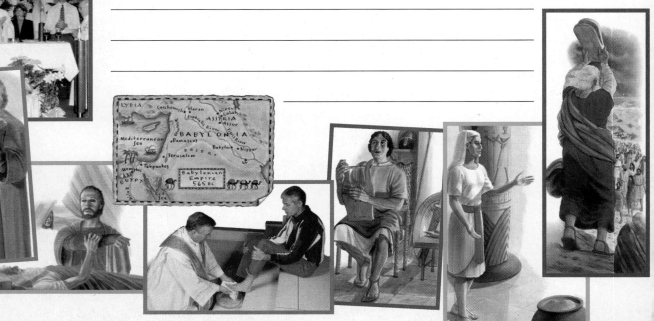

Name three things you learned about the Catholic religion that you did not know before this year.

_____

_____

_____

_____

Which saint did you most enjoy learning about? Why?

_____

_____

_____

_____

Which holy person did you most enjoy learning about? Why?

_____

_____

_____

_____

Which prayer celebration did you like most this year? Why?

_____

_____

_____

_____

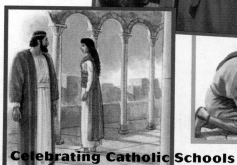

END-OF-YEAR PRAYER

A Prayer of Thanksgiving

All: In the name of the Father, and of the Son, and of the Holy Spirit.

Leader: God, our Father, you have brought us together this year to learn more about our ancestors in faith—the Hebrews. We have come to know you as the loving Creator who has gathered all people to yourself and has shown your love throughout the centuries. In the name of Jesus Christ, our Savior, and with the help of the Holy Spirit, may we grow in our faithfulness to you and honor the covenant you have made with humanity.

All: Amen.

Reader 1: A reading from the Book of Genesis.

(Read aloud Genesis 15:1–6 from the Bible.)

Reader 2: Thank you for giving us the example of Abraham, a man of great faith. May we be people of faith who are willing to seek you and believe in you.

All: We praise and thank you, Lord, for the gift of faith.

Reader 3: Another reading from the Book of Genesis.

(Read aloud Genesis 21:1–8 from the Bible.)

Reader 4: Thank you for giving Sarah the gift of faith and the gift of her son, Isaac. May our faith in the word of the Lord be as strong as Sarah's.

All: We praise and thank you, Lord, for the gift of faith.

Reader 5: A reading from the Book of Exodus.

(Read aloud Exodus 20:2–17 from the Bible.)

Reader 6: Thank you for the Ten Commandments given to Moses as a sign of your presence and care for the Israelites. May the Ten Commandments continue to guide us as we strive to lead upright Christian lives.

All: We praise and thank you, Lord, for the gift of faith.

Reader 7: A reading from the Book of Samuel.

(Read aloud 2 Samuel 5:1–5 from the Bible.)

Reader 8: Thank you for the gift of King David, the first important king of Israel. May we learn from David's life that he had great trust in God, even when he sinned and offended God. He believed that God gave him a mission and that God would help him fulfill that mission.

All: We praise and thank you, Lord, for the gift of faith.

Reader 9: A reading from the Book of Isaiah.

(Read aloud Isaiah 57:14–15 from the Bible.)

Reader 10: Thank you for the gift of the prophets, who were a sign of hope for oppressed people. May we remove the things that cause oppression for others.

All: We praise and thank you, Lord, for the gift of faith.

Reader 11: A reading from the Gospel of Matthew.

(Read aloud Matthew 1:18–25 and 2:1–6 from the Bible.)

Reader 12: Thank you for the gift of Jesus Christ, who fulfilled all the promises made to our ancestors in faith. May we continue to praise Jesus Christ, the Messiah, Wonder-Counselor, and Prince of Peace.

All: We praise and thank you, Lord, for the gift of faith.

Leader: God, our Father and Creator, we are grateful to you for the faith journey we took this year. We learned of your promises to the Israelites and your promises to us as followers of your Son, Jesus. Grant that we may be faithful followers of Jesus Christ through the power of the Holy Spirit.

All: Amen.

Credits

DESIGN: Lusignan Design, Pronk&Associates, and Scott Foresman

COVER: Gene Plaisted, OSC/The Crosiers

SCRIPTURE ART: Tim Ladwig

ILLUSTRATIONS: 1, 57, 113, 169, 198, 257, 357, 398 Elizabeth Wolf; 6, 8, 18, 20, 30, 32, 33, 42, 44, 62, 64, 76, 86, 88, 98, 118, 120, 132, 142, 144, 154, 174, 176, 188, 189, 202, 211, 212, 232, 244, 254, 256, 266, 280, 282, 287, 290, 300, 314, 330, 398 Tim Ladwig; 6 Diane Paterson; 7, 21, 156, 243, 303, 333 Heather Holbrook; 9, 231, 255, 325, 349 Barb Massey; 10, 135, 307 Martha Doty; 11 Julie Monks; 23, 103, 235 Sandy Rabinowitz; 34, 90, 234 Roman Dunets; 41, 175 Charles Shaw; 45, 316, 321, 338 David Bathurst; 52, 209 Chris Reed; 53, 109, 165, 221 Ginna Magee; 65, 157, 187, 293, 323, 339 Bernadette Lau; 66, 145, 214, 215 Paula Wendland; 66 Huy Voun Lee; 73 Claude Martinot; 75, 87, 143, 315, 349, 351 Jean and Mou-Sien Tseng; 79, 197 Marcie Hawthorne; 79, 119, 328 Cindy Rosenheim; 97 Laura Huliska-Beith; 101, 213 Jack McMaster; 122 Bernard Adnet; 129 Judy Jarrett; 131 Michael Di Giorgio; 133 Donna Perrone; 133 Arvis Stewart; 147 Suzanne Muse; 155, 265 Carla Kiwior; 159 Donna Catanese; 164, 199, 259 Deborah Pinkney; 177, 245 Heather Graham; 178 Shelley Dieterichs; 186 Freddie Levin; 201, 301, 317 John Hovell; 220, 276 Diana Magnuson; 235 Gregg Valley; 236 Linda Howard Bittner; 246 Freddie Levin; 270 Lauren Cryan; 283 Dave Whamond; 313 David Coulson; 313 Teresa Berasi; 353 Robin DeWitt.

PHOTOGRAPHS: Every effort has been made to secure permission and provide appropriate credit for photographic material. The publisher deeply regrets any omission and pledges to correct errors called to its attention in subsequent editions. Unless otherwise acknowledged, all photographs are the property of Scott Foresman, a division of Pearson Education. Photo locators denoted as follows: Top (T), Center (C), Bottom (B), Left (L), Right (R), Background (Bkgd).

vii Elizabeth Wolf; viii ©Reunion des Musees Nationaux/Art Resource, NY; x Elizabeth Wolf; xi Elizabeth Wolf; 1 Steve Maines/Stock Boston; 4 Gene Plaisted, OSC/The Crosiers; 5 Michael Newman/PhotoEdit; 12 F. Pedrick/Image Works; 16 Scala/Art Resource, NY; 17 ©David Young-Wolff/Getty Images; 18 ©James L. Shaffer; 22 Dennis MacDonald/PhotoEdit; 24 Jeff Greenberg/PhotoEdit; 28 Tom McGuire/Cathedral of Valencia; 29 Bill Gallery/Stock Boston/PictureQuest; 34 Christie's Images//SuperStock; 36 Peter Weimann/Animals Animals/Earth Scenes; 40 ©Joan Marcus; 45 ©Ian Harwood/Corbis; 46 Lee Snider/Image Works; 57 Charles Graham/eStock Photo; 60 National Maritime Museum, London; 61 Tony Freeman/PhotoEdit; 68 R. Burch/Bruce Coleman Inc.; 72 Saint Maria delle Grazzie, Milan/Canali PhotoBank/SuperStock; 73 (TR) Lawrence Migdale/Stock Boston, (CR) Joel S. Fishman/Photo Researchers, Inc.; 77 Christie's Images Ltd. 1992/©Christie's Images, New York; 78 Free the Children International; 84 ©Bill Wittman; 85 Richard Pasley/Stock Boston; 89 (TR) ©Ronnie Kaufman/Corbis, (CR) ©Myrleen Ferguson Cate/PhotoEdit, (BR) CLEO; 90 Santa Maria Della Vittoria, Rome/Canali PhotoBank, Milan/SuperStock; 92 PhotoDisc; 96 Z. Radovan, Jerusalem; 100 ©Queen of the Americas Guild; 102 Bill Aron/PhotoEdit/PictureQuest; 103 ©Lynda Richardson/Corbis; 107 Corbis; 113 Reprinted from ABC's of The Bible, ©1991 The Readers Digest Association Ltd.. Used by permission of The Readers Digest Association, Inc., Pleasantville, NY; 116 (BR) Museum of Music, Bologne, Italy/ET Archive, London/SuperStock, (CR) Thomas Coram Foundation, London/Bridgeman Art Library London/SuperStock; 117 David Young-Wolff/PhotoEdit; 122 Courtesy of the Inn Dwelling; 124 ©Patrick Ward/Corbis; 128 LucasFilm LTD/Paramount/Kobal Collection; 130 Gene Plaisted, OSC/The Crosiers; 134 Chris Sheridan; 140 Warner Brothers/Kobal Collection; 141 PhotoDisc; 146 ©Myrleen Ferguson Cate/PhotoEdit; 152 Getty Images; 153 PhotoDisc; 158 Thomas Nebbia/NGS Image Collection; 169 Photograph by Erich Lessing/Art Resource, NY; 172 ©Steve Taylor/Getty Images; 173 Jim Whitmer;

179 Michael Newman/PhotoEdit; 180 ©Myrleen Ferguson Cate/PhotoEdit; 180 ©Frank Whitney/Getty Images/The Image Bank; 185 (BL) David Young-Wolff/PhotoEdit, (TR) Mark Richards/PhotoEdit, (CR) Michael Newman/PhotoEdit; 186 Michael Newman/PhotoEdit; 190 AP/Wide World; 191 Michael Newman/PhotoEdit; 196 ©2000 Carol Rosegg; 204 Adam Jones/Dembinsky Photo Assoc. Inc.; 208 Reprinted with permission of Behrman House, Inc.; 214 ©Bill Wittman; 216 David Matherly/Visuals Unlimited; 225 (Bkgd) ©Sonia Halliday Photographs, (BR) Scala/Art Resource, NY; 228 Joel De Grand/Shrine of St. Jude Thaddeus/The Dominicans; 229 ©Ian Shaw/Getty Images; 230 Courtesy of the Father Solanus Guild/www.solanuscasey.org; 234 Joe Viesti/Viesti Collection, Inc.; 236 www.blimpphoto.com; 240 Huntington Library/Sipa Press; 242 ©Bill Wittman; 248 (CL) Jim Strawser/Grant Heilman Photography, (CC) Larry Lefever/Grant Heilman Photography, (CR) Lefever/Grushow/Grant Heilman Photography, (Bkgd) Grant Heilman/Grant Heilman Photography; 252 Ellen Dooley/Liaison Agency; 253 ©Celine Amiot/Corbis Sygma; 260 Gene Plaisted, OSC/The Crosiers; 264 Kobal Collection; 268 ©David Young-Wolff/PhotoEdit; 269 Hanan Isachar/Israelimages; 272 (Bkgd) SuperStock, (BR) Gerard Lacz/Animals Animals/Earth Scenes; 275 Homeboy Industries; 281 (BL) Gene Plaisted, OSC/The Crosiers, (CR) Photo by Jim Whitmer; 283 ©Peter Lilja/ImageState/Alamy.com; 285 ©James L. Shaffer; 286 ©Jose Luis Pelaez, Inc./Corbis; 288 H. Rogers/Art Directors & Trip Photo Library; 291 Gene Plaisted, OSC/The Crosiers; 292 Gene Plaisted, OSC/The Crosiers; 294 ©Paul Conklin/PhotoEdit; 297 Photo by Jim Whitmer; 298 Guildhall Art Gallery, Corp. of London/Bridgeman Art Library/SuperStock; 299 ©James L. Shaffer; 304 ©Bill Wittman; 305 ©Bill Wittman; 306 PhotoDisc; 310 Jim Whitmer; 311 Jim Whitmer; 312 A & F Pears Ltd., London/SuperStock; 318 ©George Goodwin/SuperStock; 319 ©George Goodwin/SuperStock; 320 AKG London Ltd.; 322 ©Erich Lessing/Art Resource, NY; 324 Scala/Art Resource, NY; 326 ©Sean Cayton/The Image Works, Inc.; 327 SuperStock; 329 (TR) ©Joe McNally/Corbis, (CR, BR) ©W.P. Wittman; 331 CLEO; 332 Gene Plaisted, OSC/The Crosiers; 334 ©Joseph Martin/AKG London Ltd.; 335 ©Jean-Francois Amelot/AKG London Ltd.; 336 ©Convent St. Joseph; 337 (TR) ©Nancy Richmond/The Image Works, Inc., (BR) ©Cindy Charles/PhotoEdit; 340 ©Bettmann/Corbis; 342 Gene Plaisted, OSC/The Crosiers; 343 ©Myrleen Ferguson Cate/PhotoEdit; 344 Gene Plaisted, OSC/The Crosiers; 345 ©Robert Fried; 346 AP/Wide World Photos; 347 AP/Wide World Photos; 348 ©Maryknoll Sisters Photos/Maryknoll Mission Archives, Maryknoll, NY; 350 ©Redemptorist Archives/The Seelos Center; 352 ©Michael St. Maur Sheil/Corbis; 358 A. Tjagny-Rjadno; 359 David Lees/LIFE Magazine/©Time Inc.; 360 Scala/Art Resource, NY; 361 ©W.P. Wittman; 362 MacDonald Photography/Unicorn Stock Photos; 363 Regina McAloney; 367 Jim Whitmer; 368 (TR) ©Greg Nikas/Corbis, (BL) Anne Hamersky; 369 David Young-Wolff/PhotoEdit; 372 David Young-Wolff/PhotoEdit; 373 Corbis; 374 Skjold Photographs; 375 ©James L. Shaffer; 377 David Young-Wolff/PhotoEdit; 380 ©Myrleen Ferguson Cate/PhotoEdit; 381 SuperStock; 396 The Granger Collection; 397 ©Ross M. Horowitz/Getty Images; 398 (CL) Gene Plaisted, OSC/The Crosiers, (BC) ©Bill Wittman; 400 ©Marie-Louise Brimberg/NGS Image Collection.